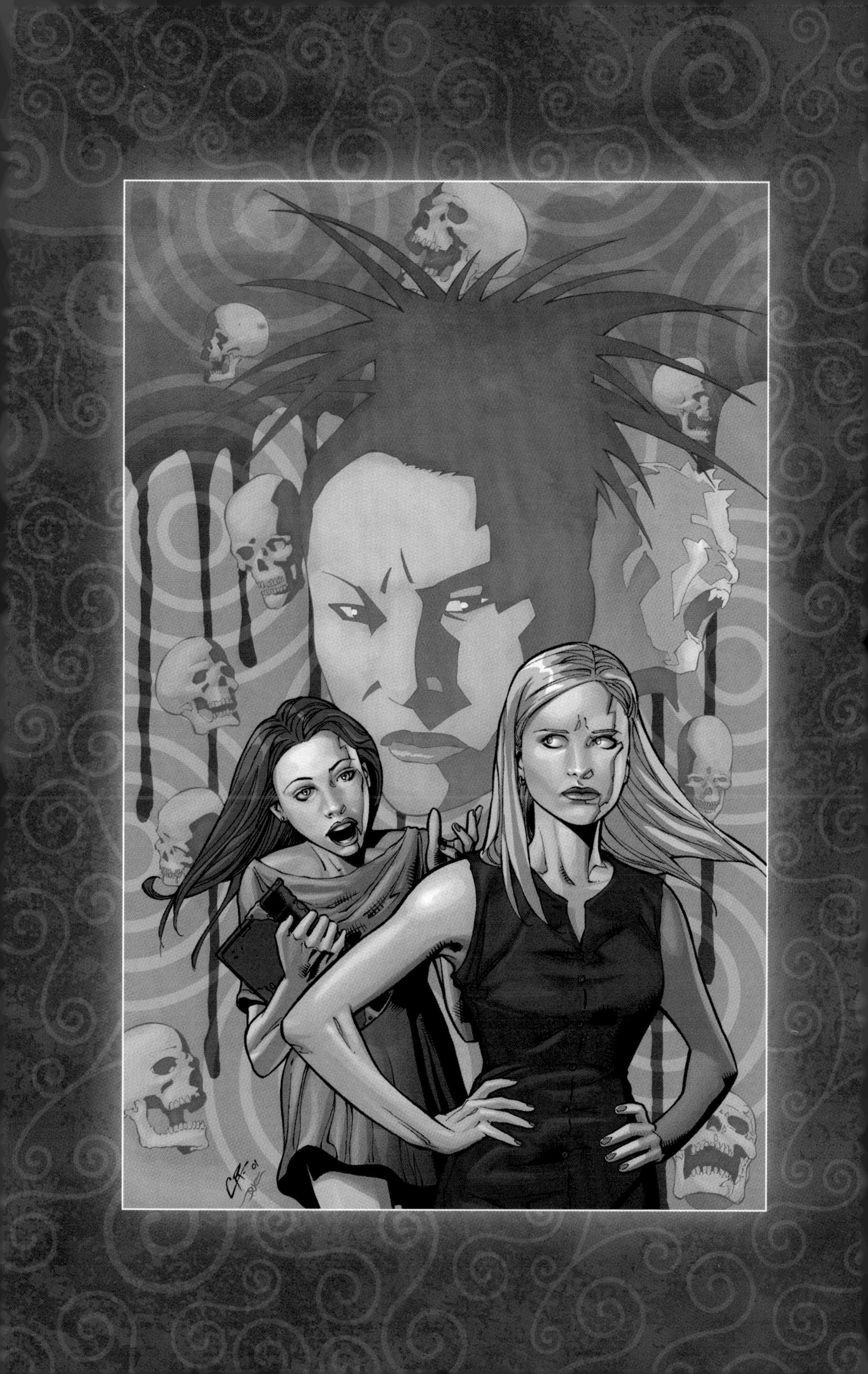

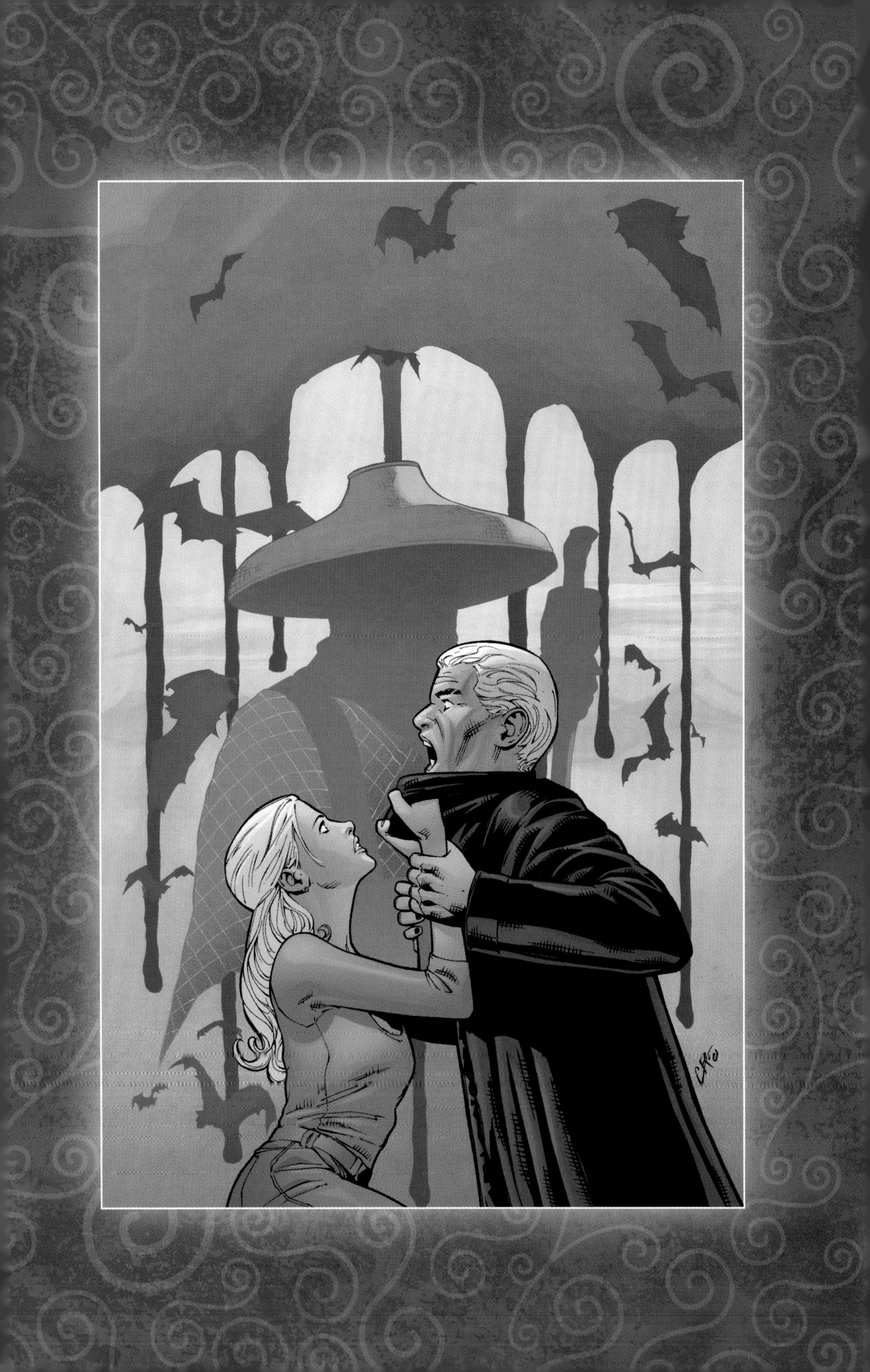

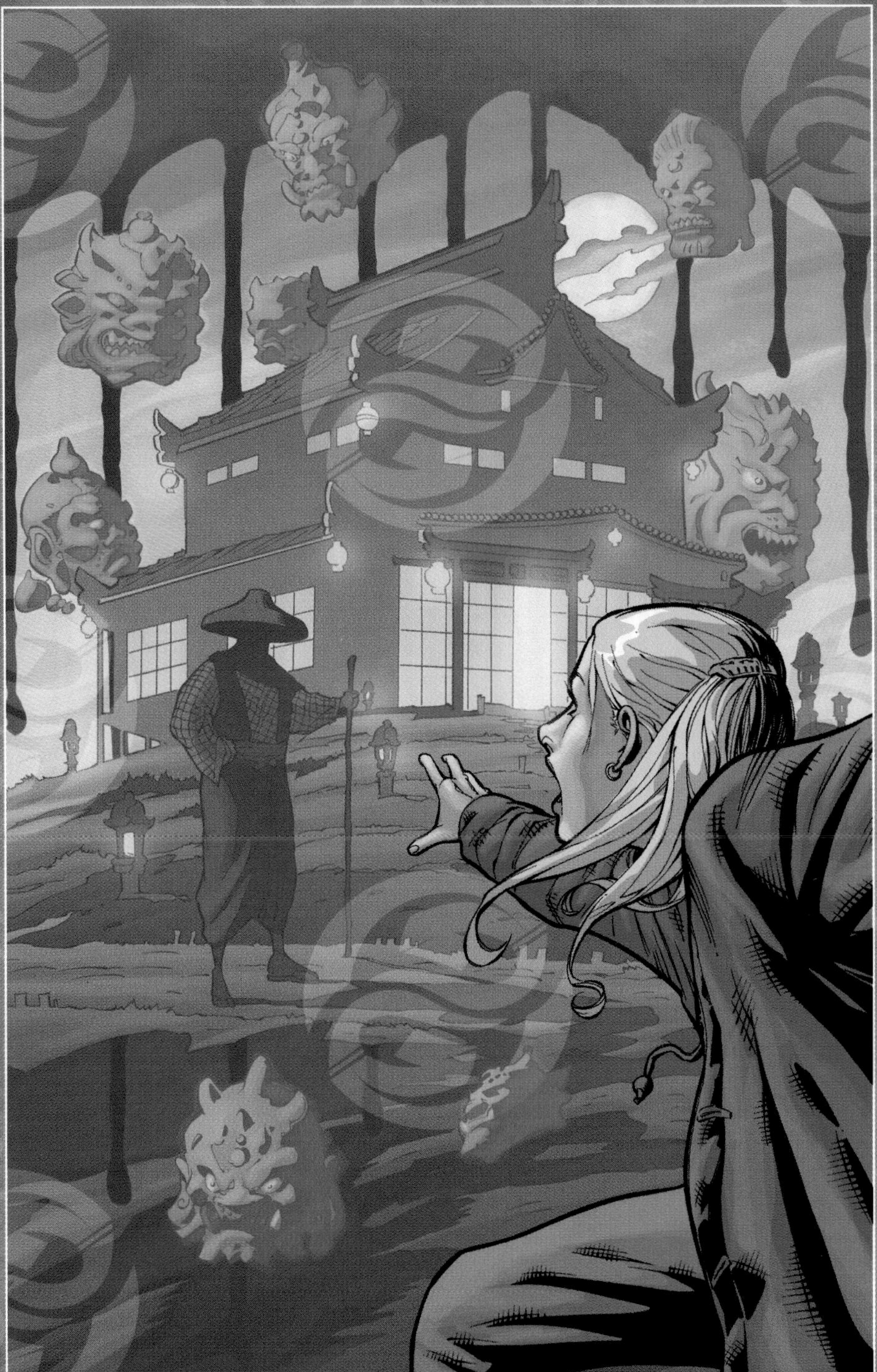

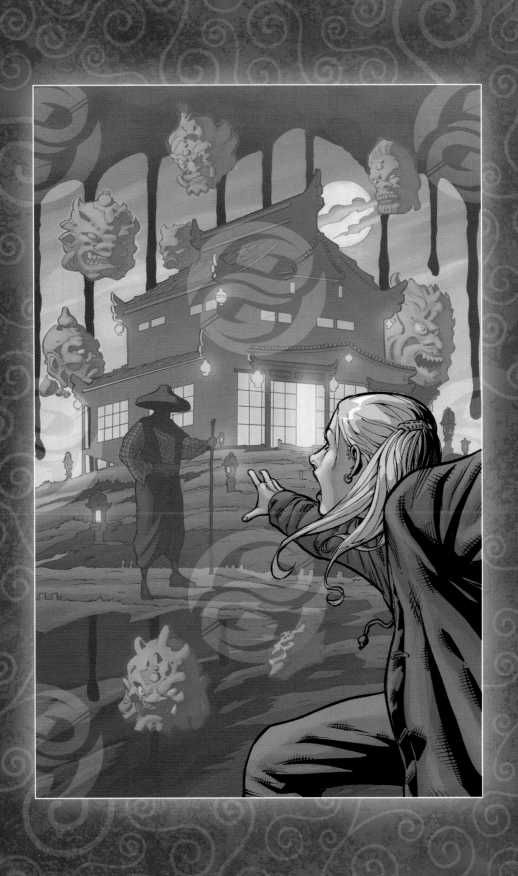

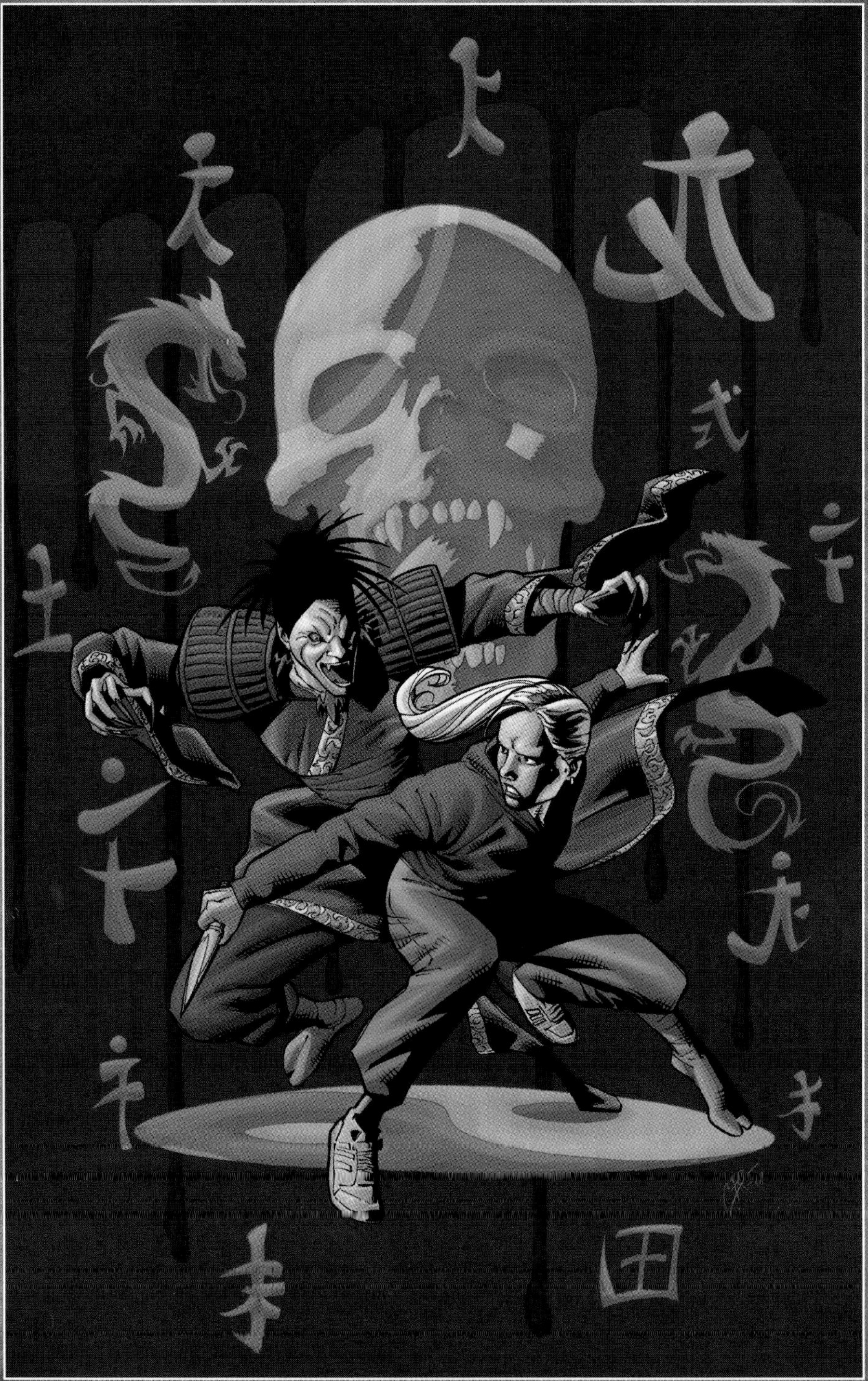

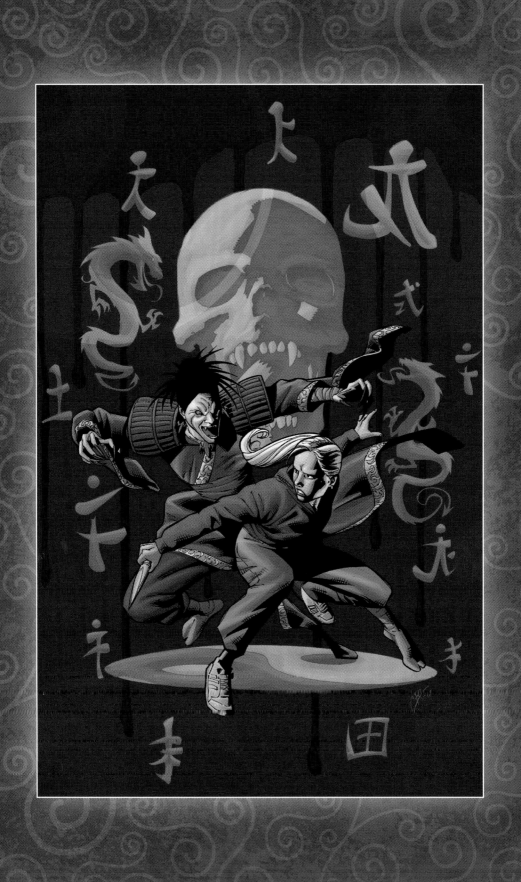

Buffy the Vampire Slayer™

False Memories

based on the television series created by
JOSS WHEDON

writers TOM FASSBENDER & JIM PASCOE

penciller CLIFF RICHARDS

inkers JOE PIMENTEL & WILL CONRAD

colorist DAVE MCCAIG

letterer CLEM ROBINS

cover image KEITH WOOD

This story takes place during Buffy the Vampire Slayer's fifth season.

Dark Horse Comics®

publisher
MIKE RICHARDSON

editor
SCOTT ALLIE
with MICHAEL CARRIGLITTO

designer
LANI SCHREIBSTEIN

art director
MARK COX

special thanks to
DEBBIE OLSHAN AT FOX LICENSING
AND DAVID CAMPITI AT GLASS HOUSE GRAPHICS

Buffy the Vampire Slayer™: False Memories. Published by Dark Horse Comics, Inc., 10956 SE Main Street, Milwaukie, OR, 97222.
Buffy the Vampire Slayer™ & © 2002 Twentieth Century Fox Film Corporation. All rights reserved.
TM designates a trademark of Twentieth Century Fox Film Corporation. The stories, institutions, and characters in this publication are fictional.
Any resemblance to actual persons, living or dead, events, institutions, or locales, without satiric intent, is purely coincidental.
No portion of this book may be reproduced, by any means, without express written permission from
the copyright holder. Dark Horse Comics® and the Dark Horse logo are trademarks of Dark Horse Comics, Inc.,
registered in various categories and countries. All rights reserved.

PUBLISHED BY
DARK HORSE COMICS, INC.
10956 SE MAIN STREET
MILWAUKIE, OR 97222

FIRST EDITION
JUNE 2002
ISBN: 1-56971-736-2

1 3 5 7 9 10 8 6 4 2

printed in china

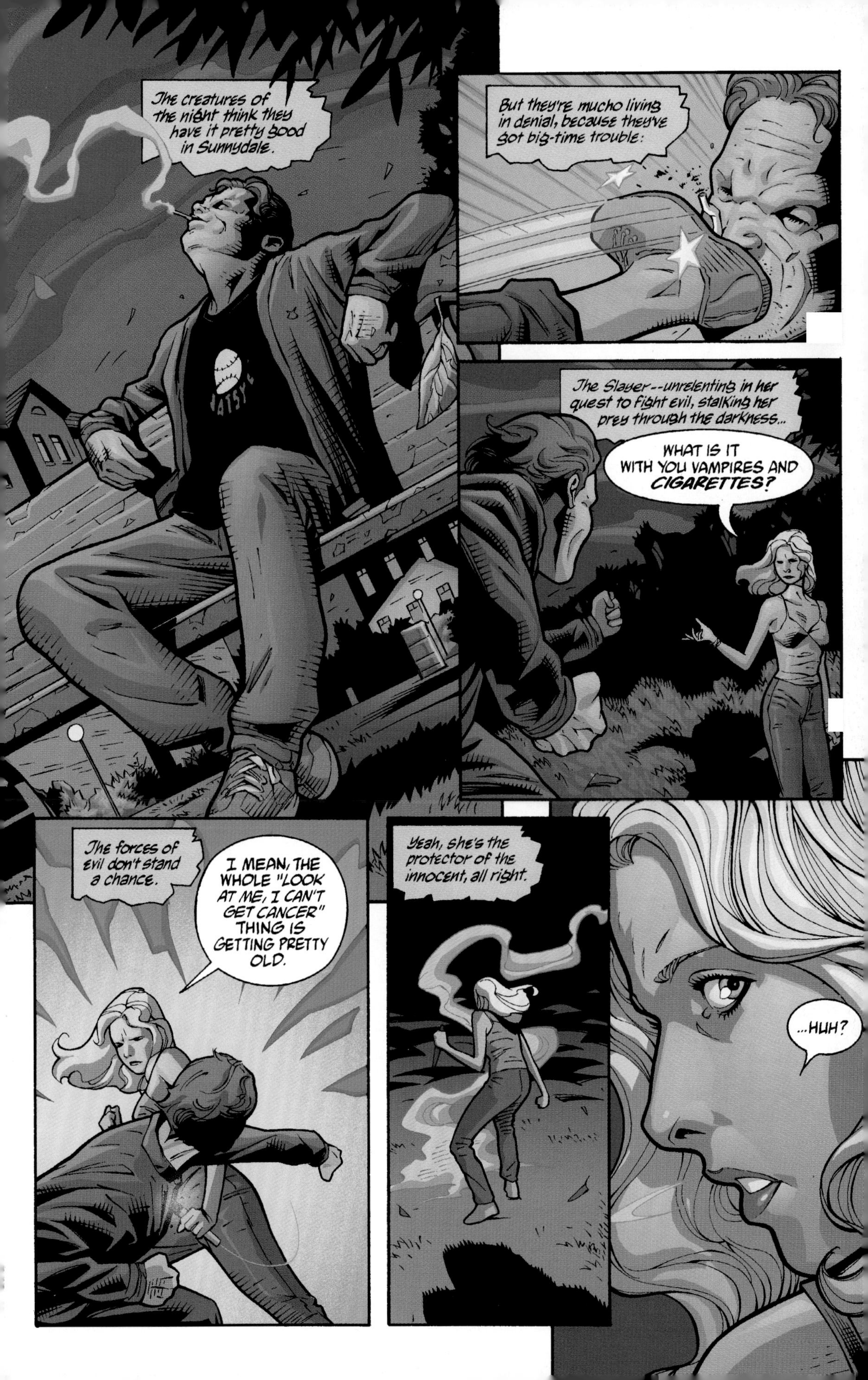

The creatures of the night think they have it pretty good in Sunnydale.
But they're mucho living in denial, because they've got big-time trouble:
The Slayer--unrelenting in her quest to fight evil, stalking her prey through the darkness...
WHAT IS IT WITH YOU VAMPIRES AND CIGARETTES?
The forces of evil don't stand a chance.
I MEAN, THE WHOLE "LOOK AT ME, I CAN'T GET CANCER" THING IS GETTING PRETTY OLD.
Yeah, she's the protector of the innocent, all right.
...HUH?

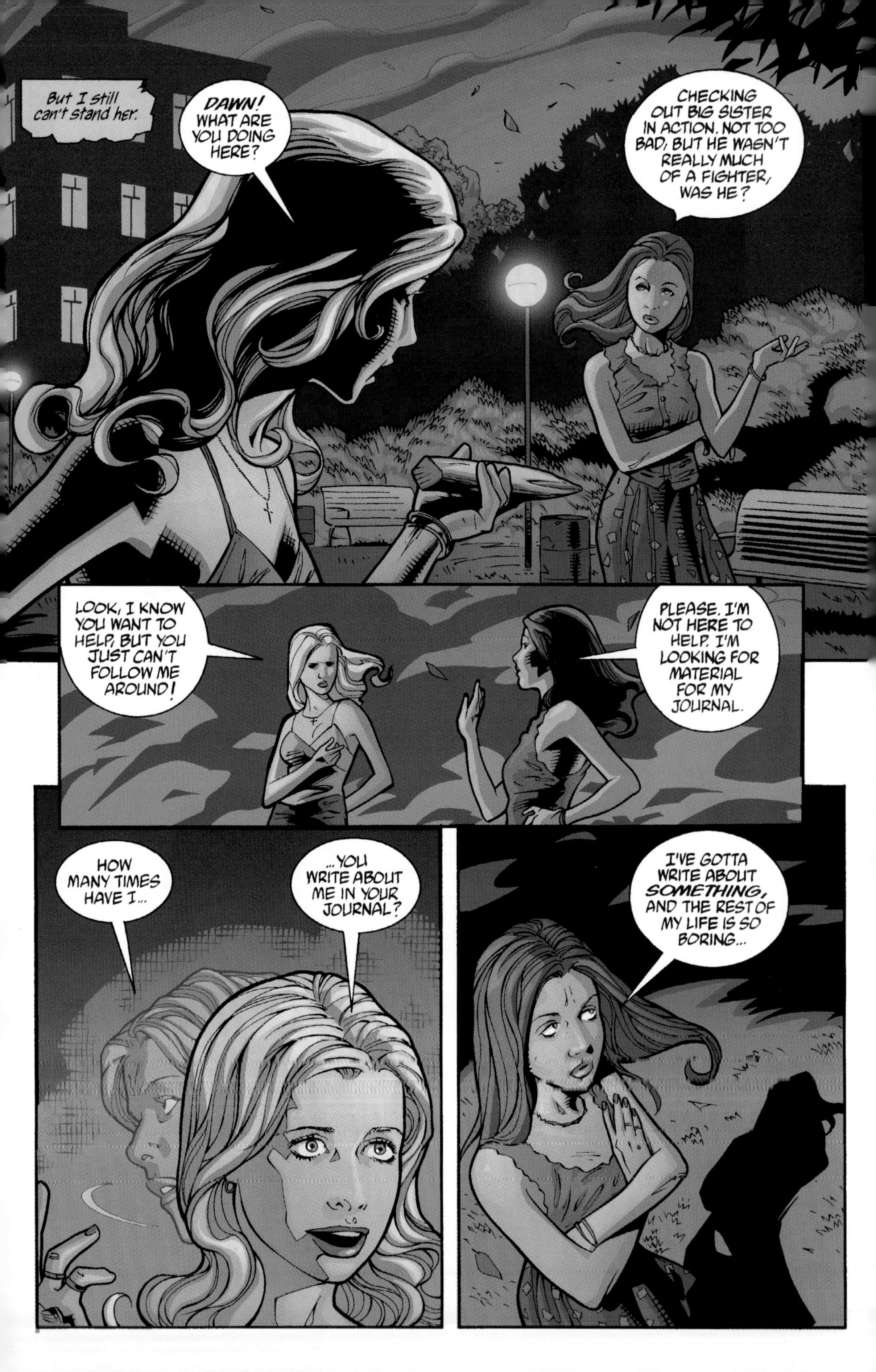

But I still can't stand her.
DAWN! WHAT ARE YOU DOING HERE?
CHECKING OUT BIG SISTER IN ACTION. NOT TOO BAD, BUT HE WASN'T REALLY MUCH OF A FIGHTER, WAS HE?
LOOK, I KNOW YOU WANT TO HELP, BUT YOU JUST CAN'T FOLLOW ME AROUND!
PLEASE. I'M NOT HERE TO HELP. I'M LOOKING FOR MATERIAL FOR MY JOURNAL.
HOW MANY TIMES HAVE I...
...YOU WRITE ABOUT ME IN YOUR JOURNAL?
I'VE GOTTA WRITE ABOUT SOMETHING, AND THE REST OF MY LIFE IS SO BORING...

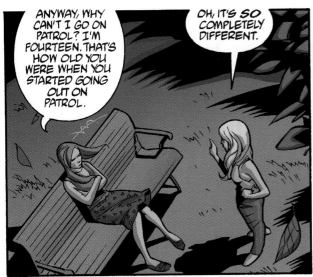

ANYWAY, WHY CAN'T I GO ON PATROL? I'M FOURTEEN. THAT'S HOW OLD YOU WERE WHEN YOU STARTED GOING OUT ON PATROL.

OH, IT'S *SO* COMPLETELY DIFFERENT.

HOW?

I'M THE *SLAYER.* YOU KNOW, SUPER STRENGTH, DAMAGE RESISTANCE.

RILEY DIDN'T HAVE SUPER-STRENGTH --AND HE SURE WASN'T DAMAGE RESISTANT. BESIDES, NOW THAT HE'S GONE, YOU'LL NEED SOMEONE TO WATCH YOUR BACK.

RILEY HAD MILITARY TRAINING, YOU DON'T. AND I DO *NOT* NEED SOMEONE TO WATCH MY BACK.

BUT RILEY ALWAYS TOLD ME HOW WORRIED HE GOT WHEN YOU WENT ON PATROL, AND NOW THAT HE'S GONE--

CAN WE *NOT* TALK ABOUT RILEY? COME ON, I'VE GOTTA GET YOU HOME BEFORE MOM FINDS OUT YOU'RE OUT HERE WANDERING AROUND. SHE'LL KILL ME.

SAY, NOW THAT CAMPUS IS CLEAR, THINK WE CAN MAKE A QUICK SWEEP THROUGH THE CEMETERY?

ABSOLUTELY NOT. NOW MOVE IT.

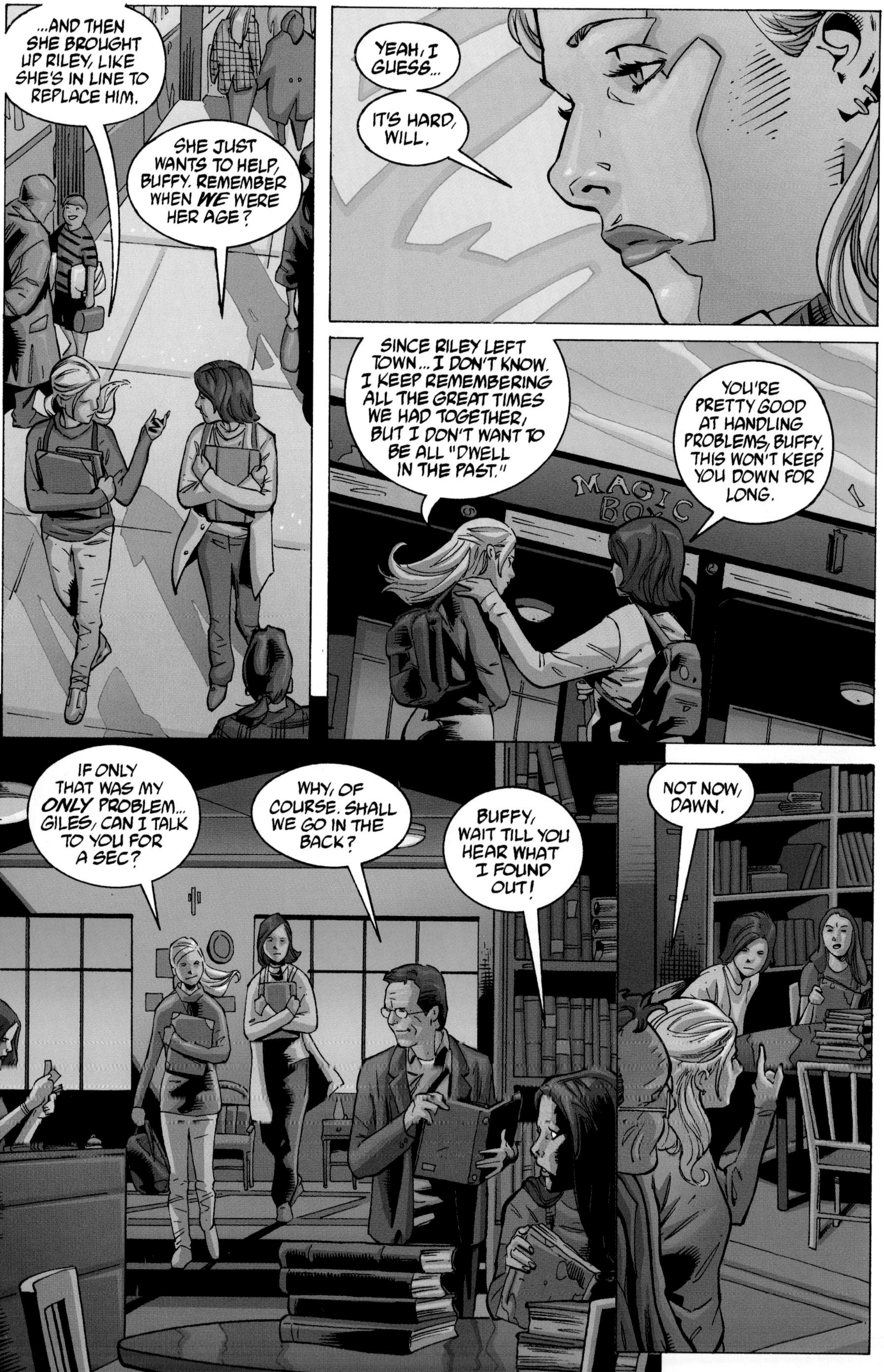
...AND THEN SHE BROUGHT UP RILEY, LIKE SHE'S IN LINE TO REPLACE HIM.
SHE JUST WANTS TO HELP, BUFFY. REMEMBER WHEN WE WERE HER AGE?
YEAH, I GUESS...
IT'S HARD, WILL.
SINCE RILEY LEFT TOWN... I DON'T KNOW. I KEEP REMEMBERING ALL THE GREAT TIMES WE HAD TOGETHER, BUT I DON'T WANT TO BE ALL "DWELL IN THE PAST."
YOU'RE PRETTY GOOD AT HANDLING PROBLEMS, BUFFY. THIS WON'T KEEP YOU DOWN FOR LONG.
MAGIC BOX
IF ONLY THAT WAS MY ONLY PROBLEM... GILES, CAN I TALK TO YOU FOR A SEC?
WHY, OF COURSE. SHALL WE GO IN THE BACK?
BUFFY, WAIT TILL YOU HEAR WHAT I FOUND OUT!
NOT NOW, DAWN.

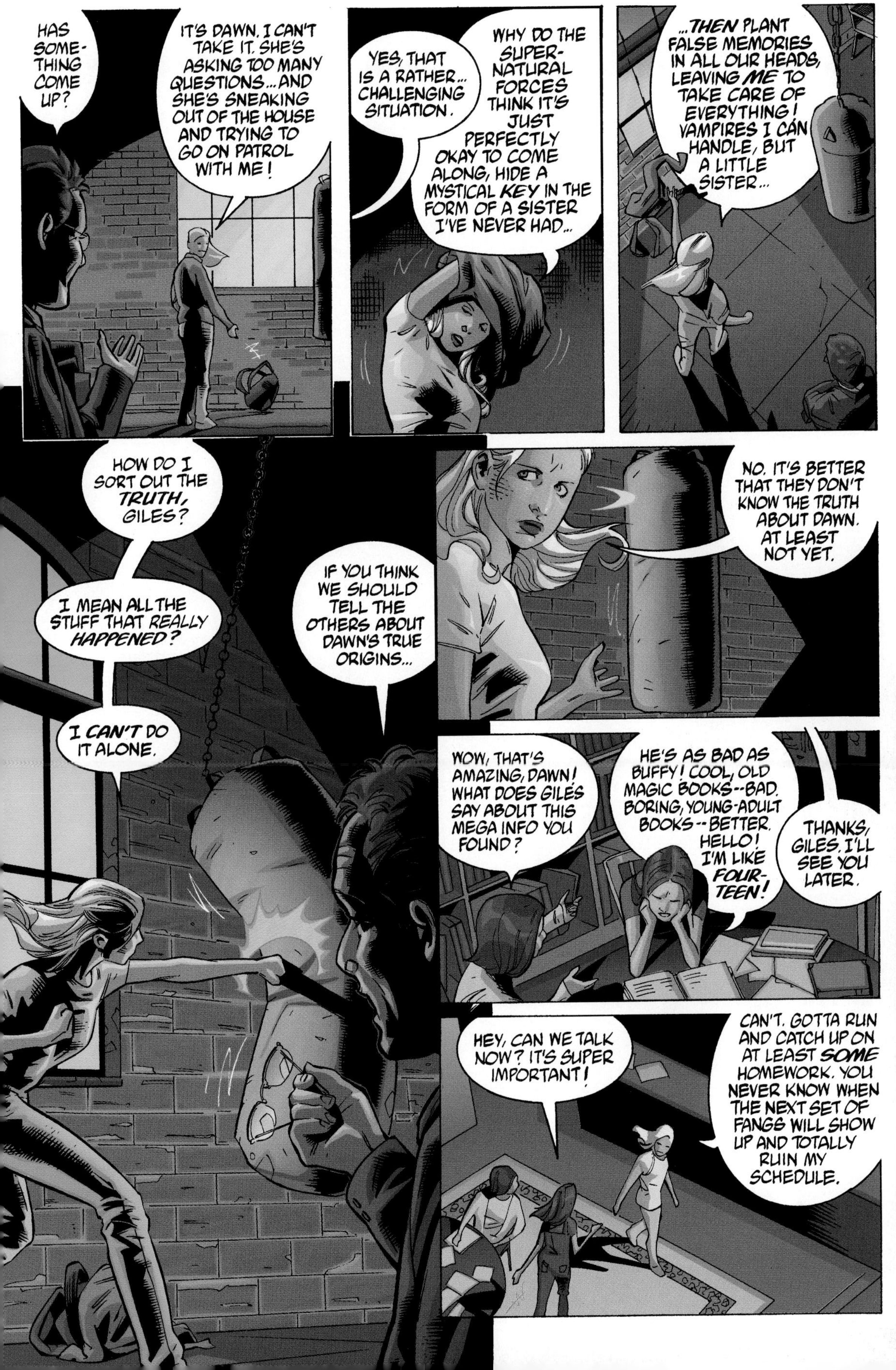
HAS SOMETHING COME UP?
IT'S DAWN. I CAN'T TAKE IT. SHE'S ASKING TOO MANY QUESTIONS... AND SHE'S SNEAKING OUT OF THE HOUSE AND TRYING TO GO ON PATROL WITH ME!
YES, THAT IS A RATHER... CHALLENGING SITUATION.
WHY DO THE SUPER-NATURAL FORCES THINK IT'S JUST PERFECTLY OKAY TO COME ALONG, HIDE A MYSTICAL KEY IN THE FORM OF A SISTER I'VE NEVER HAD...
...THEN PLANT FALSE MEMORIES IN ALL OUR HEADS, LEAVING ME TO TAKE CARE OF EVERYTHING! VAMPIRES I CAN HANDLE, BUT A LITTLE SISTER...
HOW DO I SORT OUT THE TRUTH, GILES?
I MEAN ALL THE STUFF THAT REALLY HAPPENED?
I CAN'T DO IT ALONE.
IF YOU THINK WE SHOULD TELL THE OTHERS ABOUT DAWN'S TRUE ORIGINS...
NO. IT'S BETTER THAT THEY DON'T KNOW THE TRUTH ABOUT DAWN. AT LEAST NOT YET.
WOW, THAT'S AMAZING, DAWN! WHAT DOES GILES SAY ABOUT THIS MEGA INFO YOU FOUND?
HE'S AS BAD AS BUFFY! COOL, OLD MAGIC BOOKS--BAD. BORING, YOUNG-ADULT BOOKS--BETTER. HELLO! I'M LIKE FOURTEEN!
THANKS, GILES. I'LL SEE YOU LATER.
HEY, CAN WE TALK NOW? IT'S SUPER IMPORTANT!
CAN'T. GOTTA RUN AND CATCH UP ON AT LEAST SOME HOMEWORK. YOU NEVER KNOW WHEN THE NEXT SET OF FANGS WILL SHOW UP AND TOTALLY RUIN MY SCHEDULE.

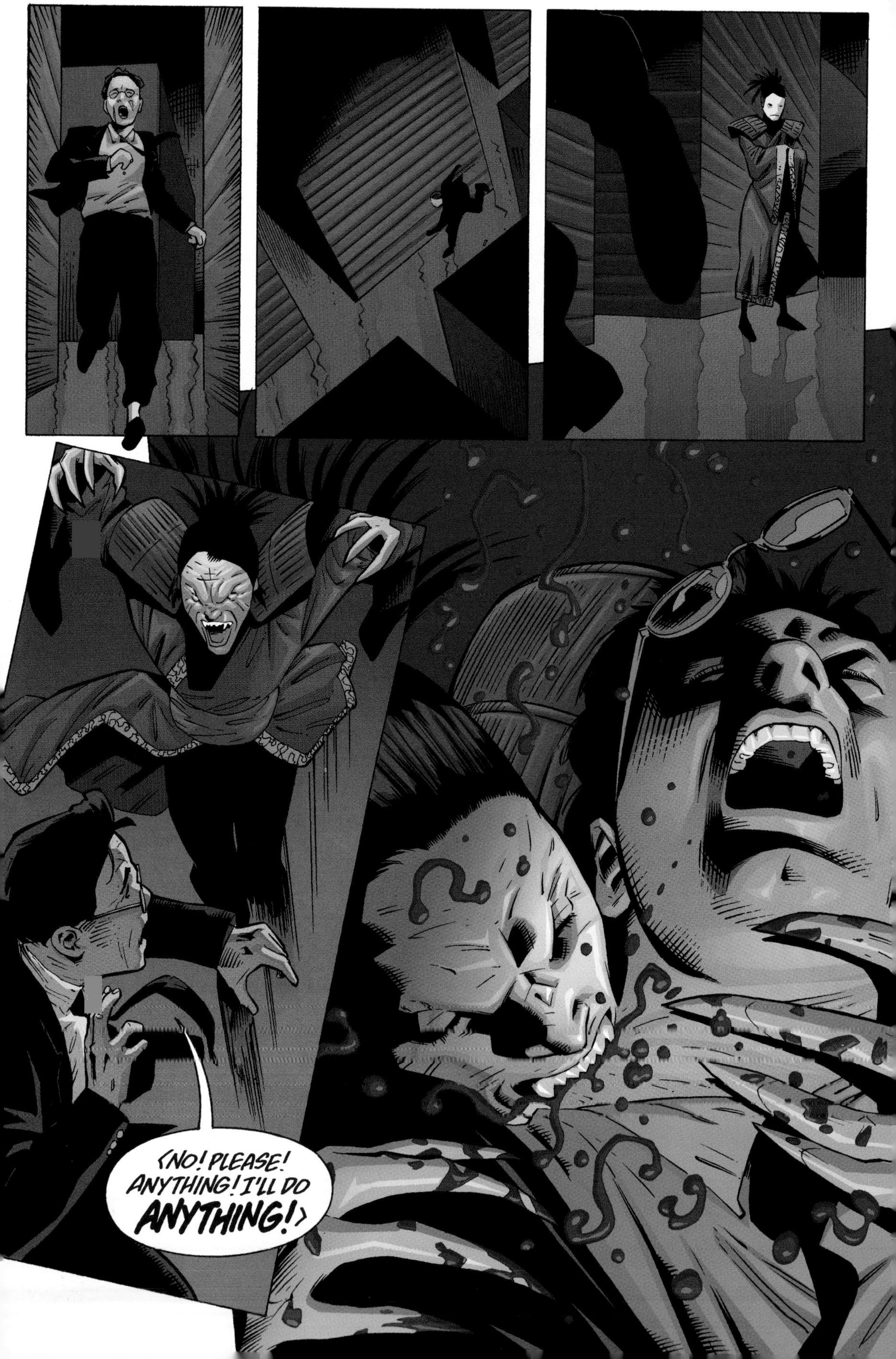
<NO! PLEASE! ANYTHING! I'LL DO ANYTHING!>

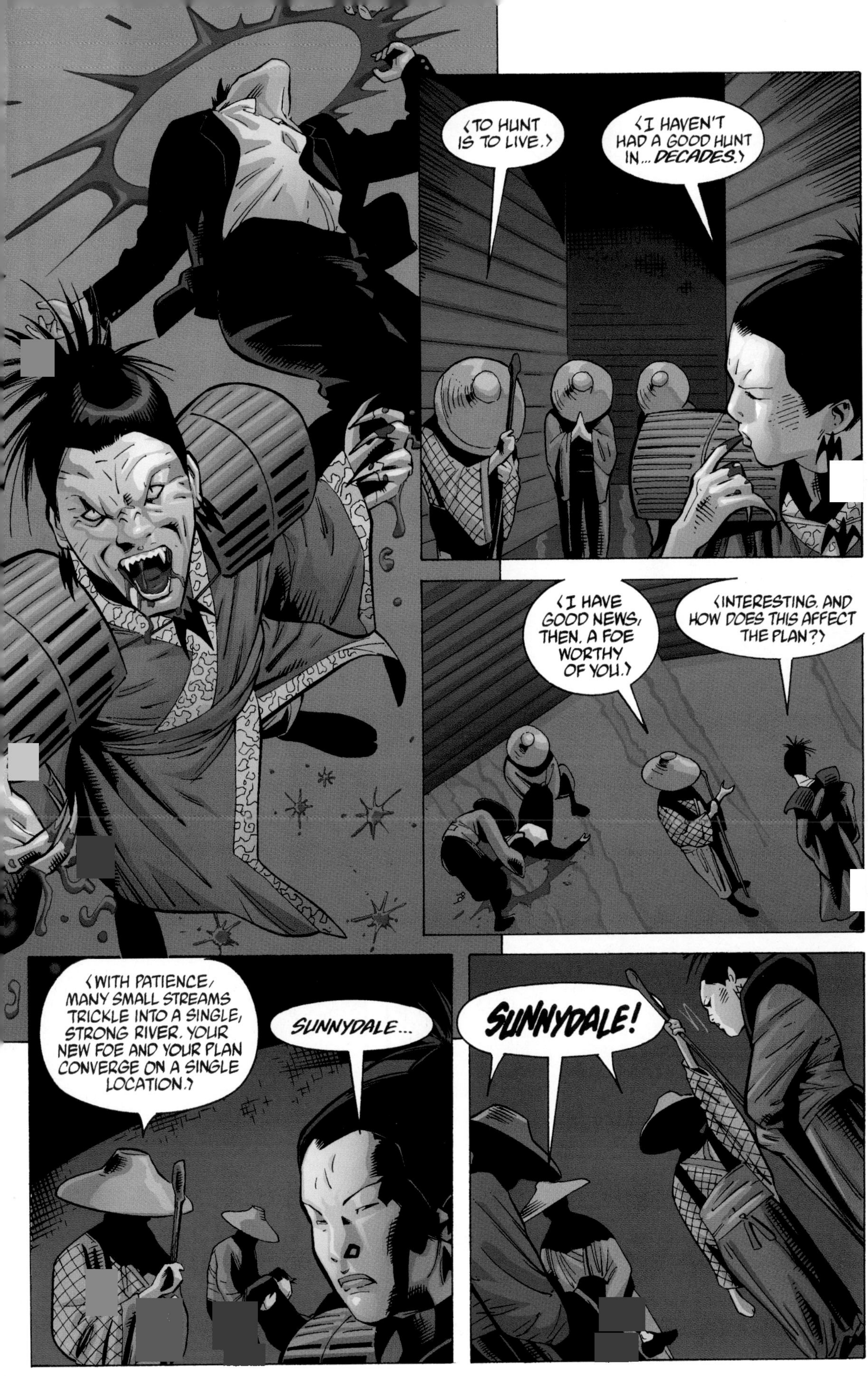
‹TO HUNT IS TO LIVE.›
‹I HAVEN'T HAD A GOOD HUNT IN... *DECADES.*›
‹I HAVE GOOD NEWS, THEN. A FOE WORTHY OF YOU.›
‹INTERESTING. AND HOW DOES THIS AFFECT THE PLAN?›
‹WITH PATIENCE, MANY SMALL STREAMS TRICKLE INTO A SINGLE, STRONG RIVER. YOUR NEW FOE AND YOUR PLAN CONVERGE ON A SINGLE LOCATION.›
SUNNYDALE...
SUNNYDALE!

BUFFY? ARE YOU BUSY?

VERY BUSY. OVERWHELMINGLY BUSY. DON'T YOU HAVE HOME-WORK?

ALL DONE. DON'T YOU HAVE PATROL?

NOT TONIGHT. IT'S BEEN PRETTY QUIET LATELY, SO I THOUGHT I'D CATCH UP ON MY SLEEP.

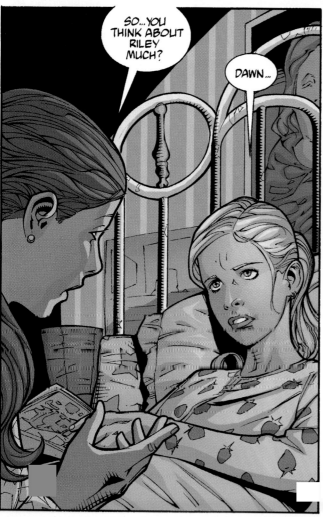

SO...YOU THINK ABOUT RILEY MUCH?

DAWN...

...YES. I THINK ABOUT HIM A LOT.

HE WAS REALLY NICE, HUH? I MEAN, REMEMBER WHEN YOU FIRST STARTED GOING OUT, WHEN WE ALL WENT TO THE PARK AND RODE THE CAROUSEL?

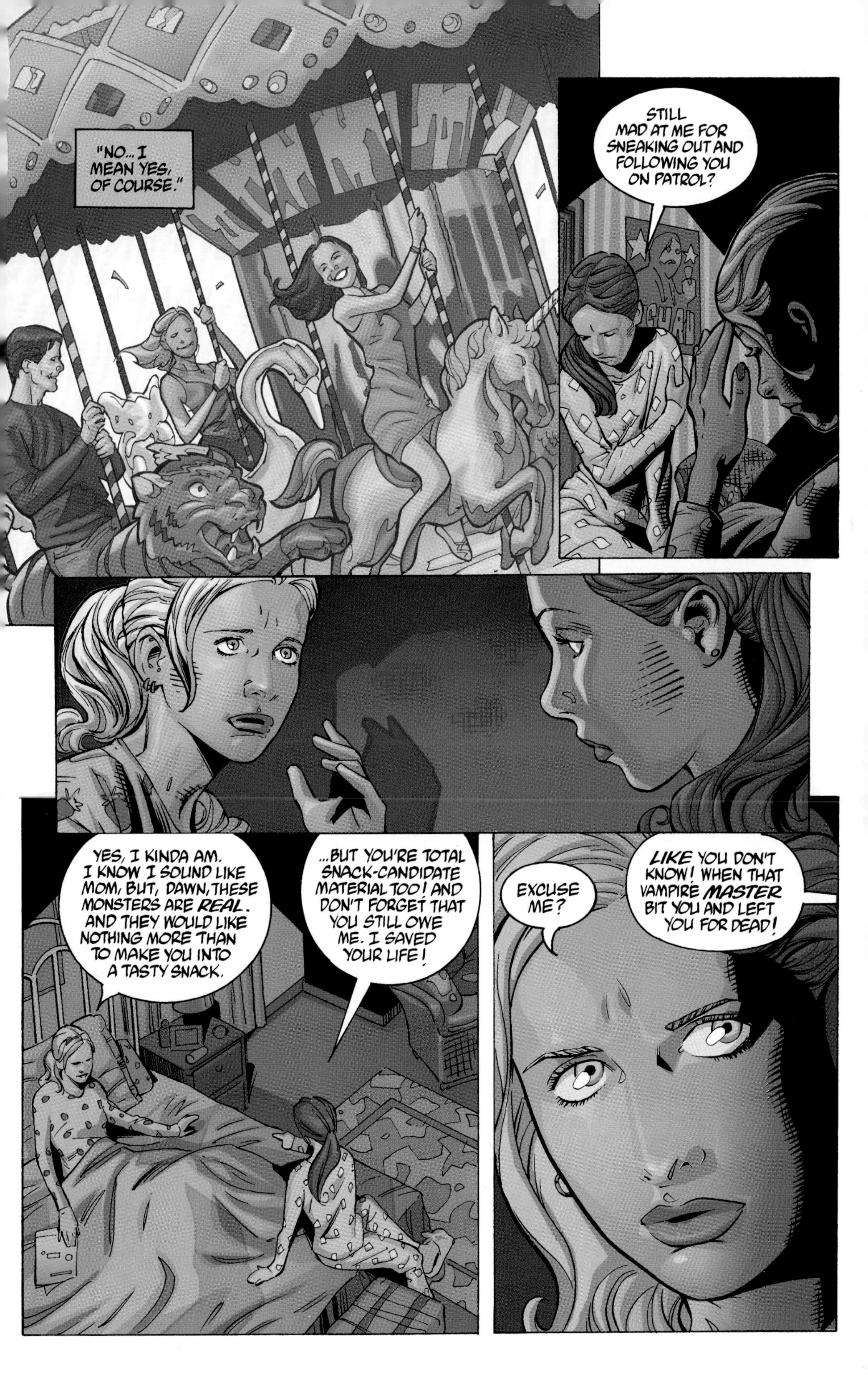
"NO... I MEAN YES, OF COURSE."
STILL MAD AT ME FOR SNEAKING OUT AND FOLLOWING YOU ON PATROL?
YES, I KINDA AM. I KNOW I SOUND LIKE MOM, BUT, DAWN, THESE MONSTERS ARE *REAL*. AND THEY WOULD LIKE NOTHING MORE THAN TO MAKE YOU INTO A TASTY SNACK.
...BUT YOU'RE TOTAL SNACK-CANDIDATE MATERIAL TOO! AND DON'T FORGET THAT YOU STILL OWE ME. I SAVED YOUR LIFE!
EXCUSE ME?
LIKE YOU DON'T KNOW! WHEN THAT VAMPIRE *MASTER* BIT YOU AND LEFT YOU FOR DEAD!

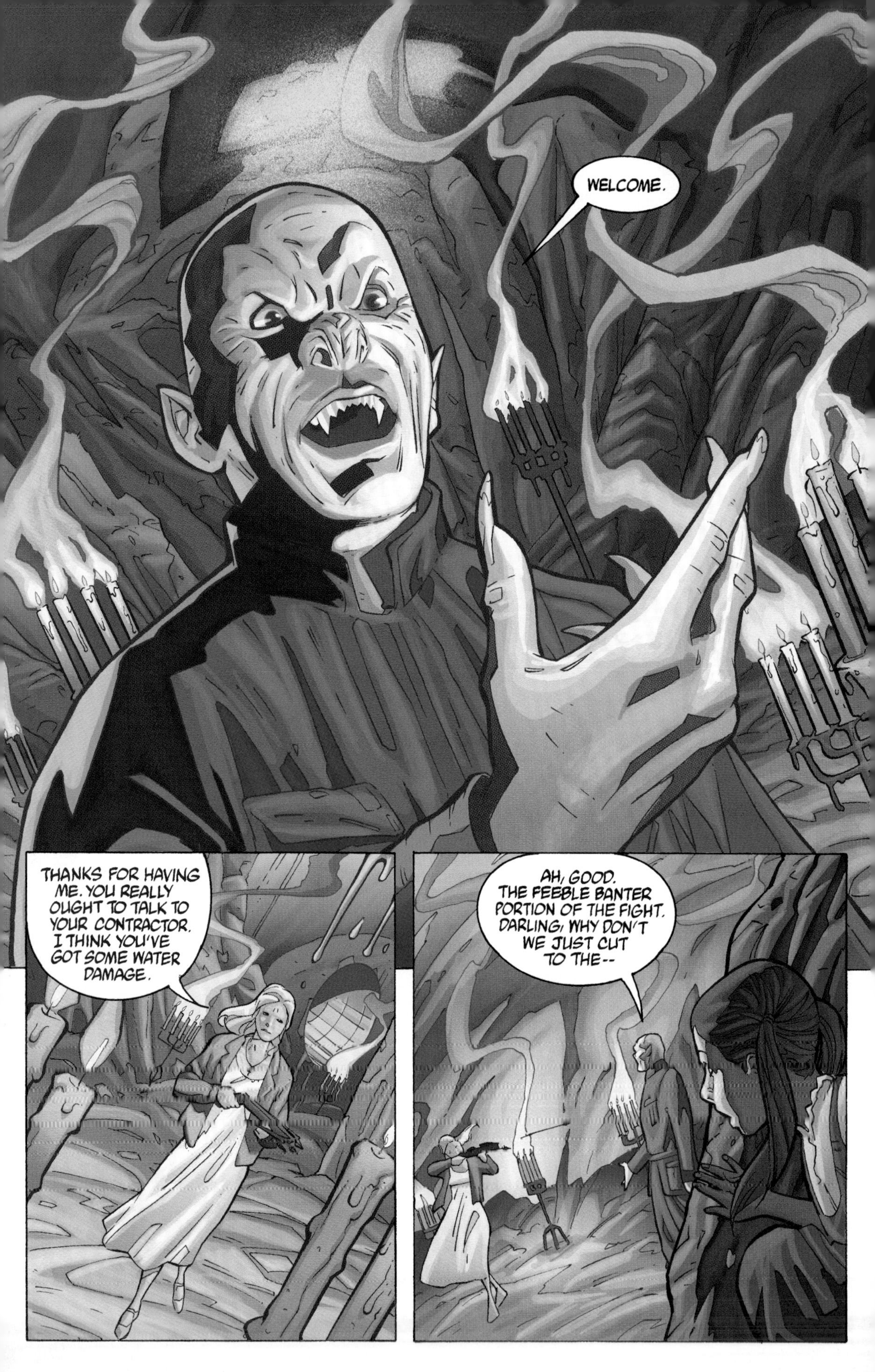
WELCOME.
THANKS FOR HAVING ME. YOU REALLY OUGHT TO TALK TO YOUR CONTRACTOR. I THINK YOU'VE GOT SOME WATER DAMAGE.
AH, GOOD. THE FEEBLE BANTER PORTION OF THE FIGHT. DARLING, WHY DON'T WE JUST CUT TO THE--

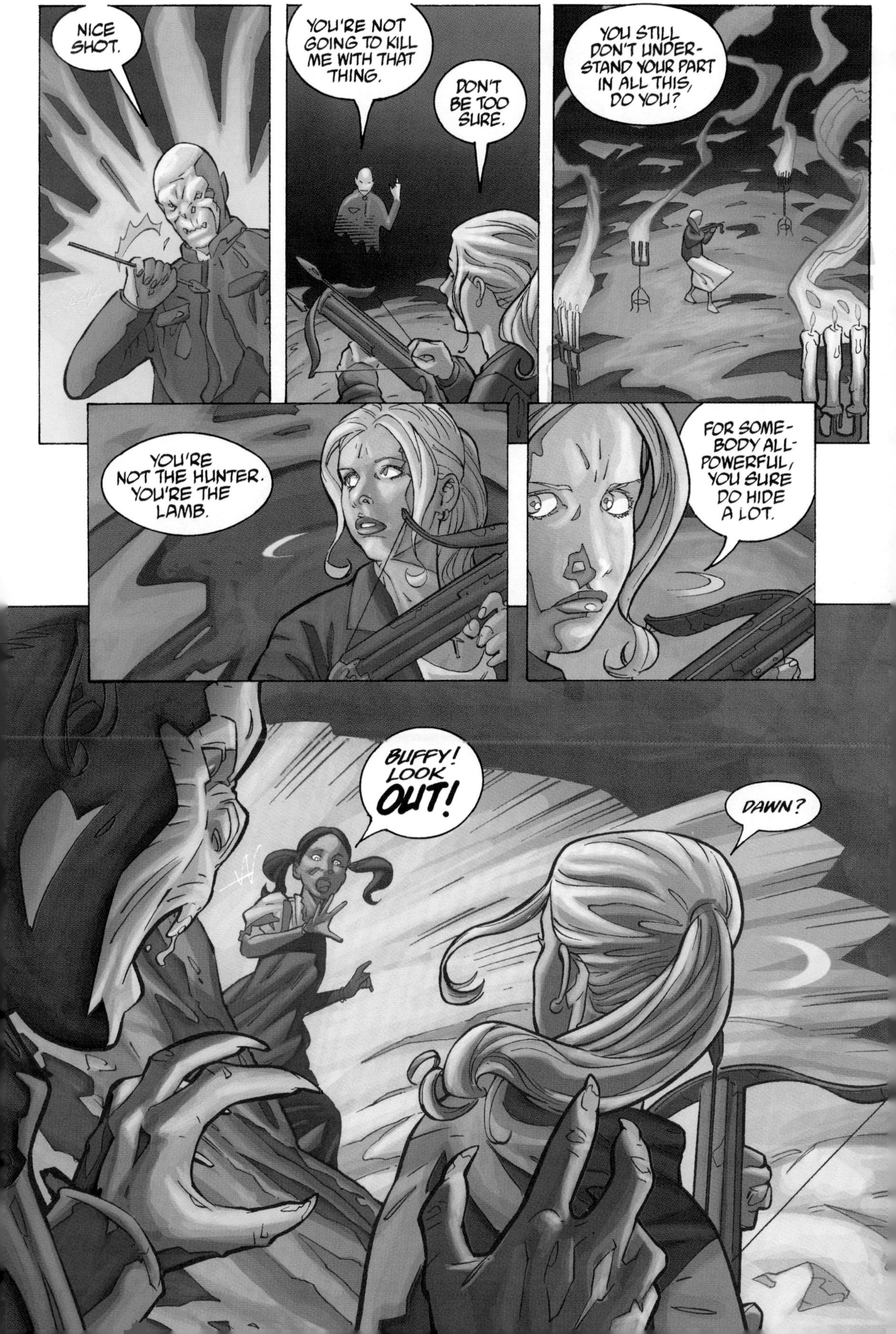
NICE SHOT.
YOU'RE NOT GOING TO KILL ME WITH THAT THING.
DON'T BE TOO SURE.
YOU STILL DON'T UNDER-STAND YOUR PART IN ALL THIS, DO YOU?
YOU'RE NOT THE HUNTER. YOU'RE THE LAMB.
FOR SOME-BODY ALL-POWERFUL, YOU SURE DO HIDE A LOT.
BUFFY! LOOK OUT!
DAWN?

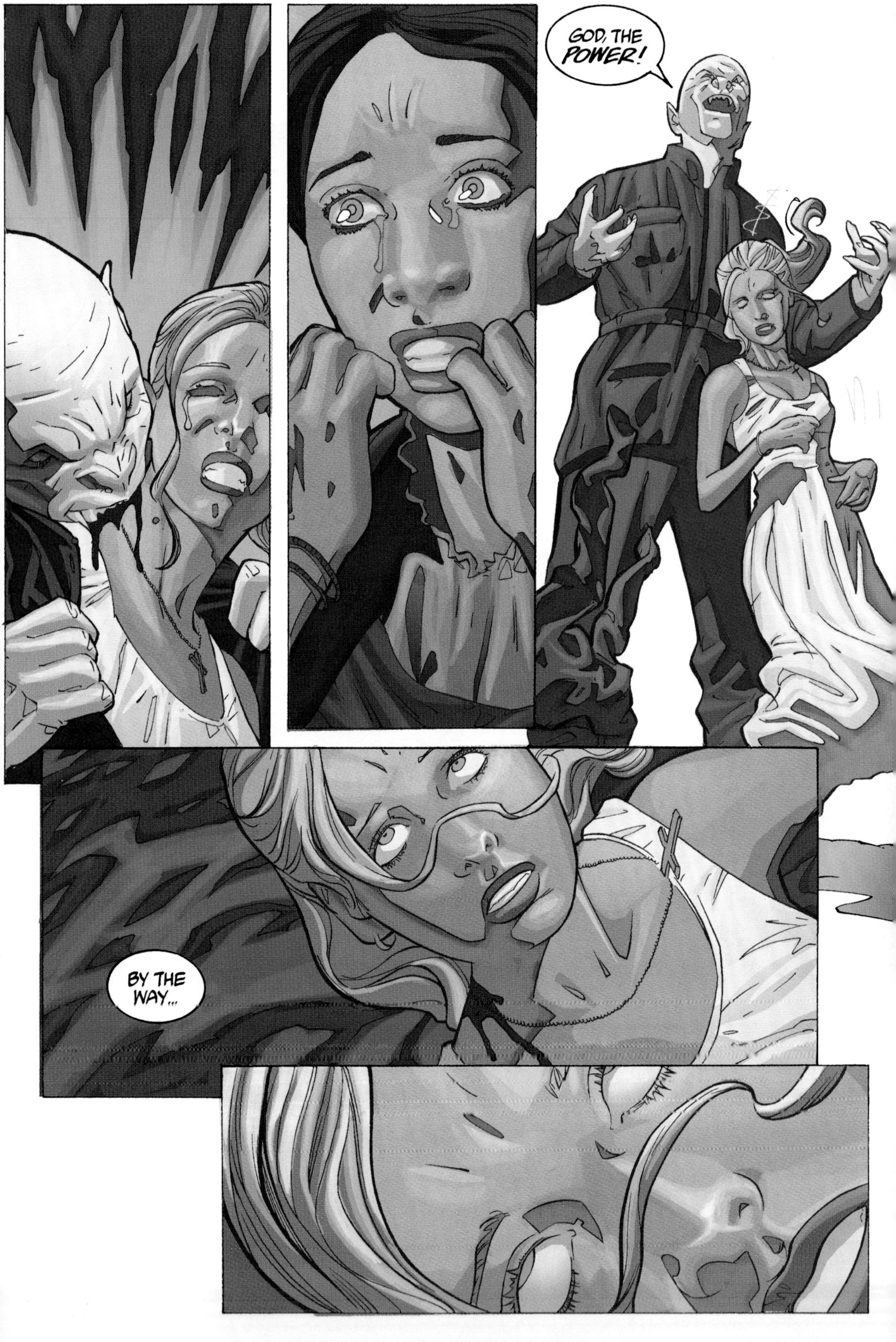
GOD, THE POWER!
BY THE WAY...

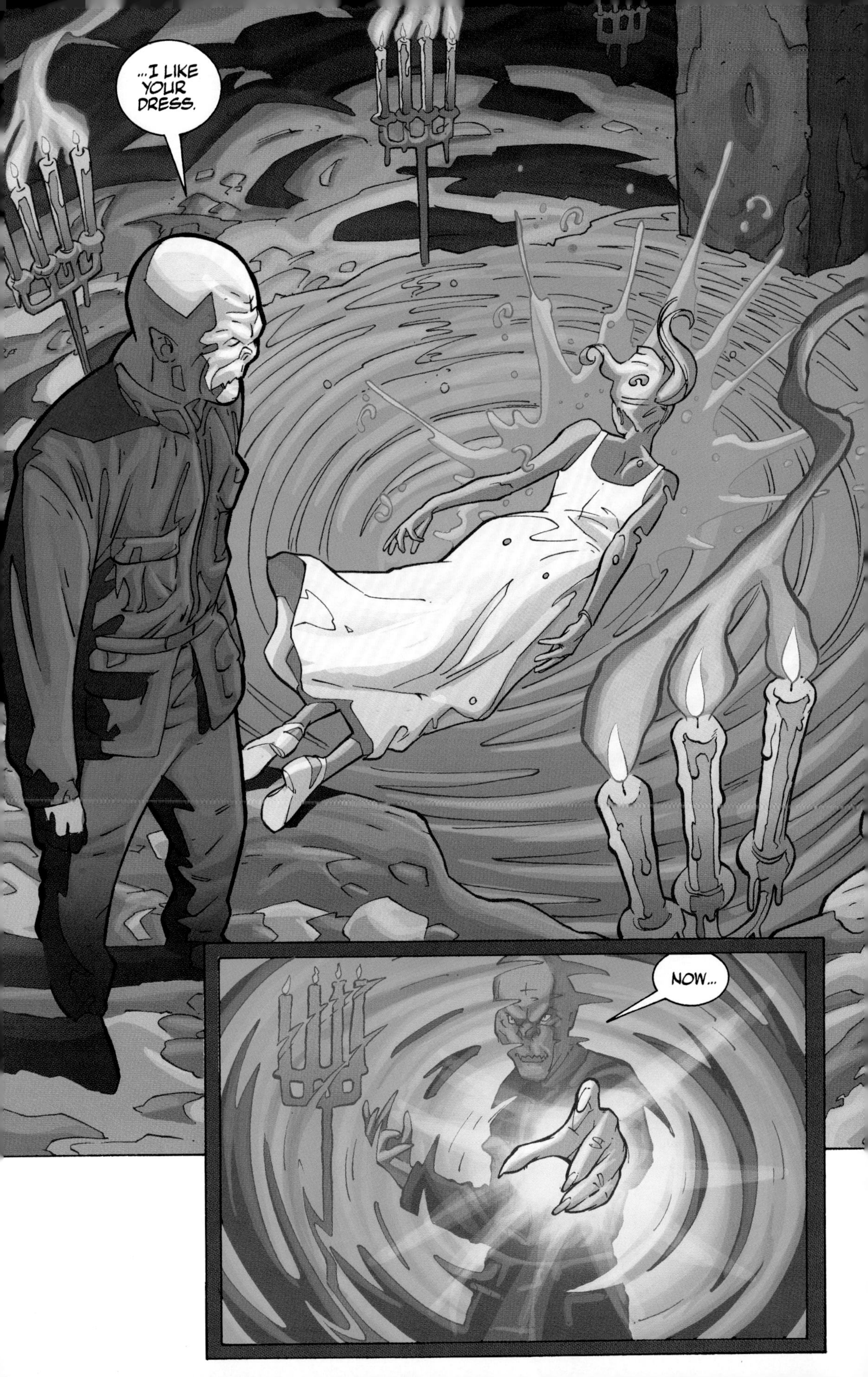
...I LIKE YOUR DRESS.
NOW...

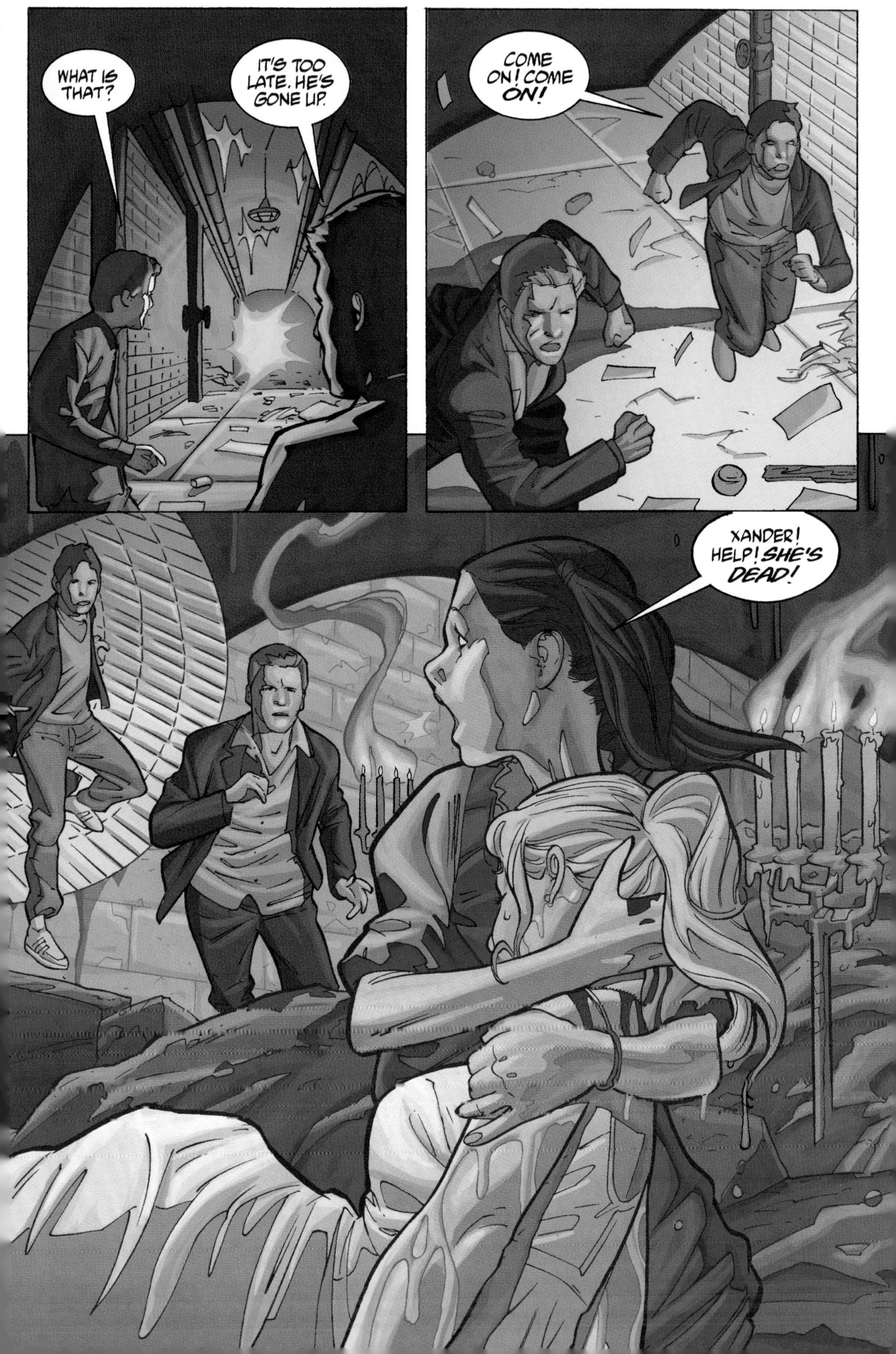
WHAT IS THAT?
IT'S TOO LATE. HE'S GONE UP.
COME ON! COME ON!
XANDER! HELP! SHE'S DEAD!

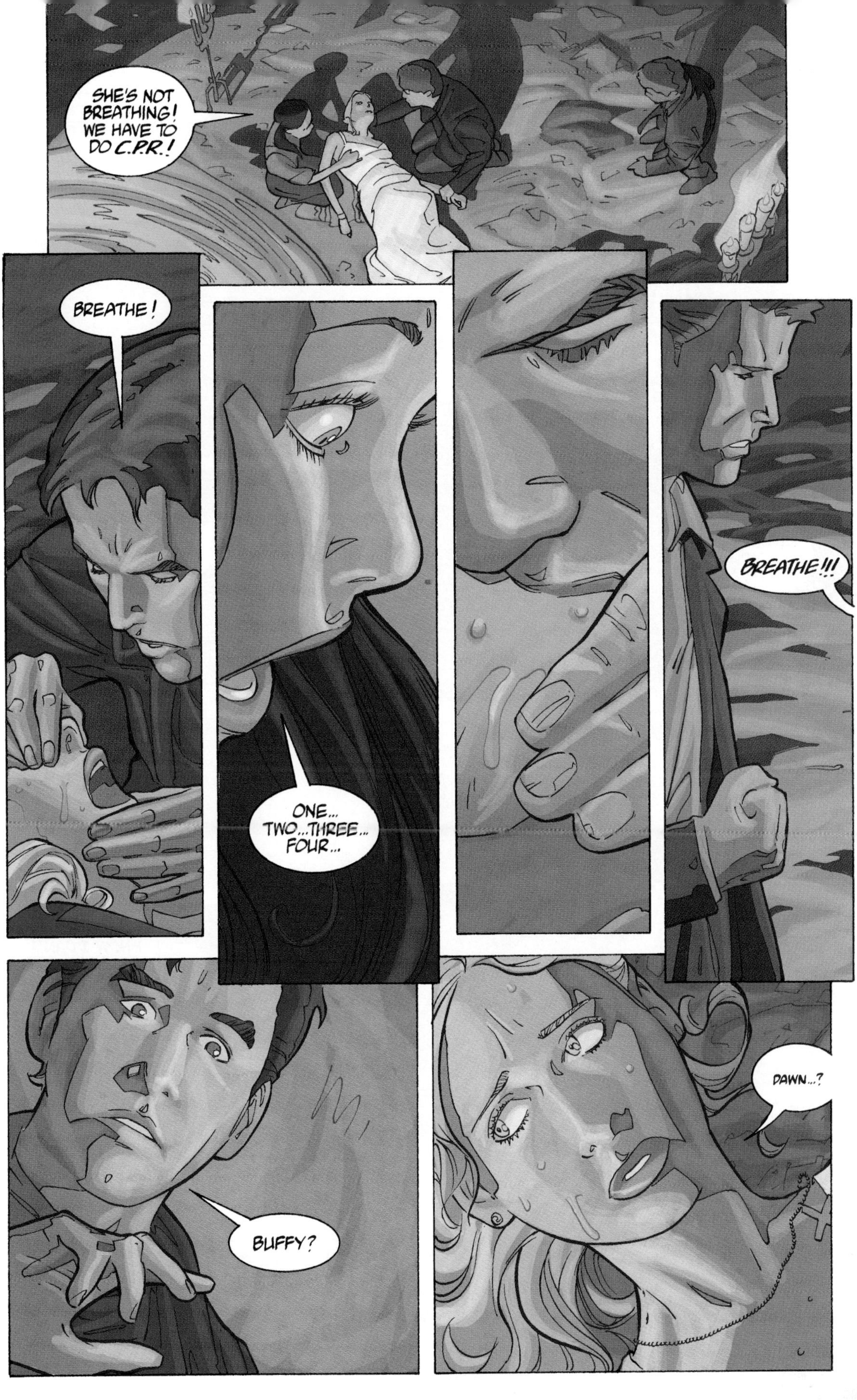
SHE'S NOT BREATHING! WE HAVE TO DO C.P.R.!
BREATHE!
ONE... TWO...THREE... FOUR...
BREATHE!!!
BUFFY?
DAWN...?

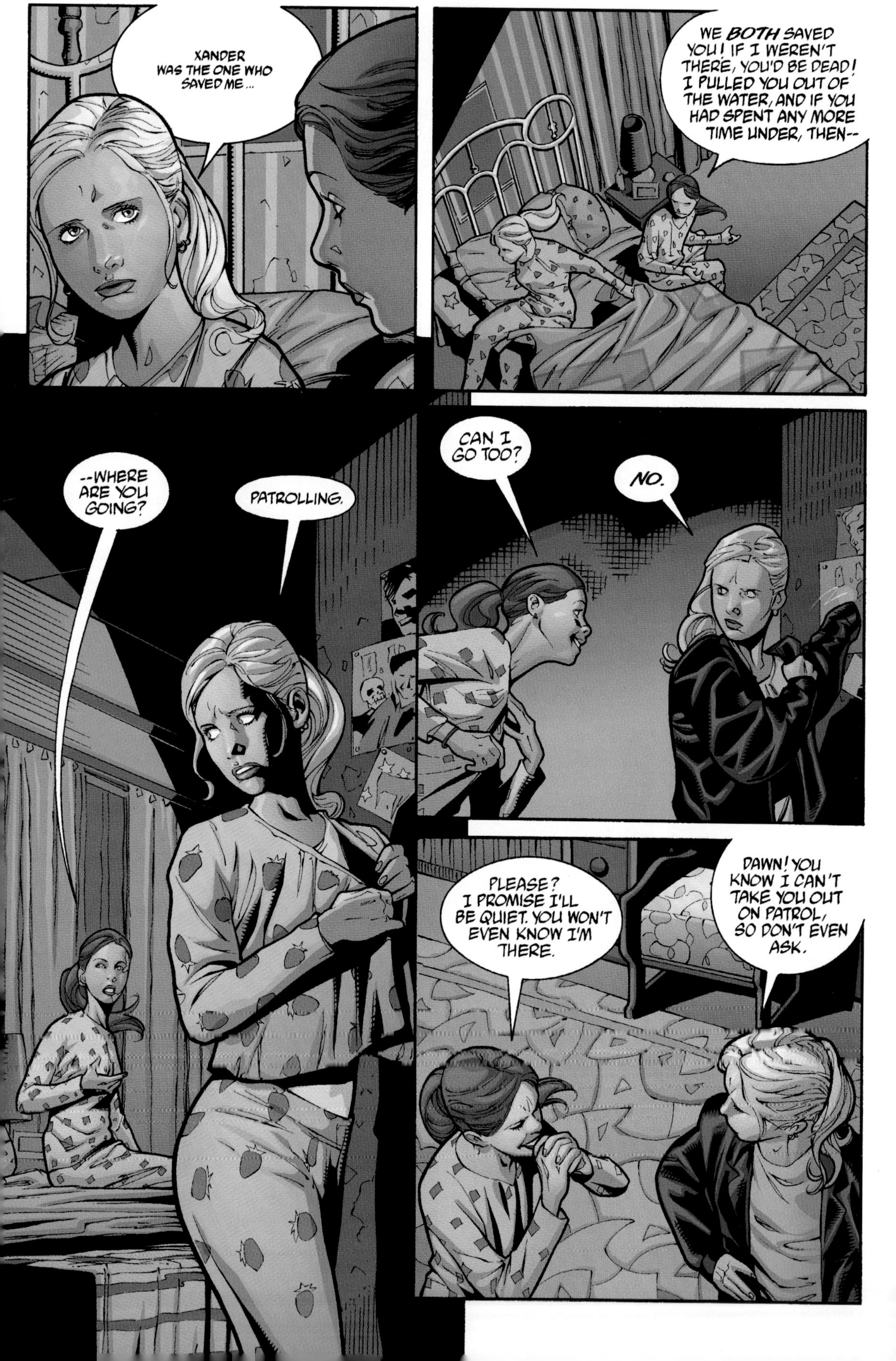
XANDER WAS THE ONE WHO SAVED ME...
WE *BOTH* SAVED YOU! IF I WEREN'T THERE, YOU'D BE DEAD! I PULLED YOU OUT OF THE WATER, AND IF YOU HAD SPENT ANY MORE TIME UNDER, THEN--
--WHERE ARE YOU GOING?
PATROLLING.
CAN I GO TOO?
NO.
PLEASE? I PROMISE I'LL BE QUIET. YOU WON'T EVEN KNOW I'M THERE.
DAWN! YOU KNOW I CAN'T TAKE YOU OUT ON PATROL, SO DON'T EVEN ASK.

IF I TELL YOU A SECRET WILL YOU LET ME COME?

NO.

CAN I POSSIBLY BE OUT OF STAKES?

YOU NEVER LISTEN TO ME. YOU DON'T CARE! NO ONE DOES!

I'M SORRY. I'VE HAD A LOT ON MY MIND, AND I HAVEN'T BEEN THE BEST LISTENER LATELY.

YOU'VE NEVER BEEN A GOOD LISTENER. NOT TO ME, ANYWAY.

I'M LISTENING NOW.

WHAT IF I DON'T WANT TO TELL YOU ANYMORE?

PAREN
ADV

COME ON, DAWN, I'M TRYING.

OKAY. WHEN I WAS READING TODAY, IN THE SHOP, I FOUND THIS BIG SLAYER TIMELINE IN ONE OF THE BOOKS. PRETTY COOL. BUT I SAW THIS ONE TIME, LIKE TWO HUNDRED YEARS AGO--NO SLAYER.

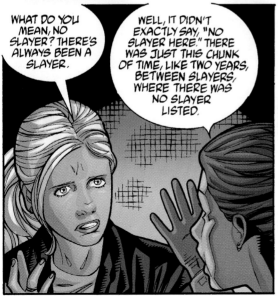

WHAT DO YOU MEAN, NO SLAYER? THERE'S ALWAYS BEEN A SLAYER.

WELL, IT DIDN'T EXACTLY SAY, "NO SLAYER HERE." THERE WAS JUST THIS CHUNK OF TIME, LIKE TWO YEARS, BETWEEN SLAYERS, WHERE THERE WAS NO SLAYER LISTED.

THERE'S GOT TO BE SOME SORT OF EXPLANATION. I'LL CHECK WITH GILES IN THE MORNING.

WHY DON'T YOU LET ME--

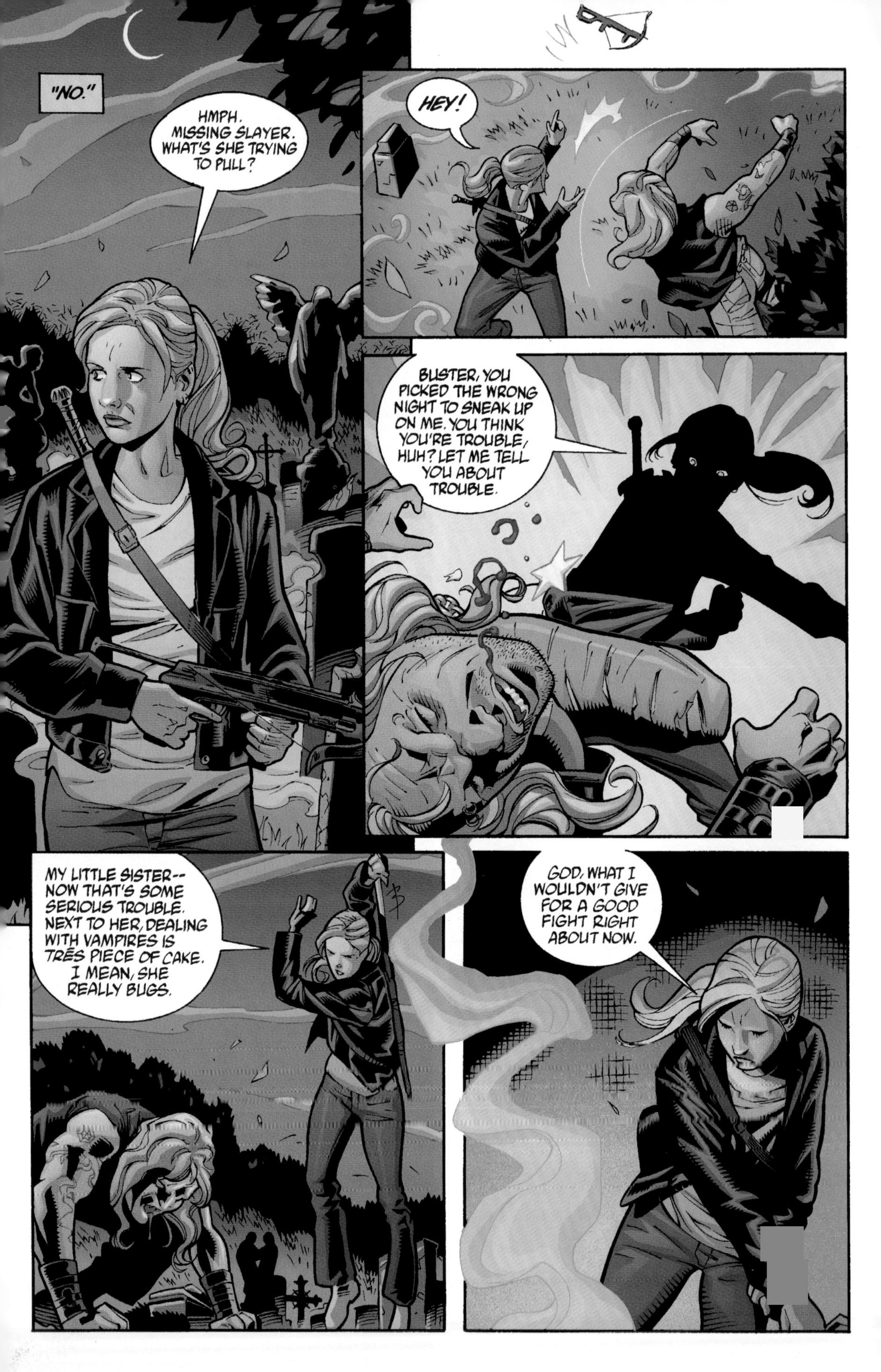
"NO."
HMPH. MISSING SLAYER. WHAT'S SHE TRYING TO PULL?
HEY!
BUSTER, YOU PICKED THE WRONG NIGHT TO SNEAK UP ON ME. YOU THINK YOU'RE TROUBLE, HUH? LET ME TELL YOU ABOUT TROUBLE.
MY LITTLE SISTER-- NOW THAT'S SOME SERIOUS TROUBLE. NEXT TO HER, DEALING WITH VAMPIRES IS TRÈS PIECE OF CAKE. I MEAN, SHE REALLY BUGS.
GOD, WHAT I WOULDN'T GIVE FOR A GOOD FIGHT RIGHT ABOUT NOW.

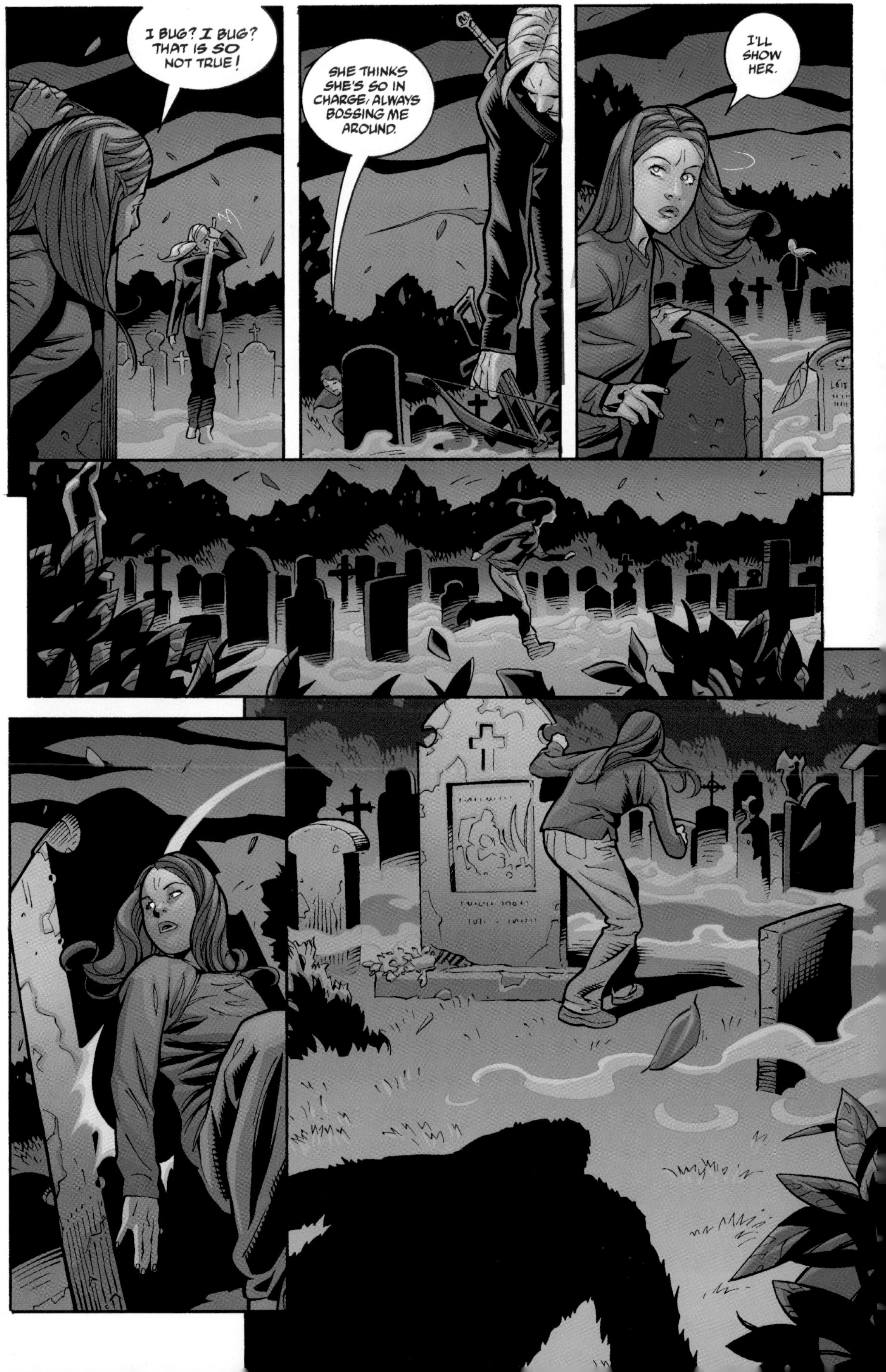
I BUG? I BUG? THAT IS SO NOT TRUE!
SHE THINKS SHE'S SO IN CHARGE, ALWAYS BOSSING ME AROUND.
I'LL SHOW HER.

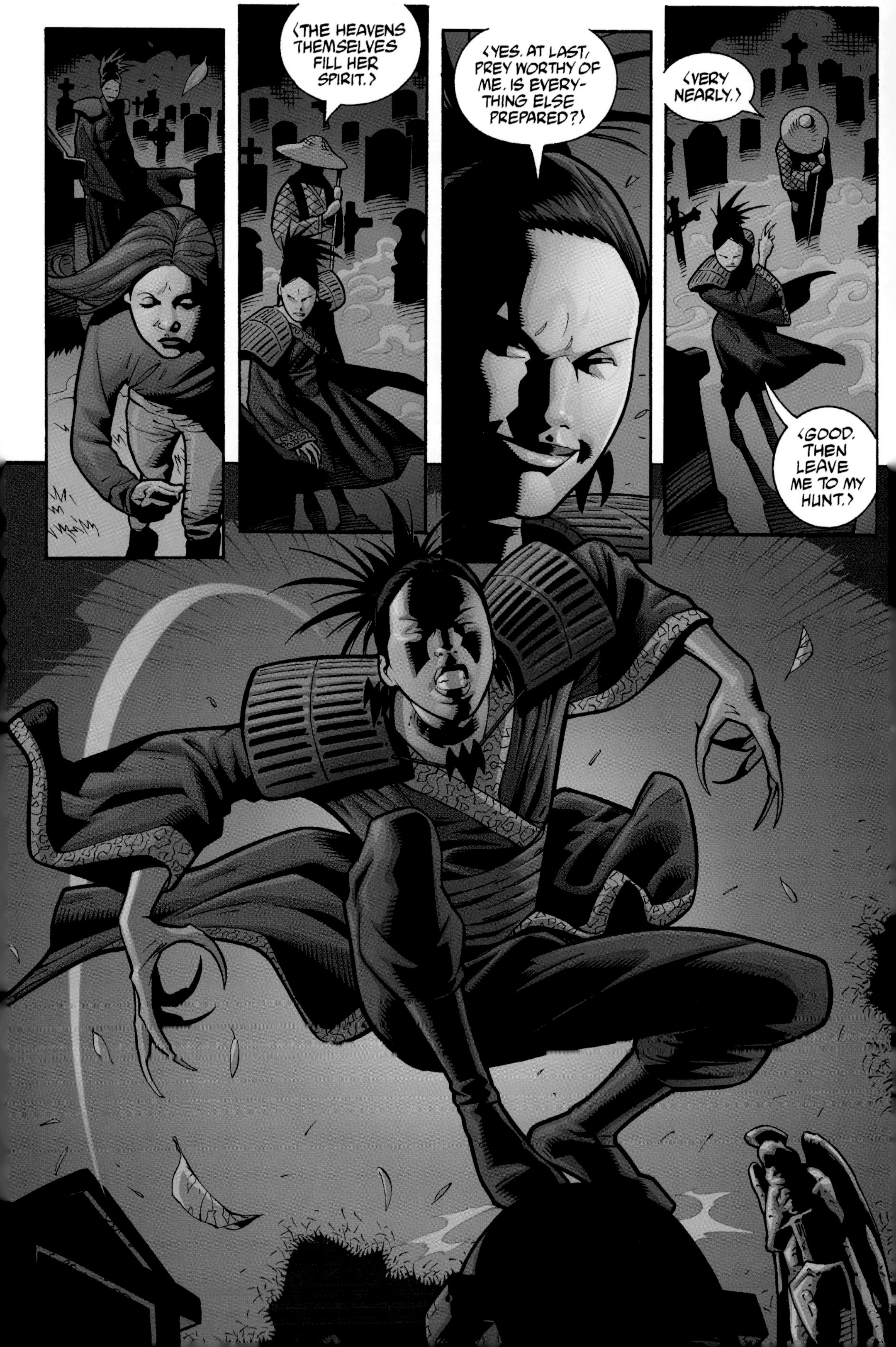

‹THE HEAVENS THEMSELVES FILL HER SPIRIT.›
‹YES. AT LAST, PREY WORTHY OF ME. IS EVERYTHING ELSE PREPARED?›
‹VERY NEARLY.›
‹GOOD. THEN LEAVE ME TO MY HUNT.›

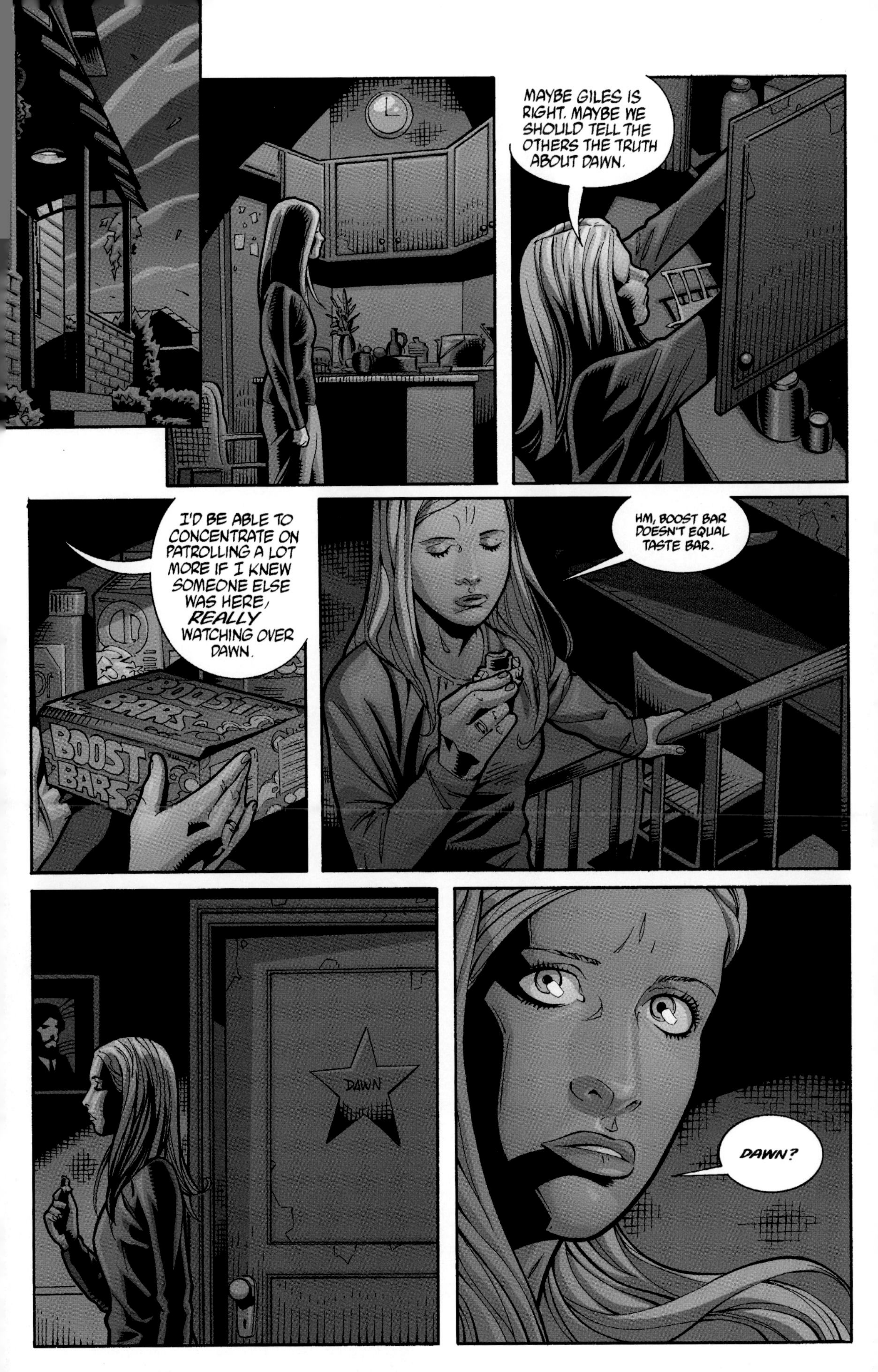
MAYBE GILES IS RIGHT. MAYBE WE SHOULD TELL THE OTHERS THE TRUTH ABOUT DAWN.
I'D BE ABLE TO CONCENTRATE ON PATROLLING A LOT MORE IF I KNEW SOMEONE ELSE WAS HERE, REALLY WATCHING OVER DAWN.
BOOST BARS
HM, BOOST BAR DOESN'T EQUAL TASTE BAR.
DAWN
DAWN?

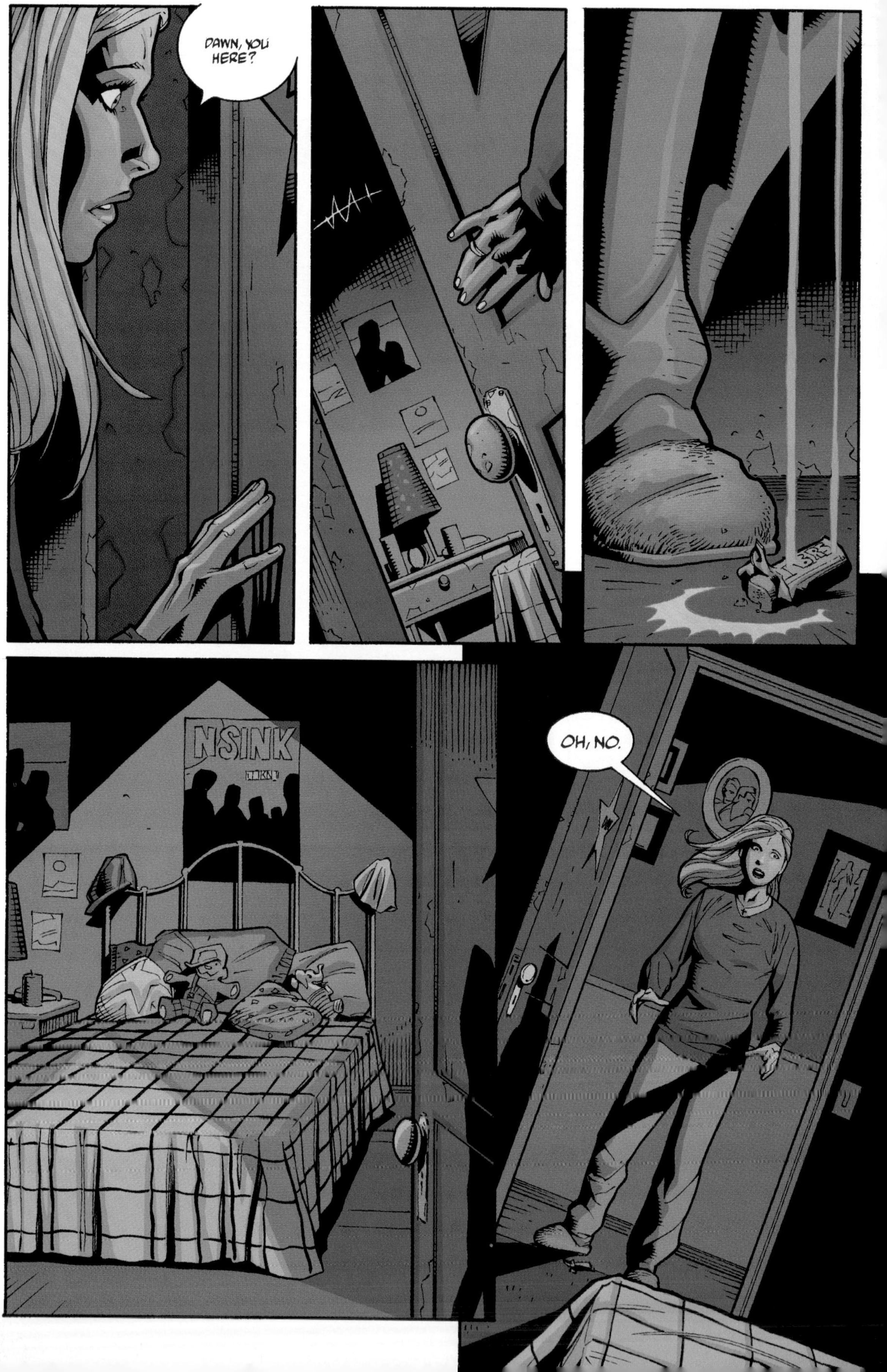
DAWN, YOU HERE?
OH, NO.
NSINK

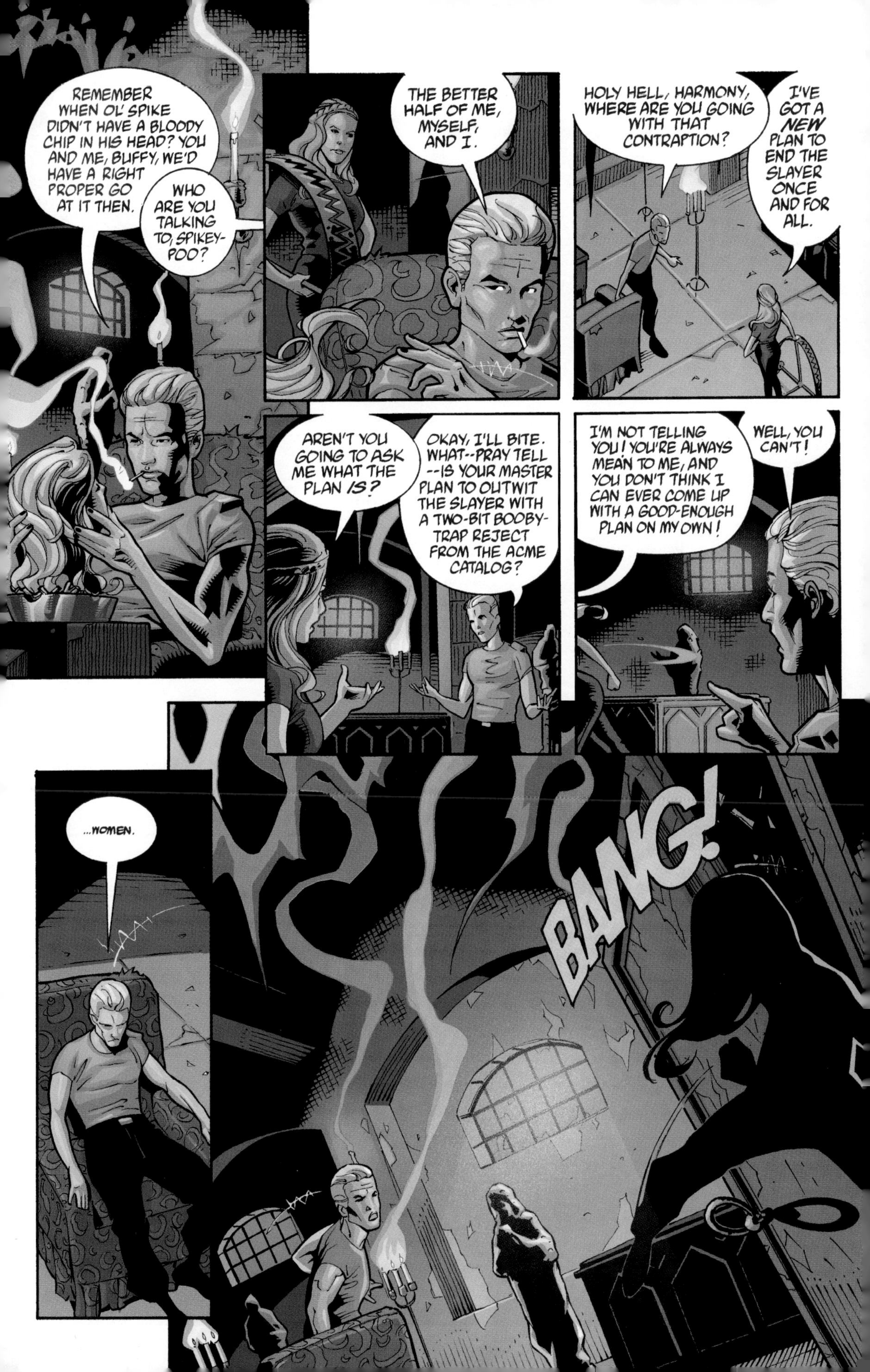

REMEMBER WHEN OL' SPIKE DIDN'T HAVE A BLOODY CHIP IN HIS HEAD? YOU AND ME, BUFFY, WE'D HAVE A RIGHT PROPER GO AT IT THEN.
WHO ARE YOU TALKING TO, SPIKEY-POO?
THE BETTER HALF OF ME, MYSELF, AND I.
HOLY HELL, HARMONY, WHERE ARE YOU GOING WITH THAT CONTRAPTION?
I'VE GOT A NEW PLAN TO END THE SLAYER ONCE AND FOR ALL.
AREN'T YOU GOING TO ASK ME WHAT THE PLAN IS?
OKAY, I'LL BITE. WHAT--PRAY TELL --IS YOUR MASTER PLAN TO OUTWIT THE SLAYER WITH A TWO-BIT BOOBY-TRAP REJECT FROM THE ACME CATALOG?
I'M NOT TELLING YOU! YOU'RE ALWAYS MEAN TO ME, AND YOU DON'T THINK I CAN EVER COME UP WITH A GOOD-ENOUGH PLAN ON MY OWN!
WELL, YOU CAN'T!
BANG!
...WOMEN.

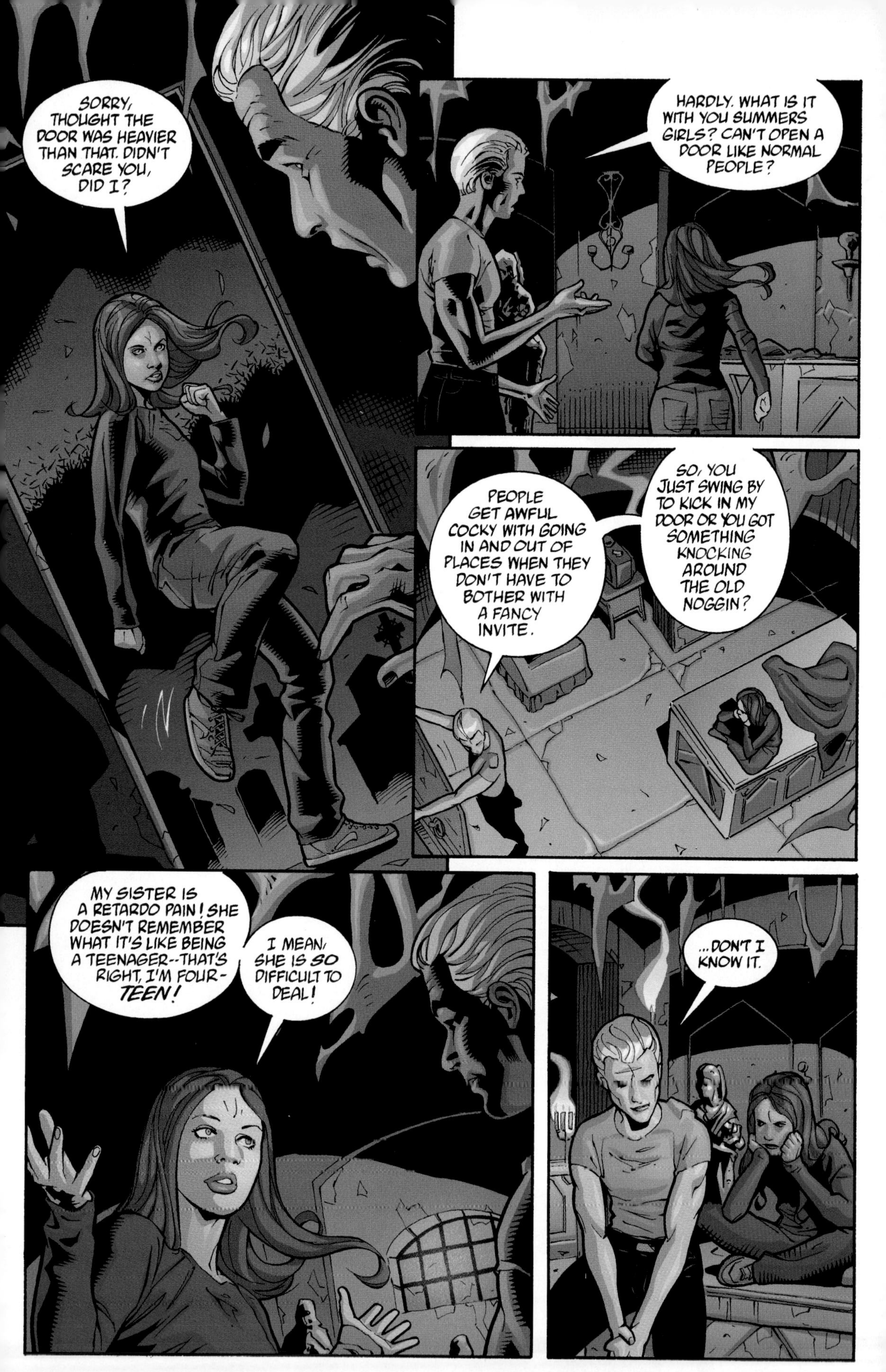
SORRY, THOUGHT THE DOOR WAS HEAVIER THAN THAT. DIDN'T SCARE YOU, DID I?
HARDLY. WHAT IS IT WITH YOU SUMMERS GIRLS? CAN'T OPEN A DOOR LIKE NORMAL PEOPLE?
PEOPLE GET AWFUL COCKY WITH GOING IN AND OUT OF PLACES WHEN THEY DON'T HAVE TO BOTHER WITH A FANCY INVITE.
SO, YOU JUST SWING BY TO KICK IN MY DOOR OR YOU GOT SOMETHING KNOCKING AROUND THE OLD NOGGIN?
MY SISTER IS A RETARDO PAIN! SHE DOESN'T REMEMBER WHAT IT'S LIKE BEING A TEENAGER--THAT'S RIGHT, I'M FOUR-TEEN!
I MEAN, SHE IS SO DIFFICULT TO DEAL!
...DON'T I KNOW IT.

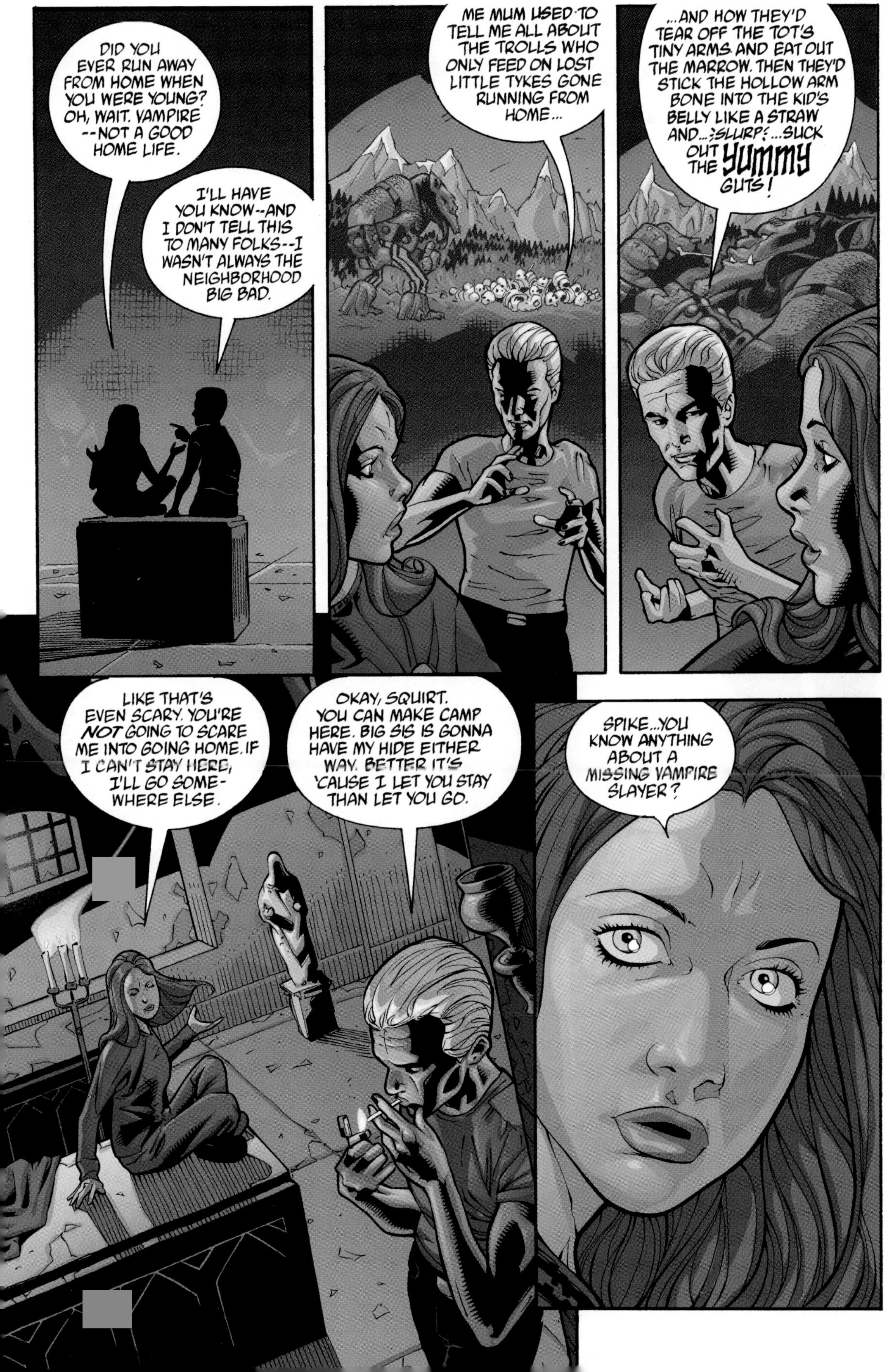
DID YOU EVER RUN AWAY FROM HOME WHEN YOU WERE YOUNG? OH, WAIT. VAMPIRE --NOT A GOOD HOME LIFE.
I'LL HAVE YOU KNOW--AND I DON'T TELL THIS TO MANY FOLKS--I WASN'T ALWAYS THE NEIGHBORHOOD BIG BAD.
ME MUM USED TO TELL ME ALL ABOUT THE TROLLS WHO ONLY FEED ON LOST LITTLE TYKES GONE RUNNING FROM HOME...
...AND HOW THEY'D TEAR OFF THE TOT'S TINY ARMS AND EAT OUT THE MARROW. THEN THEY'D STICK THE HOLLOW ARM BONE INTO THE KID'S BELLY LIKE A STRAW AND...¿SLURP¿...SUCK OUT THE YUMMY GUTS!
LIKE THAT'S EVEN SCARY. YOU'RE NOT GOING TO SCARE ME INTO GOING HOME. IF I CAN'T STAY HERE, I'LL GO SOME-WHERE ELSE.
OKAY, SQUIRT. YOU CAN MAKE CAMP HERE. BIG SIS IS GONNA HAVE MY HIDE EITHER WAY. BETTER IT'S 'CAUSE I LET YOU STAY THAN LET YOU GO.
SPIKE...YOU KNOW ANYTHING ABOUT A MISSING VAMPIRE SLAYER?

...A MISSING SLAYER, YOU SAY? THAT'S... PREPOSTEROUS...

WHATEVER. I'M NOT WORRIED ABOUT A SLAYER THAT MAY OR MAY NOT HAVE DISAPPEARED OFF THE BOOKS A CENTURY AGO. I'M WORRIED ABOUT DAWN DISAPPEARING IN REAL LIFE, RIGHT NOW.

YES, THAT IS GREATER CAUSE FOR ALARM. TELL ME AGAIN, WHEN WAS THE LAST TIME YOU SAW HER?

HOW MANY TIMES DO I HAVE TO GO OVER IT? I WENT ON PATROL LAST NIGHT, AND WHEN I CAME BACK HOME-- NO DAWN. HER BED WAS STILL MADE, EVEN.

HER BED WAS MADE... WOW, THAT IS TOTALLY WEIRD.

WILL! I NEED YOU ON MY SIDE!

COME ON, BUFFY. THIS ISN'T THE FIRST TIME DAWN'S GONE MISSING. AND FACE IT, YOU RIDE HER PRETTY HARD-- SOMETIMES YOU'RE MORE MOM THAN SISTER.

I KNOW YOU'RE WORRIED, BUT DAWN'S SMART. SHE CAN TAKE CARE OF HERSELF. I'M SURE SHE'LL BE BACK AS SOON AS SHE BLOWS OFF A LITTLE ADOLESCENT STEAM.

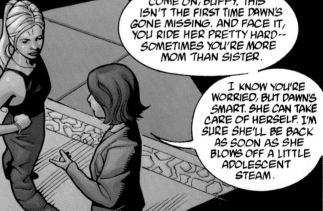

I SUSPECT WE SHOULD ORGANIZE A SEARCH--

HAVE YOU LOOKED AT SCHOOL? I HEARD THAT WHEN YOU LOSE SOMETHING, YOU'RE SUPPOSED TO LOOK IN THE PLACE YOU'D MOST EXPECT...

OR IS IT THE PLACE YOU'D LEAST EXPECT?

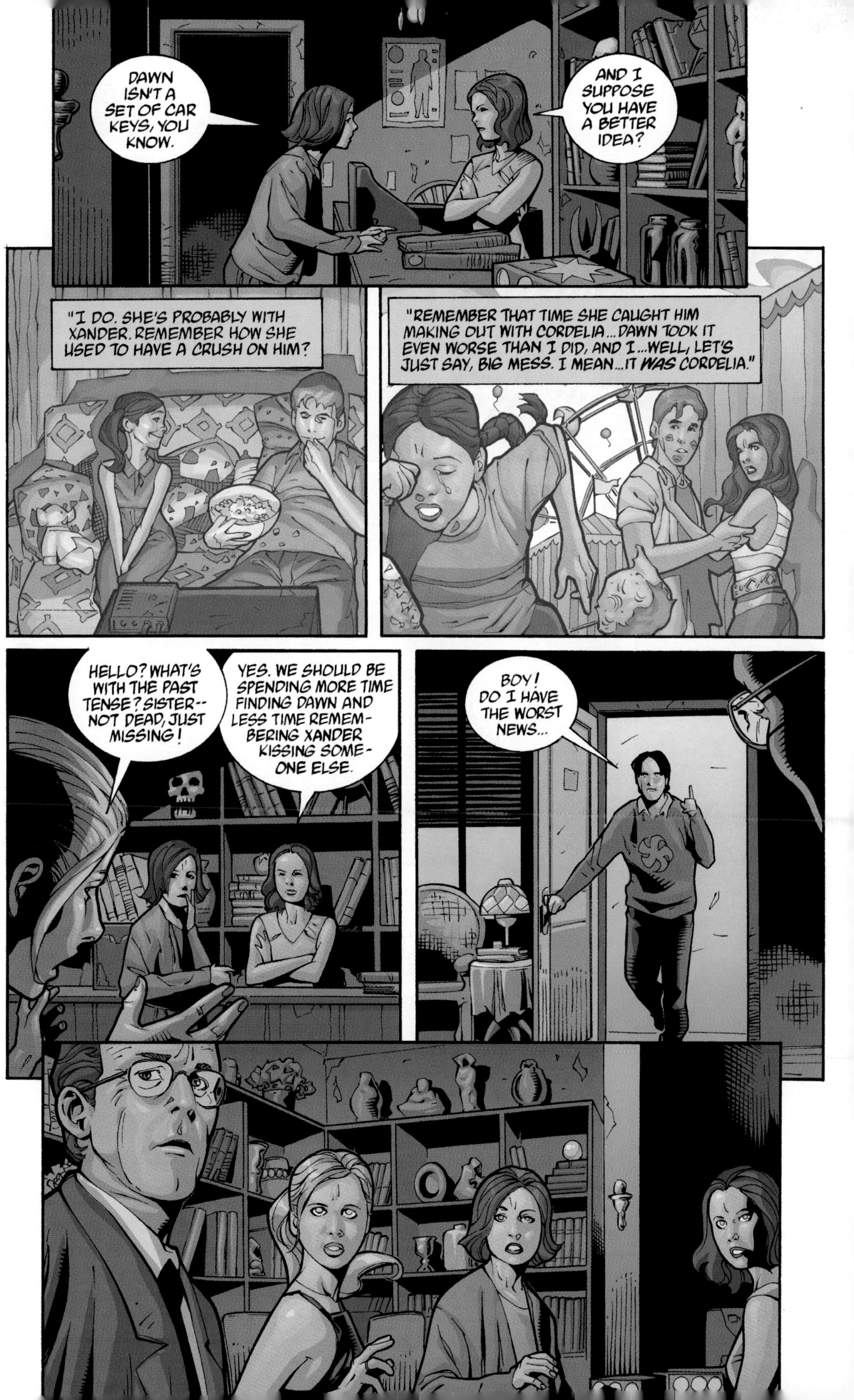
DAWN ISN'T A SET OF CAR KEYS, YOU KNOW.
AND I SUPPOSE YOU HAVE A BETTER IDEA?
"I DO. SHE'S PROBABLY WITH XANDER. REMEMBER HOW SHE USED TO HAVE A CRUSH ON HIM?
"REMEMBER THAT TIME SHE CAUGHT HIM MAKING OUT WITH CORDELIA... DAWN TOOK IT EVEN WORSE THAN I DID, AND I... WELL, LET'S JUST SAY, BIG MESS. I MEAN... IT WAS CORDELIA."
HELLO? WHAT'S WITH THE PAST TENSE? SISTER-- NOT DEAD, JUST MISSING!
YES. WE SHOULD BE SPENDING MORE TIME FINDING DAWN AND LESS TIME REMEMBERING XANDER KISSING SOMEONE ELSE.
BOY! DO I HAVE THE WORST NEWS...

WORK SUCKS!

XANDER! WAY TO DRIVE US ALL TO SCARED CITY!

WHAT? WHAT'D I SAY?

WE'VE LOST DAWN!

LOST AS IN MISSING? OR LOST AS IN--

SHE'S MISSING.

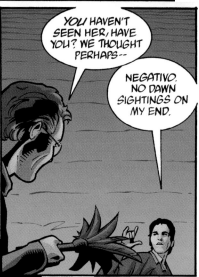

YOU HAVEN'T SEEN HER, HAVE YOU? WE THOUGHT PERHAPS--

NEGATIVO. NO DAWN SIGHTINGS ON MY END.

I DON'T SUPPOSE ANY-ONE CHECKED SCHOOL?

I'M THINKING SHE'S PUTTING ON A LITTLE RUNAWAY ACT ...YOU KNOW, TO GET OUT FROM UNDER BUFFY'S THUMB.

SHE'S NOT UNDER MY THUMB!

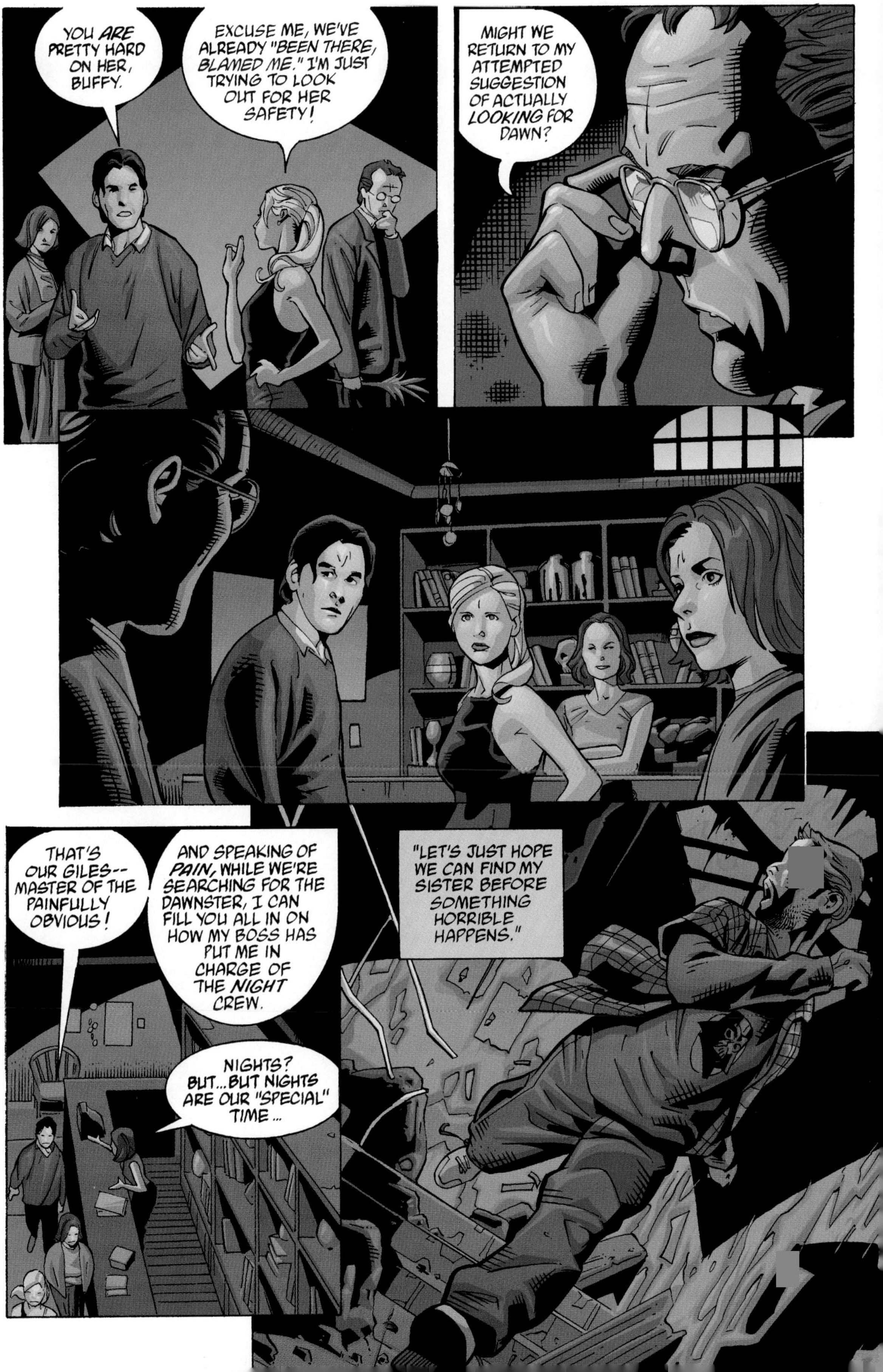
YOU *ARE* PRETTY HARD ON HER, BUFFY.
EXCUSE ME, WE'VE ALREADY "BEEN THERE, *BLAMED ME.*" I'M JUST TRYING TO LOOK OUT FOR HER SAFETY!
MIGHT WE RETURN TO MY ATTEMPTED SUGGESTION OF ACTUALLY *LOOKING* FOR DAWN?
THAT'S OUR GILES-- MASTER OF THE PAINFULLY OBVIOUS!
AND SPEAKING OF *PAIN,* WHILE WE'RE SEARCHING FOR THE DAWNSTER, I CAN FILL YOU ALL IN ON HOW MY BOSS HAS PUT ME IN CHARGE OF THE *NIGHT* CREW.
NIGHTS? BUT...BUT NIGHTS ARE OUR "SPECIAL" TIME...
"LET'S JUST HOPE WE CAN FIND MY SISTER BEFORE SOMETHING HORRIBLE HAPPENS."

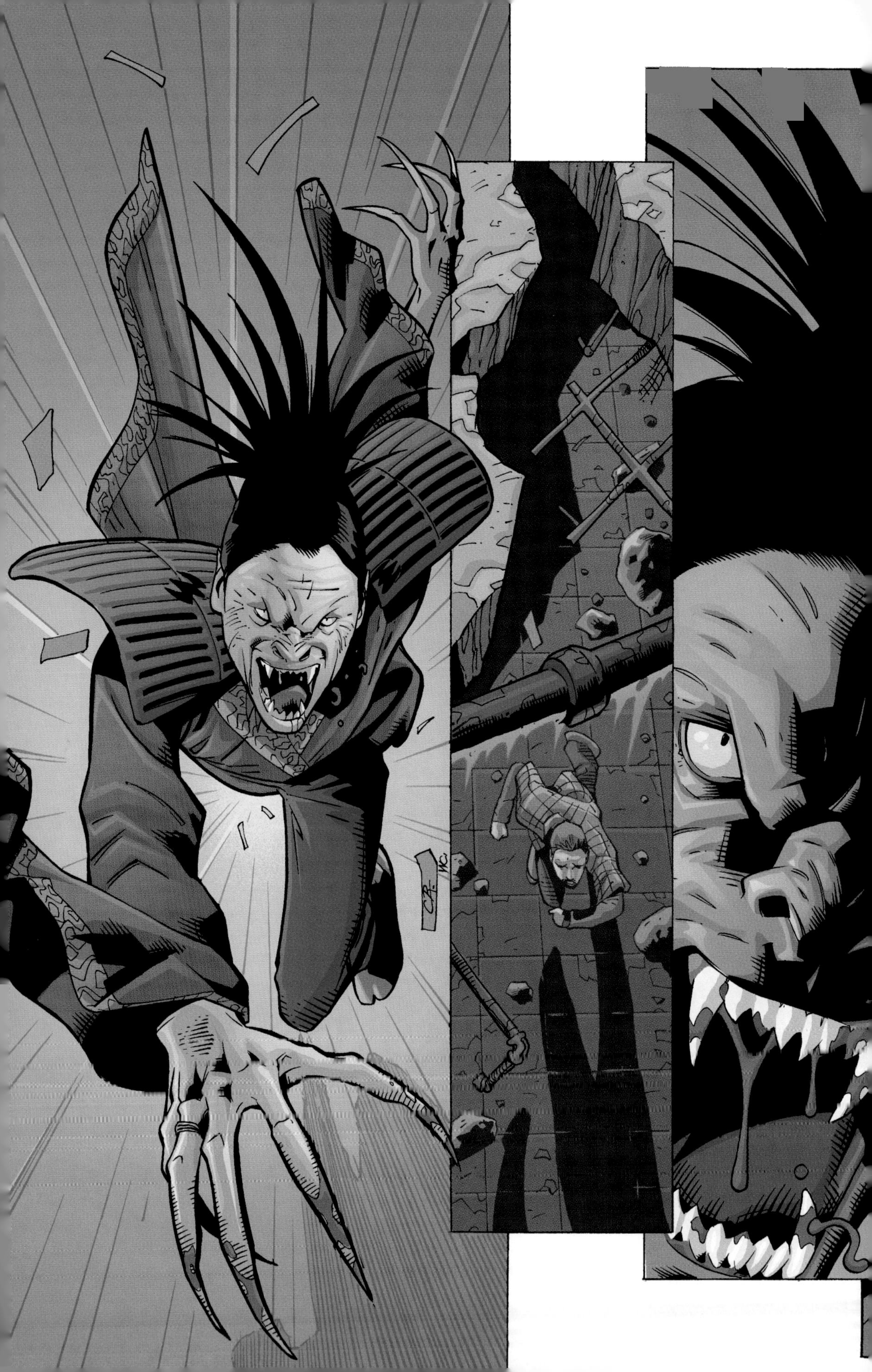

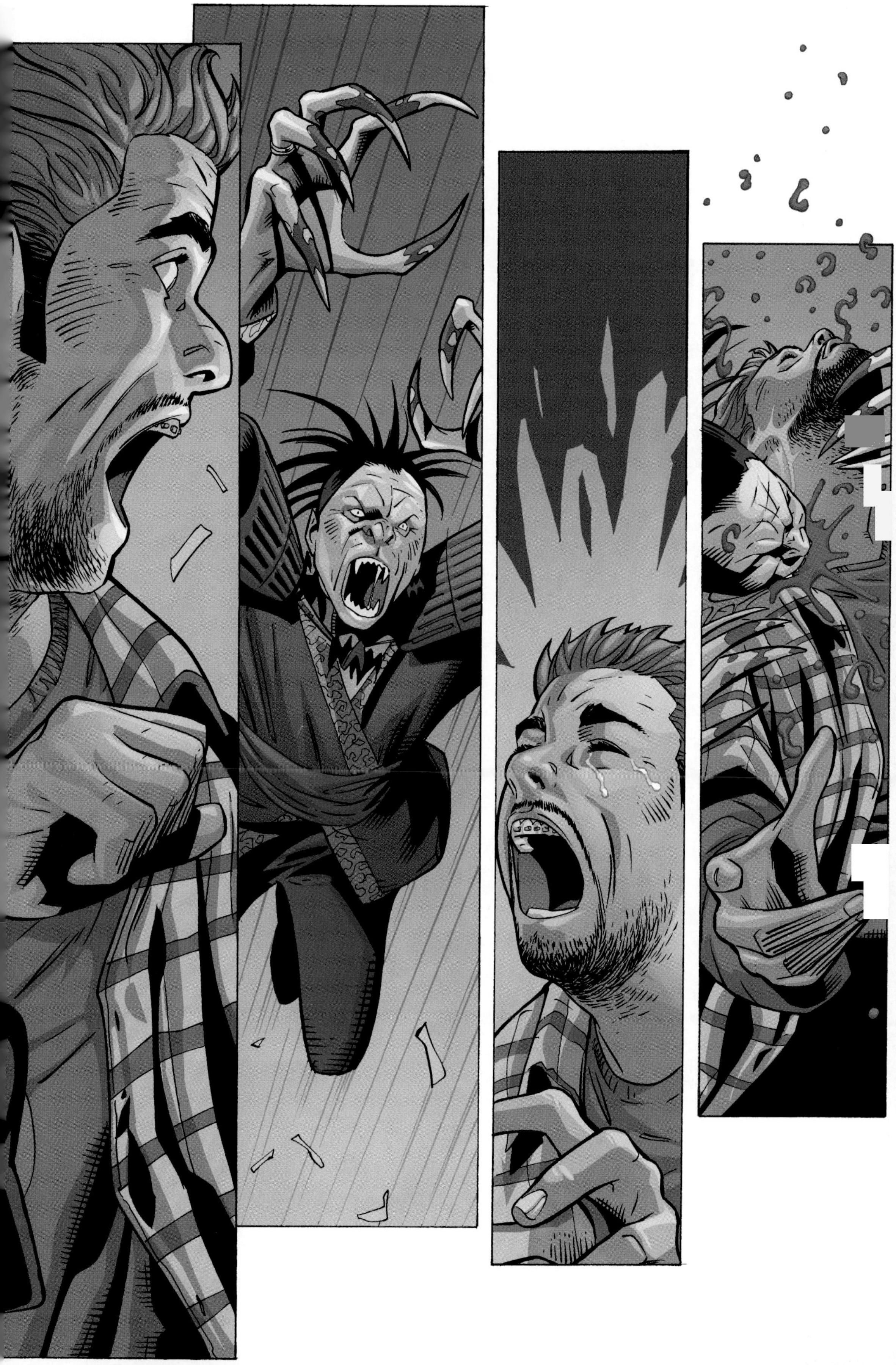

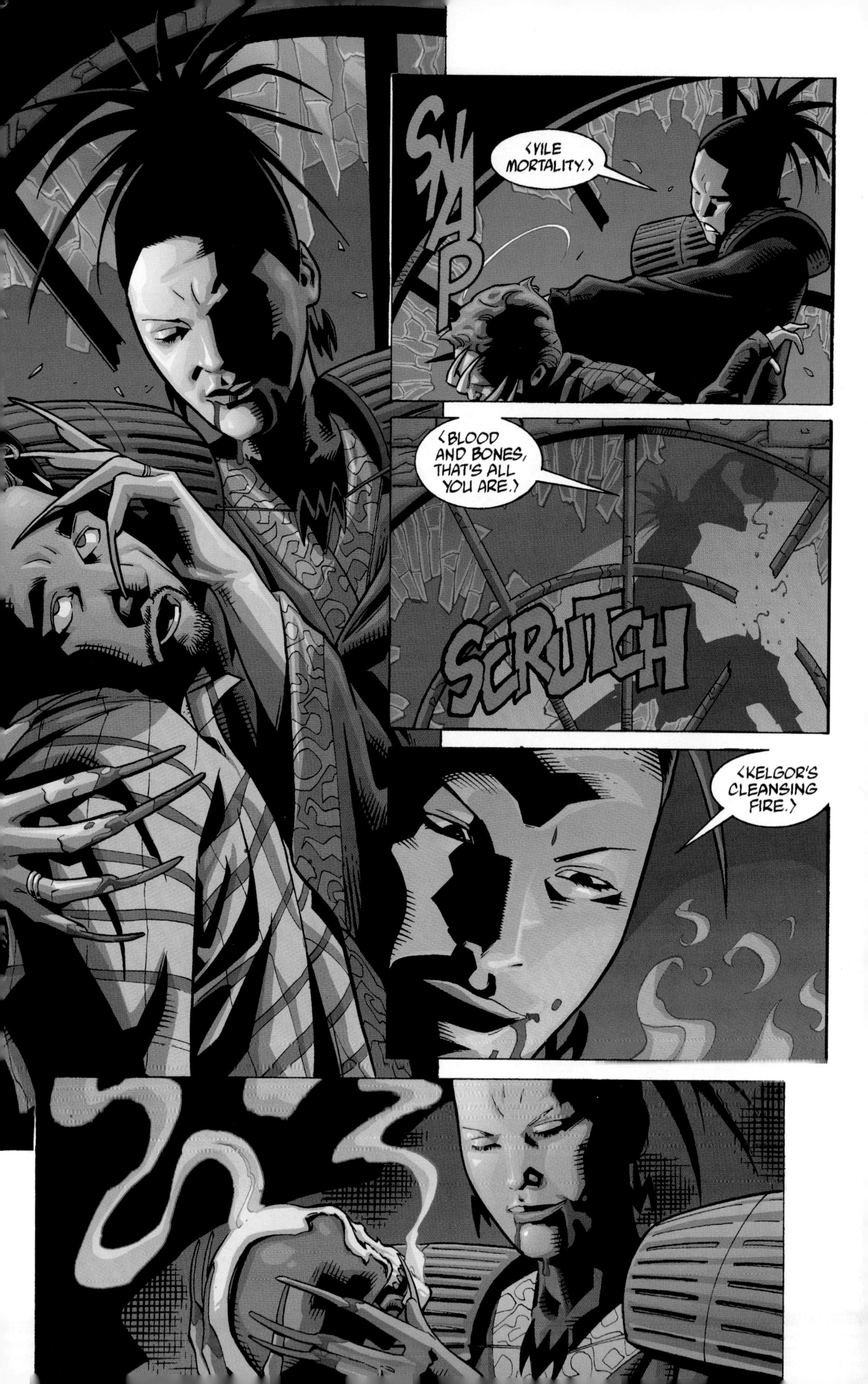
SNAP
<VILE MORTALITY.>
<BLOOD AND BONES, THAT'S ALL YOU ARE.>
SCRUTCH
<KELGOR'S CLEANSING FIRE.>

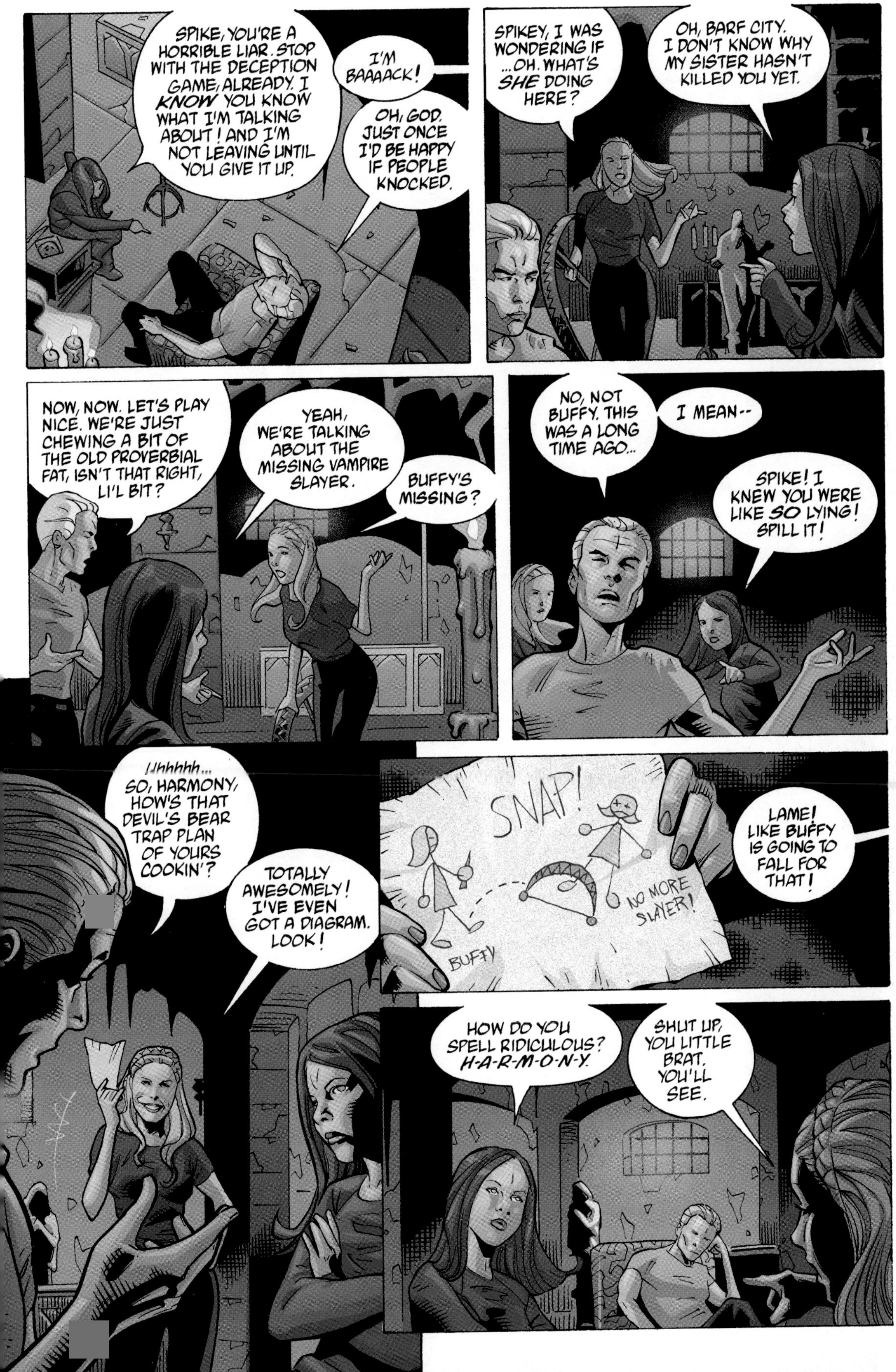
SPIKE, YOU'RE A HORRIBLE LIAR. STOP WITH THE DECEPTION GAME, ALREADY. I KNOW YOU KNOW WHAT I'M TALKING ABOUT! AND I'M NOT LEAVING UNTIL YOU GIVE IT UP.
I'M BAAAACK!
OH, GOD. JUST ONCE I'D BE HAPPY IF PEOPLE KNOCKED.
SPIKEY, I WAS WONDERING IF ...OH. WHAT'S SHE DOING HERE?
OH, BARF CITY. I DON'T KNOW WHY MY SISTER HASN'T KILLED YOU YET.
NOW, NOW. LET'S PLAY NICE. WE'RE JUST CHEWING A BIT OF THE OLD PROVERBIAL FAT, ISN'T THAT RIGHT, LI'L BIT?
YEAH, WE'RE TALKING ABOUT THE MISSING VAMPIRE SLAYER.
BUFFY'S MISSING?
NO, NOT BUFFY. THIS WAS A LONG TIME AGO...
I MEAN--
SPIKE! I KNEW YOU WERE LIKE SO LYING! SPILL IT!
Uhhhhh... SO, HARMONY, HOW'S THAT DEVIL'S BEAR TRAP PLAN OF YOURS COOKIN'?
TOTALLY AWESOMELY! I'VE EVEN GOT A DIAGRAM. LOOK!
SNAP!
BUFFY
NO MORE SLAYER!
LAME! LIKE BUFFY IS GOING TO FALL FOR THAT!
HOW DO YOU SPELL RIDICULOUS? H-A-R-M-O-N-Y.
SHUT UP, YOU LITTLE BRAT. YOU'LL SEE.

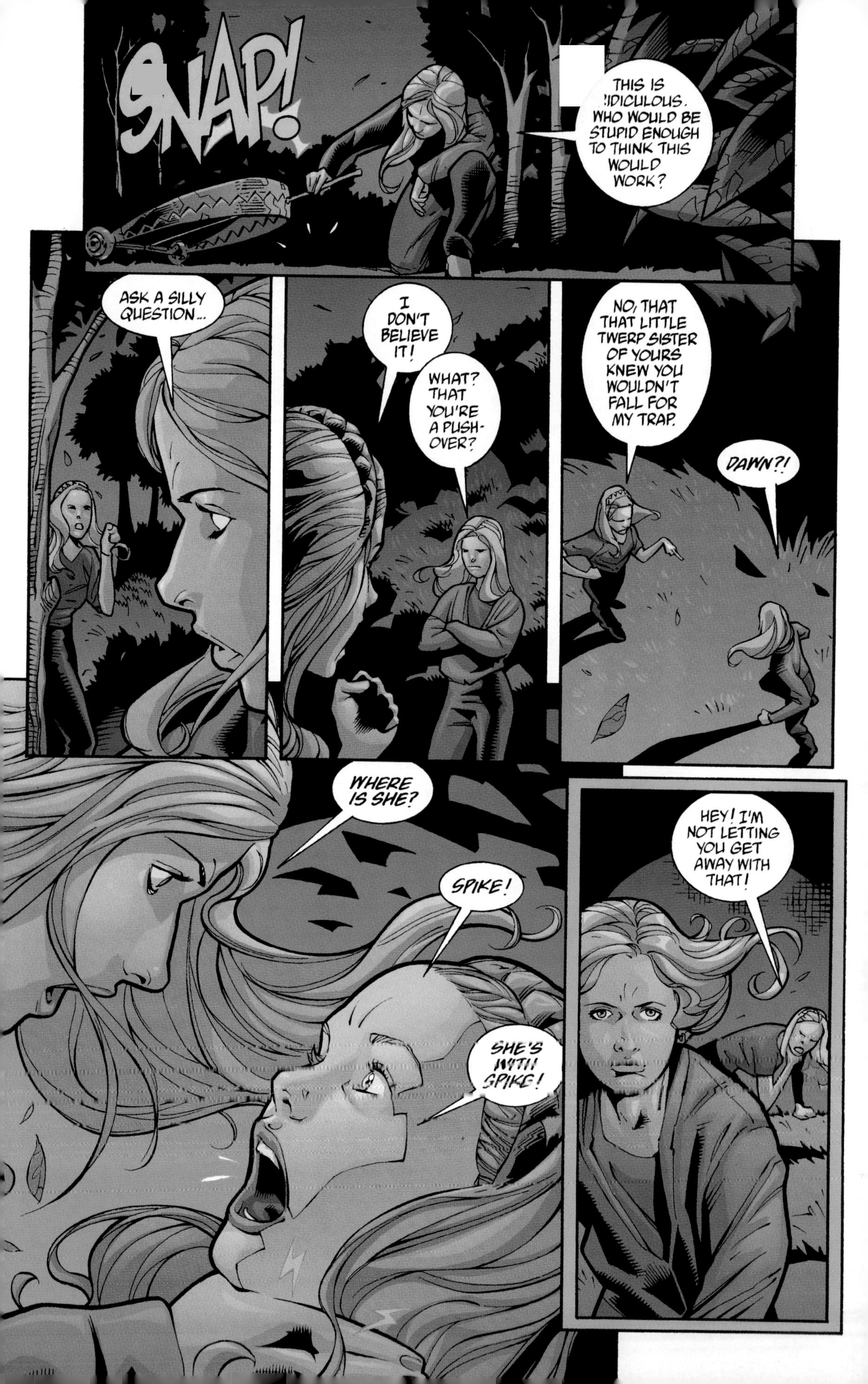
SNAP!
THIS IS IDICULOUS. WHO WOULD BE STUPID ENOUGH TO THINK THIS WOULD WORK?
ASK A SILLY QUESTION...
I DON'T BELIEVE IT!
WHAT? THAT YOU'RE A PUSH-OVER?
NO, THAT THAT LITTLE TWERP SISTER OF YOURS KNEW YOU WOULDN'T FALL FOR MY TRAP.
DAWN?!
WHERE IS SHE?
SPIKE!
SHE'S WITH SPIKE!
HEY! I'M NOT LETTING YOU GET AWAY WITH THAT!

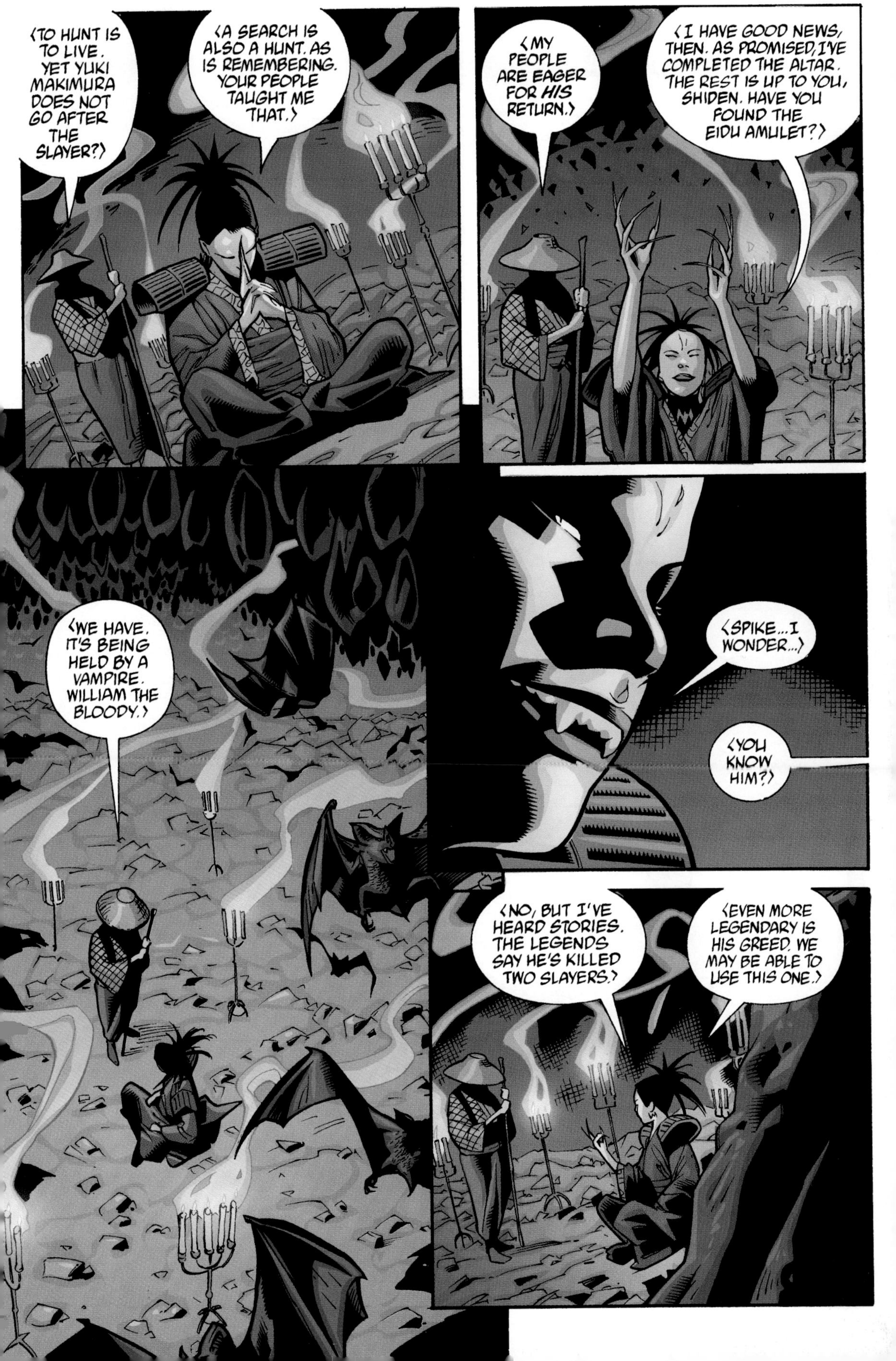
⟨TO HUNT IS TO LIVE. YET YUKI MAKIMURA DOES NOT GO AFTER THE SLAYER?⟩
⟨A SEARCH IS ALSO A HUNT. AS IS REMEMBERING. YOUR PEOPLE TAUGHT ME THAT.⟩
⟨MY PEOPLE ARE EAGER FOR *HIS* RETURN.⟩
⟨I HAVE GOOD NEWS, THEN. AS PROMISED, I'VE COMPLETED THE ALTAR. THE REST IS UP TO YOU, SHIDEN. HAVE YOU FOUND THE EIDU AMULET?⟩
⟨WE HAVE. IT'S BEING HELD BY A VAMPIRE. WILLIAM THE BLOODY.⟩
⟨SPIKE... I WONDER...⟩
⟨YOU KNOW HIM?⟩
⟨NO, BUT I'VE HEARD STORIES. THE LEGENDS SAY HE'S KILLED TWO SLAYERS.⟩
⟨EVEN MORE LEGENDARY IS HIS GREED. WE MAY BE ABLE TO USE THIS ONE.⟩

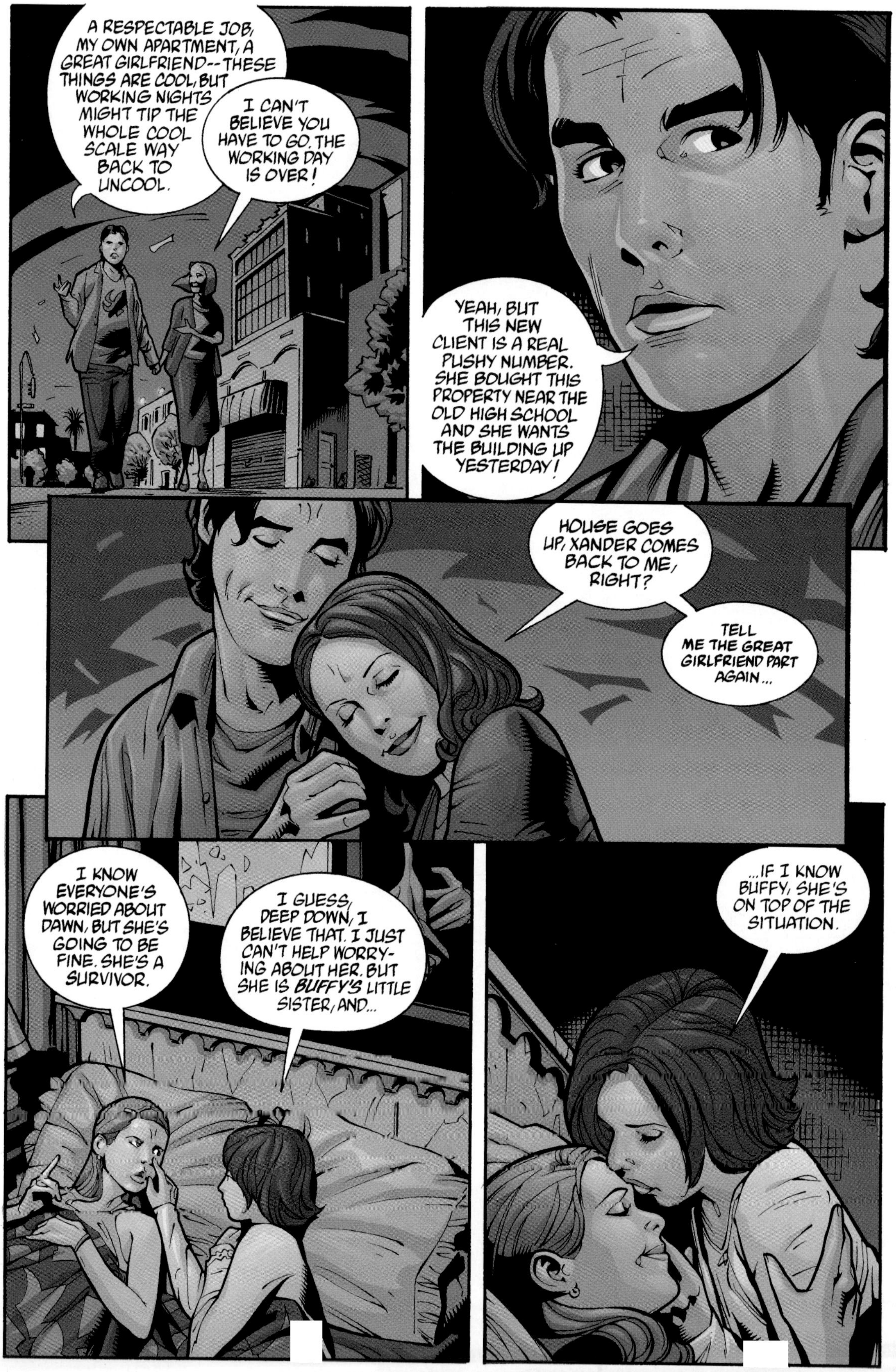
A RESPECTABLE JOB, MY OWN APARTMENT, A GREAT GIRLFRIEND--THESE THINGS ARE COOL, BUT WORKING NIGHTS MIGHT TIP THE WHOLE COOL SCALE WAY BACK TO UNCOOL.
I CAN'T BELIEVE YOU HAVE TO GO. THE WORKING DAY IS OVER!
YEAH, BUT THIS NEW CLIENT IS A REAL PUSHY NUMBER. SHE BOUGHT THIS PROPERTY NEAR THE OLD HIGH SCHOOL AND SHE WANTS THE BUILDING UP YESTERDAY!
HOUSE GOES UP, XANDER COMES BACK TO ME, RIGHT?
TELL ME THE GREAT GIRLFRIEND PART AGAIN...
I KNOW EVERYONE'S WORRIED ABOUT DAWN, BUT SHE'S GOING TO BE FINE. SHE'S A SURVIVOR.
I GUESS, DEEP DOWN, I BELIEVE THAT. I JUST CAN'T HELP WORRYING ABOUT HER. BUT SHE IS BUFFY'S LITTLE SISTER, AND...
...IF I KNOW BUFFY, SHE'S ON TOP OF THE SITUATION.

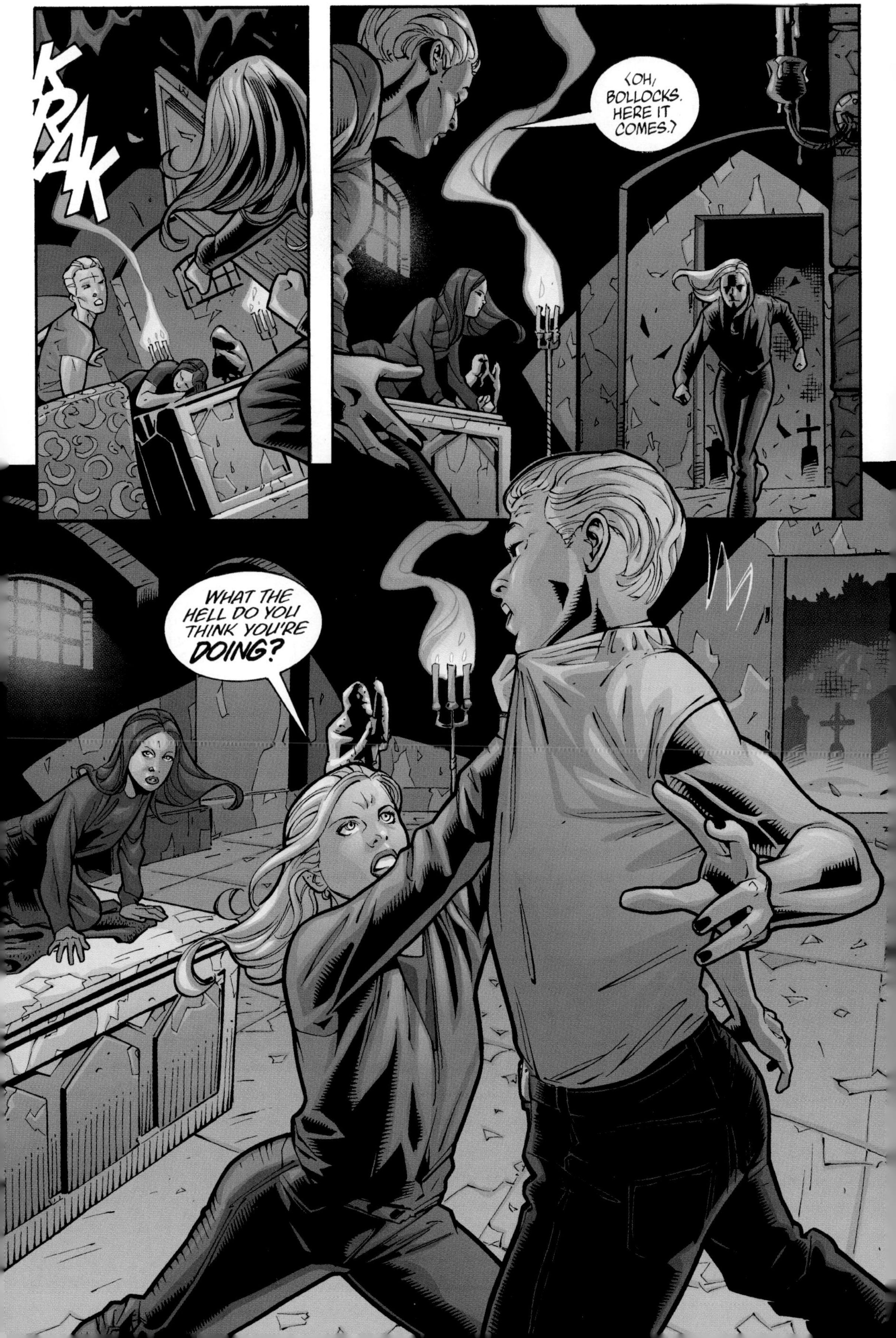
KRAK
‹OH, BOLLOCKS. HERE IT COMES.›
WHAT THE HELL DO YOU THINK YOU'RE DOING?

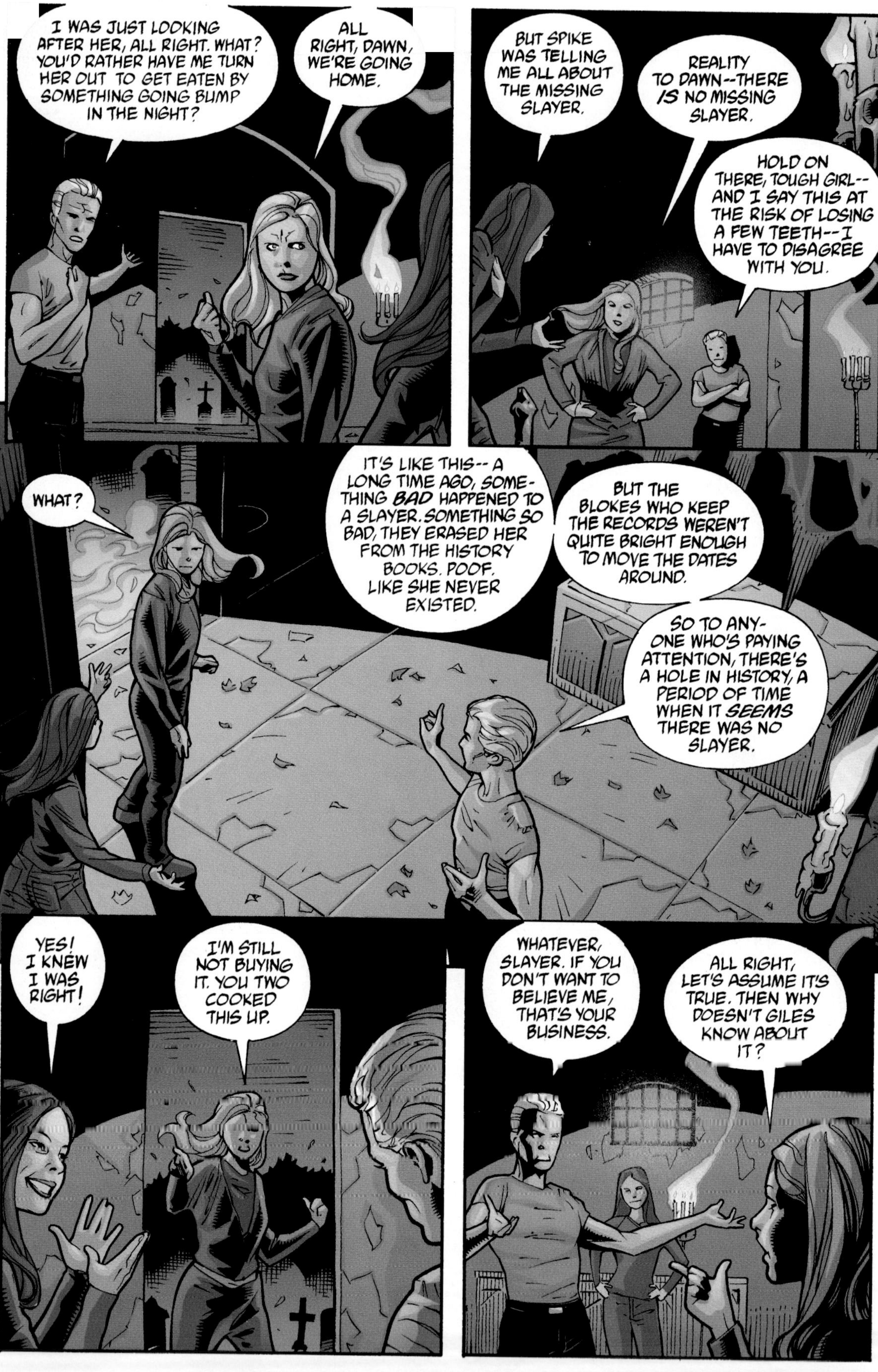
I WAS JUST LOOKING AFTER HER, ALL RIGHT. WHAT? YOU'D RATHER HAVE ME TURN HER OUT TO GET EATEN BY SOMETHING GOING BUMP IN THE NIGHT?
ALL RIGHT, DAWN, WE'RE GOING HOME.
BUT SPIKE WAS TELLING ME ALL ABOUT THE MISSING SLAYER.
REALITY TO DAWN--THERE *IS* NO MISSING SLAYER.
HOLD ON THERE, TOUGH GIRL--AND I SAY THIS AT THE RISK OF LOSING A FEW TEETH--I HAVE TO DISAGREE WITH YOU.
WHAT?
IT'S LIKE THIS-- A LONG TIME AGO, SOMETHING *BAD* HAPPENED TO A SLAYER. SOMETHING *SO* BAD, THEY ERASED HER FROM THE HISTORY BOOKS. POOF. LIKE SHE NEVER EXISTED.
BUT THE BLOKES WHO KEEP THE RECORDS WEREN'T QUITE BRIGHT ENOUGH TO MOVE THE DATES AROUND.
SO TO ANYONE WHO'S PAYING ATTENTION, THERE'S A HOLE IN HISTORY, A PERIOD OF TIME WHEN IT *SEEMS* THERE WAS NO SLAYER.
YES! I KNEW I WAS RIGHT!
I'M STILL NOT BUYING IT. YOU TWO COOKED THIS UP.
WHATEVER, SLAYER. IF YOU DON'T WANT TO BELIEVE ME, THAT'S YOUR BUSINESS.
ALL RIGHT, LET'S ASSUME IT'S TRUE. THEN WHY DOESN'T GILES KNOW ABOUT IT?

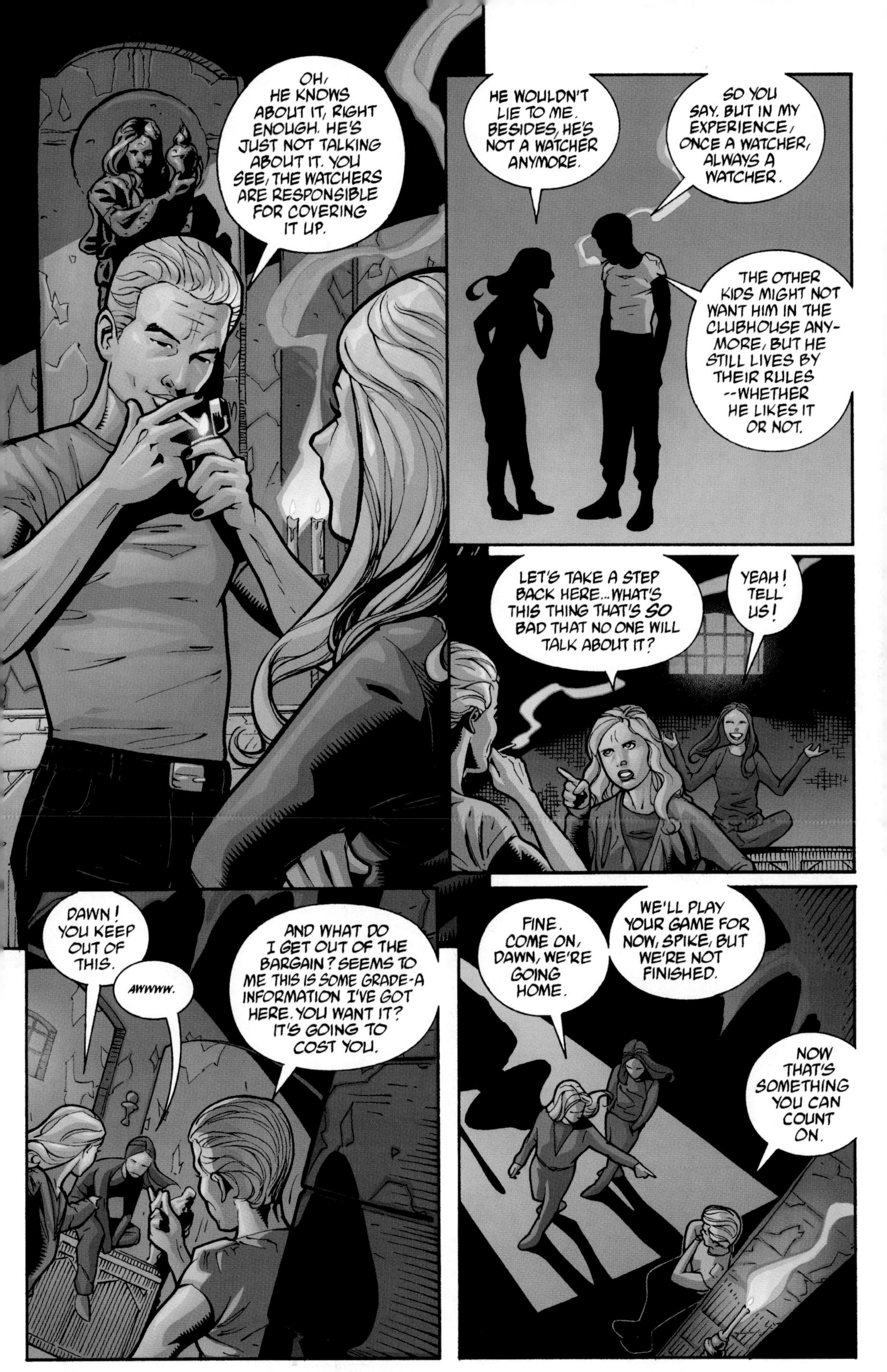
OH, HE KNOWS ABOUT IT, RIGHT ENOUGH. HE'S JUST NOT TALKING ABOUT IT. YOU SEE, THE WATCHERS ARE RESPONSIBLE FOR COVERING IT UP.
HE WOULDN'T LIE TO ME. BESIDES, HE'S NOT A WATCHER ANYMORE.
SO YOU SAY. BUT IN MY EXPERIENCE, ONCE A WATCHER, ALWAYS A WATCHER.
THE OTHER KIDS MIGHT NOT WANT HIM IN THE CLUBHOUSE ANY-MORE, BUT HE STILL LIVES BY THEIR RULES --WHETHER HE LIKES IT OR NOT.
LET'S TAKE A STEP BACK HERE... WHAT'S THIS THING THAT'S SO BAD THAT NO ONE WILL TALK ABOUT IT?
YEAH! TELL US!
DAWN! YOU KEEP OUT OF THIS.
AWWWW.
AND WHAT DO I GET OUT OF THE BARGAIN? SEEMS TO ME THIS IS SOME GRADE-A INFORMATION I'VE GOT HERE. YOU WANT IT? IT'S GOING TO COST YOU.
FINE. COME ON, DAWN, WE'RE GOING HOME.
WE'LL PLAY YOUR GAME FOR NOW, SPIKE, BUT WE'RE NOT FINISHED.
NOW THAT'S SOMETHING YOU CAN COUNT ON.

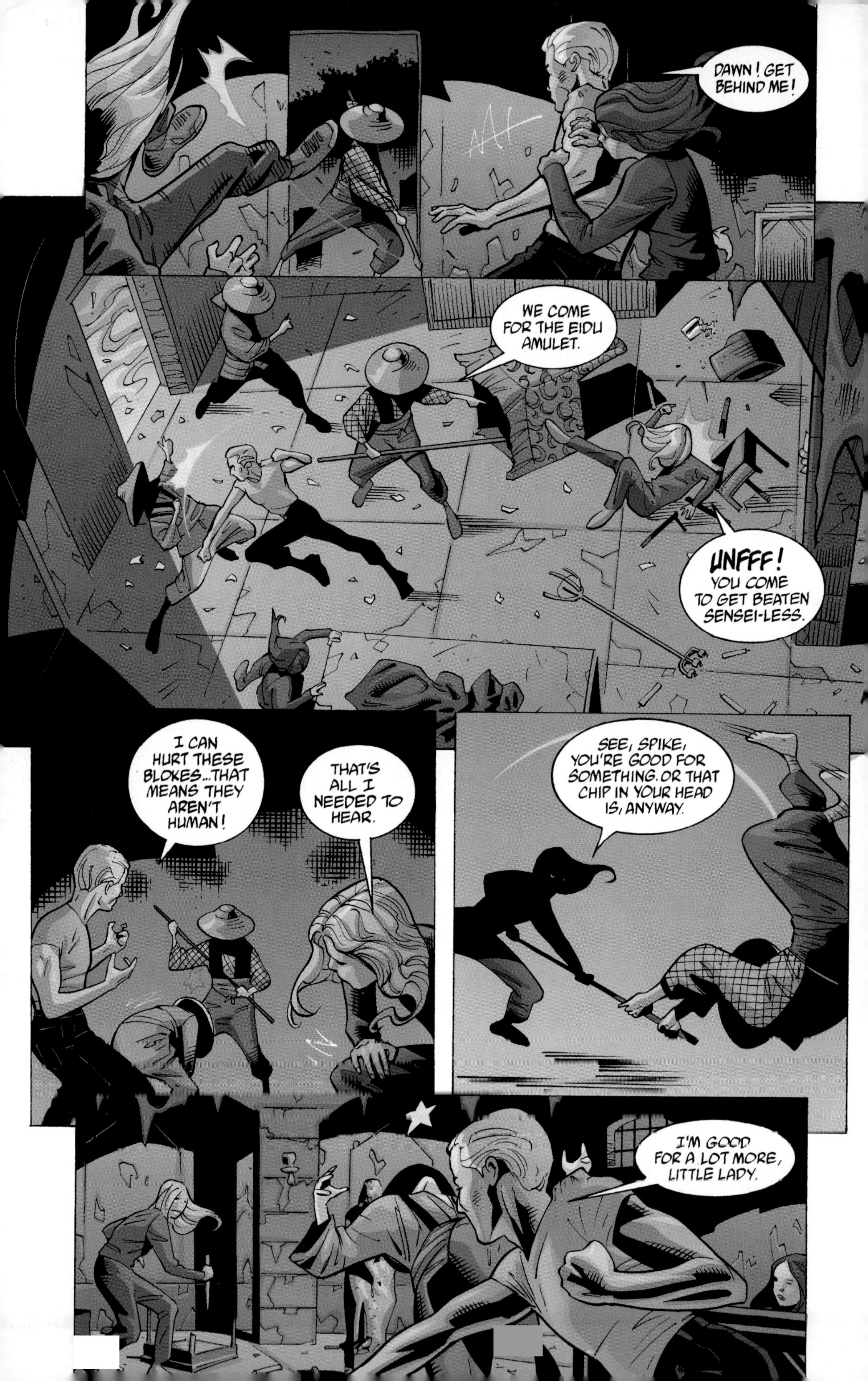
DAWN! GET BEHIND ME!
WE COME FOR THE EIDU AMULET.
UNFFF! YOU COME TO GET BEATEN SENSEI-LESS.
I CAN HURT THESE BLOKES...THAT MEANS THEY AREN'T HUMAN!
THAT'S ALL I NEEDED TO HEAR.
SEE, SPIKE, YOU'RE GOOD FOR SOMETHING. OR THAT CHIP IN YOUR HEAD IS, ANYWAY.
I'M GOOD FOR A LOT MORE, LITTLE LADY.

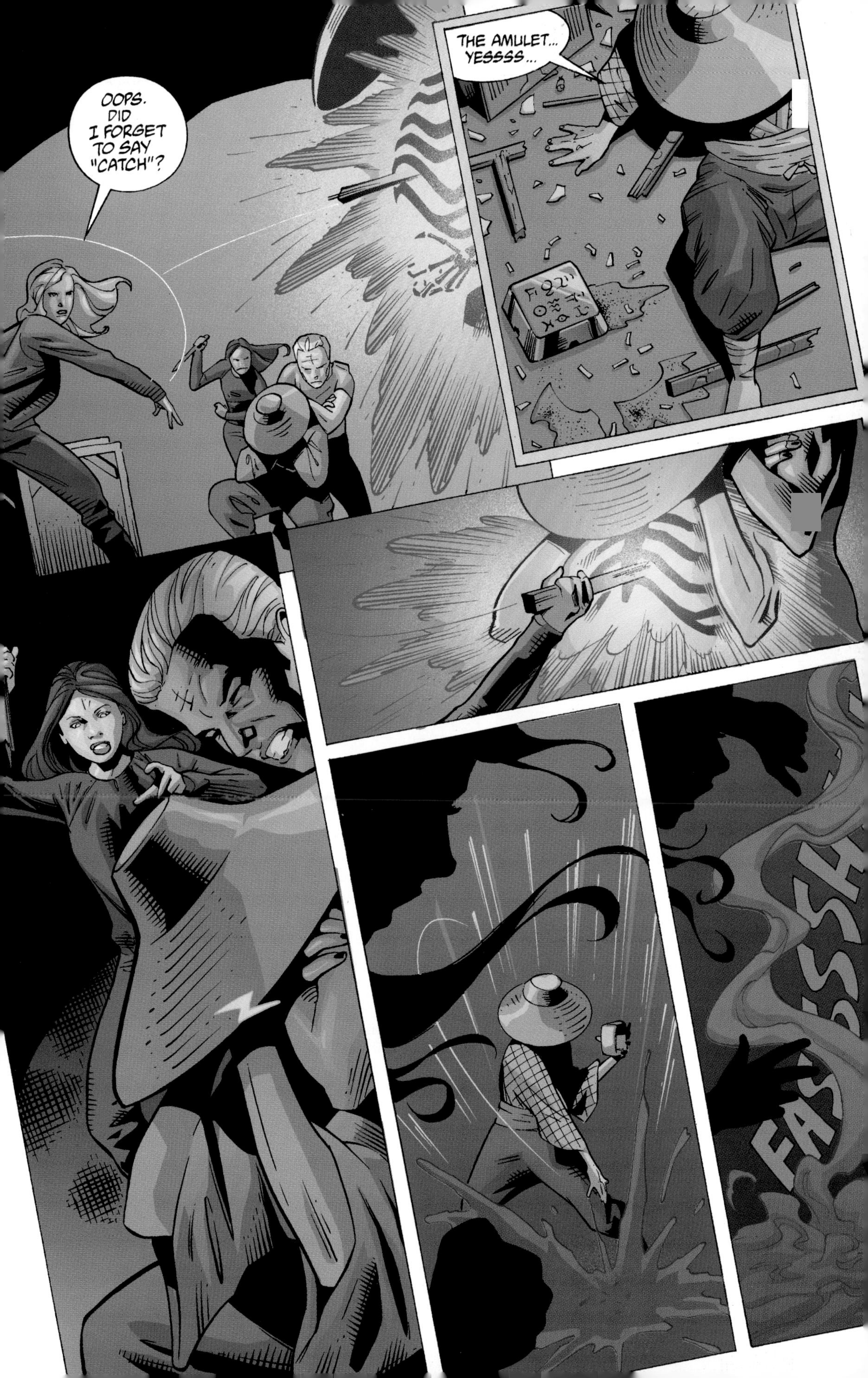
OOPS. DID I FORGET TO SAY "CATCH"?
THE AMULET... YESSSS...
FASSSH

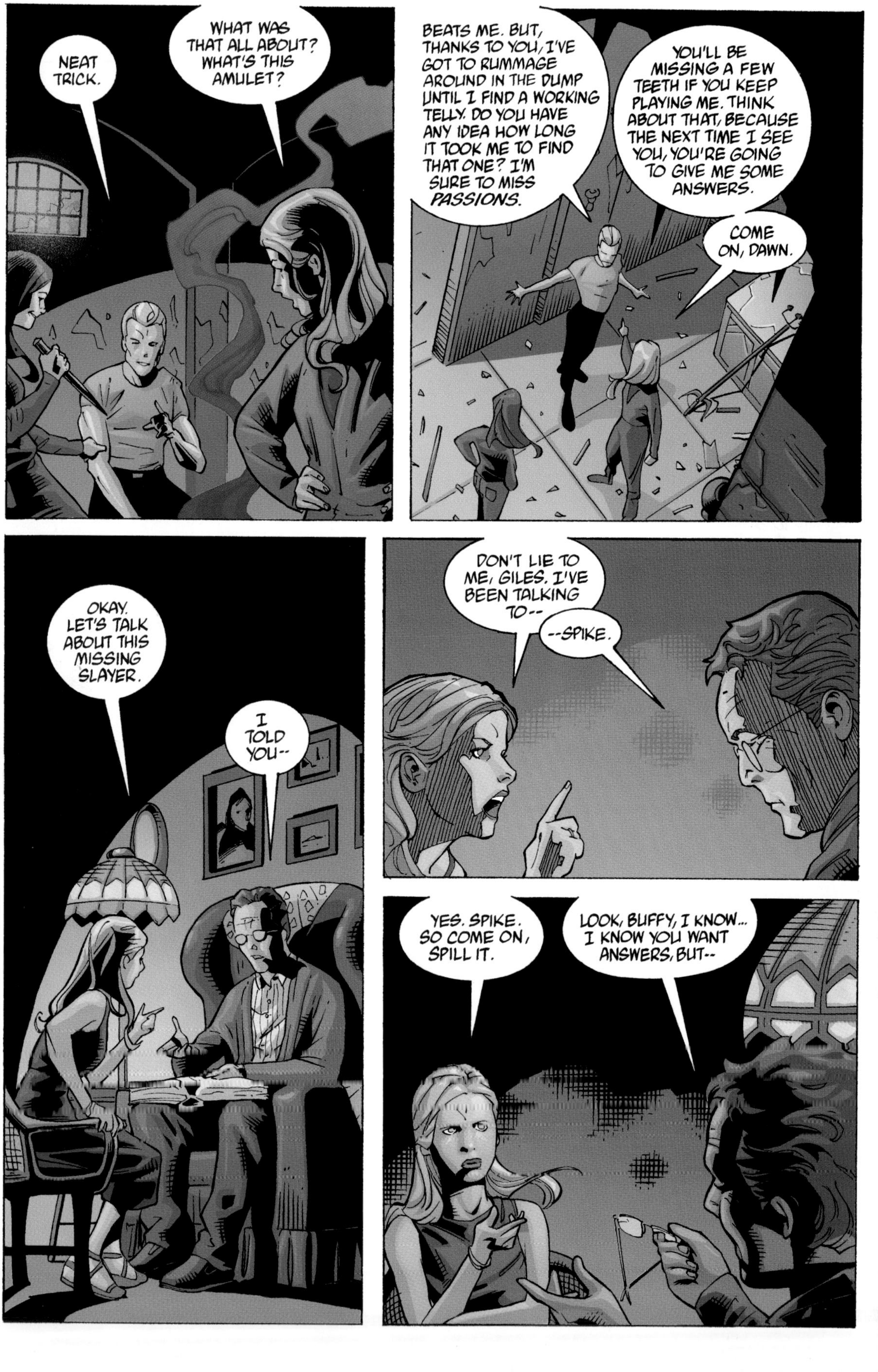
NEAT TRICK.
WHAT WAS THAT ALL ABOUT? WHAT'S THIS AMULET?
BEATS ME. BUT, THANKS TO YOU, I'VE GOT TO RUMMAGE AROUND IN THE DUMP UNTIL I FIND A WORKING TELLY. DO YOU HAVE ANY IDEA HOW LONG IT TOOK ME TO FIND THAT ONE? I'M SURE TO MISS *PASSIONS*.
YOU'LL BE MISSING A FEW TEETH IF YOU KEEP PLAYING ME. THINK ABOUT THAT, BECAUSE THE NEXT TIME I SEE YOU, YOU'RE GOING TO GIVE ME SOME ANSWERS.
COME ON, DAWN.
OKAY. LET'S TALK ABOUT THIS MISSING SLAYER.
I TOLD YOU--
DON'T LIE TO ME, GILES. I'VE BEEN TALKING TO--
--SPIKE.
YES. SPIKE. SO COME ON, SPILL IT.
LOOK, BUFFY, I KNOW... I KNOW YOU WANT ANSWERS, BUT--

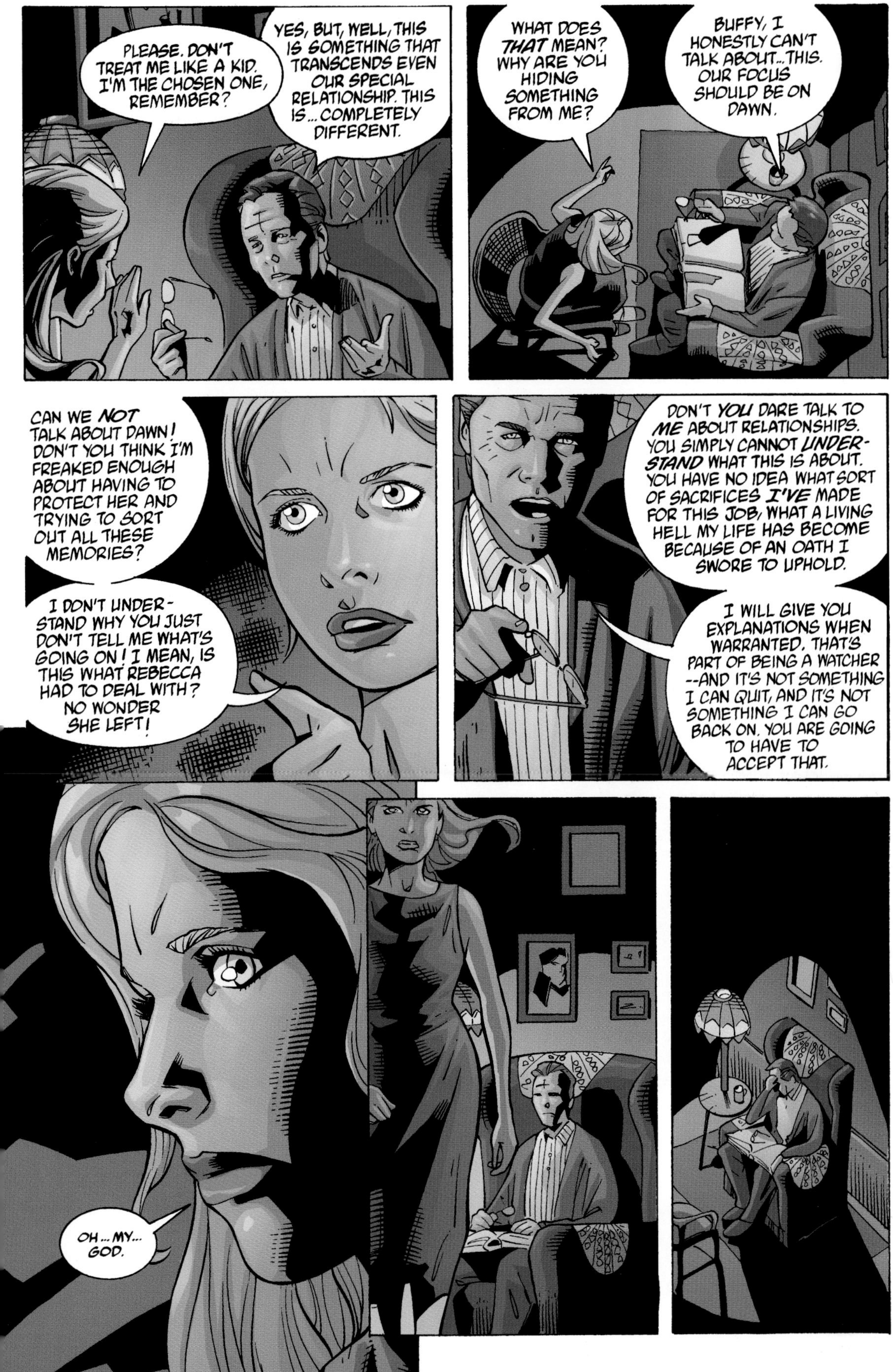
PLEASE. DON'T TREAT ME LIKE A KID. I'M THE CHOSEN ONE, REMEMBER?
YES, BUT, WELL, THIS IS SOMETHING THAT TRANSCENDS EVEN OUR SPECIAL RELATIONSHIP. THIS IS... COMPLETELY DIFFERENT.
WHAT DOES THAT MEAN? WHY ARE YOU HIDING SOMETHING FROM ME?
BUFFY, I HONESTLY CAN'T TALK ABOUT... THIS. OUR FOCUS SHOULD BE ON DAWN.
CAN WE NOT TALK ABOUT DAWN! DON'T YOU THINK I'M FREAKED ENOUGH ABOUT HAVING TO PROTECT HER AND TRYING TO SORT OUT ALL THESE MEMORIES?
I DON'T UNDER-STAND WHY YOU JUST DON'T TELL ME WHAT'S GOING ON! I MEAN, IS THIS WHAT REBECCA HAD TO DEAL WITH? NO WONDER SHE LEFT!
DON'T YOU DARE TALK TO ME ABOUT RELATIONSHIPS. YOU SIMPLY CANNOT UNDER-STAND WHAT THIS IS ABOUT. YOU HAVE NO IDEA WHAT SORT OF SACRIFICES I'VE MADE FOR THIS JOB, WHAT A LIVING HELL MY LIFE HAS BECOME BECAUSE OF AN OATH I SWORE TO UPHOLD.
I WILL GIVE YOU EXPLANATIONS WHEN WARRANTED. THAT'S PART OF BEING A WATCHER --AND IT'S NOT SOMETHING I CAN QUIT, AND IT'S NOT SOMETHING I CAN GO BACK ON. YOU ARE GOING TO HAVE TO ACCEPT THAT.
OH... MY... GOD.

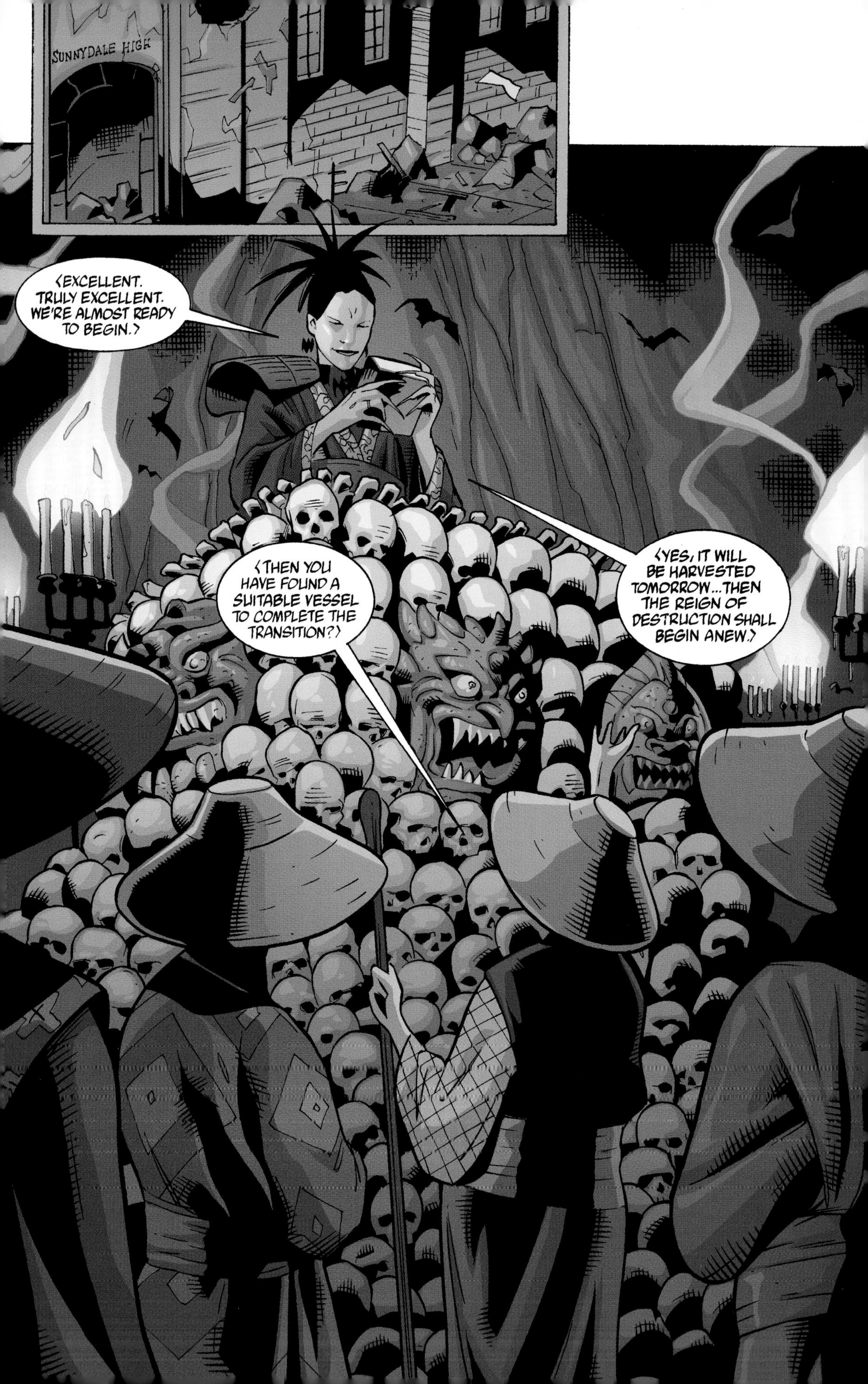
SUNNYDALE HIGH
<EXCELLENT. TRULY EXCELLENT. WE'RE ALMOST READY TO BEGIN.>
<THEN YOU HAVE FOUND A SUITABLE VESSEL TO COMPLETE THE TRANSITION?>
<YES, IT WILL BE HARVESTED TOMORROW...THEN THE REIGN OF DESTRUCTION SHALL BEGIN ANEW.>

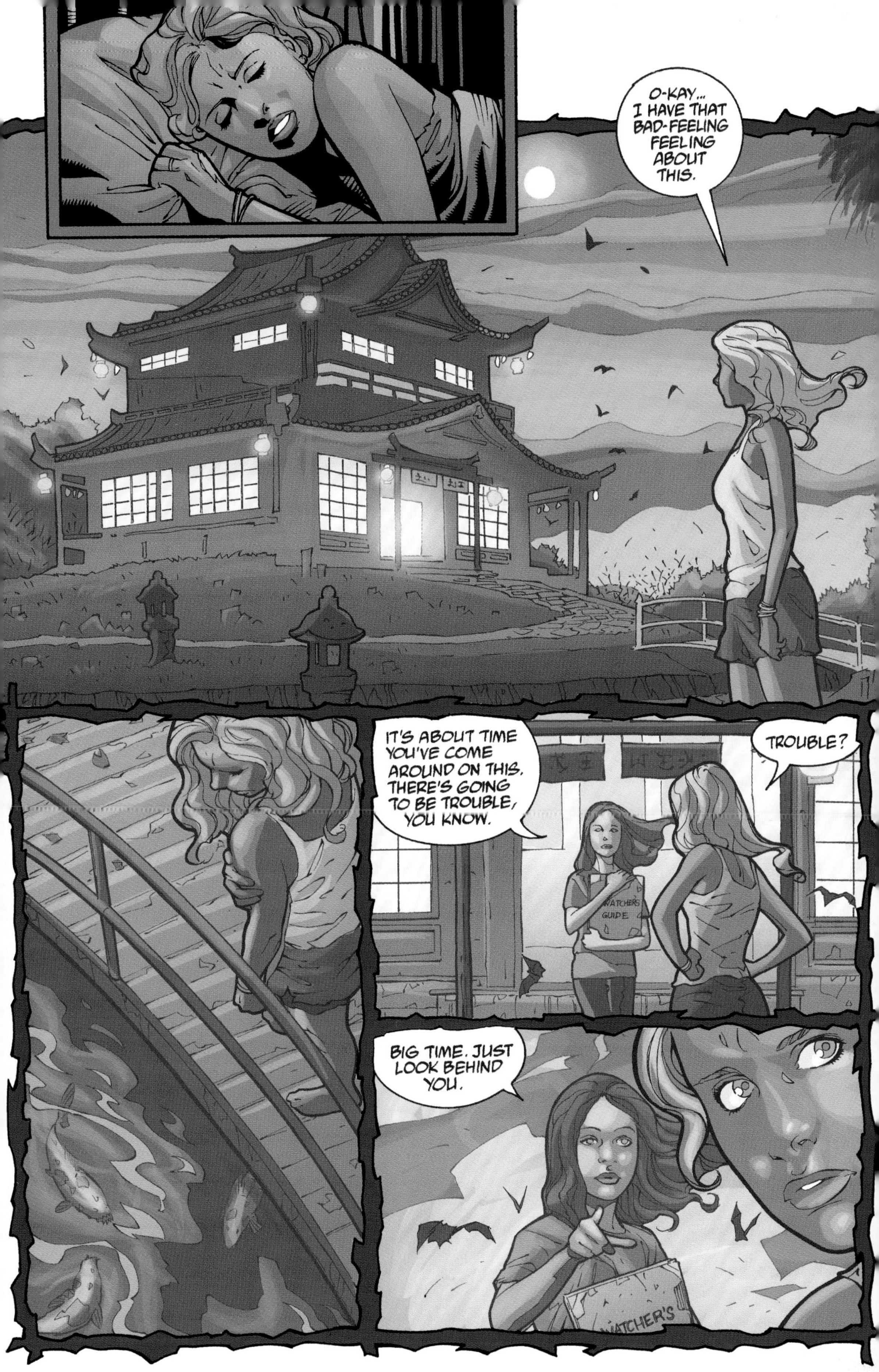
O-KAY... I HAVE THAT BAD-FEELING FEELING ABOUT THIS.
IT'S ABOUT TIME YOU'VE COME AROUND ON THIS. THERE'S GOING TO BE TROUBLE, YOU KNOW.
TROUBLE?
WATCHER'S GUIDE
BIG TIME. JUST LOOK BEHIND YOU.
WATCHER'S

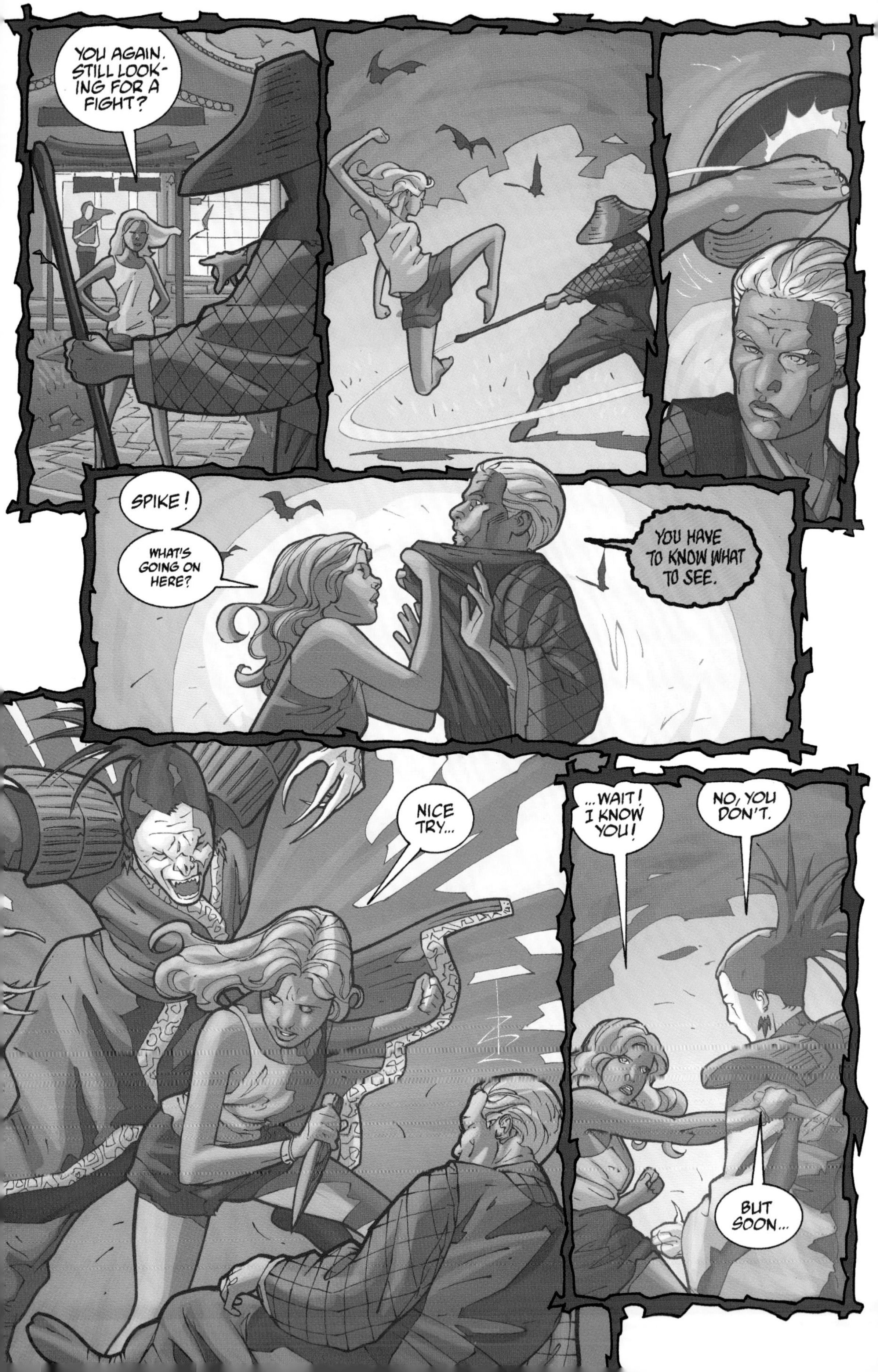
YOU AGAIN. STILL LOOK-ING FOR A FIGHT?
SPIKE!
WHAT'S GOING ON HERE?
YOU HAVE TO KNOW WHAT TO SEE.
NICE TRY...
...WAIT! I KNOW YOU!
NO, YOU DON'T.
BUT SOON...

OH!

DAWN...WHAT ARE YOU DOING?

I HEARD VOICES...I WANTED TO SEE IF YOU'RE OKAY.

AND YOU CAME IN TO CHECK ON ME? I DON'T THINK SO. WHAT'S THE REAL DEAL?

UM...WELL...I KNOW YOU'RE STILL MAD AT ME FOR RUNNING AWAY...

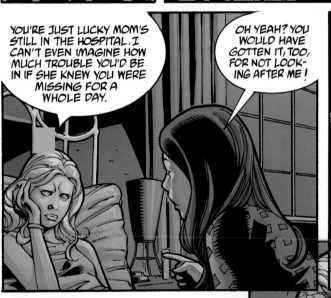

YOU'RE JUST LUCKY MOM'S STILL IN THE HOSPITAL. I CAN'T EVEN IMAGINE HOW MUCH TROUBLE YOU'D BE IN IF SHE KNEW YOU WERE MISSING FOR A WHOLE DAY.

OH YEAH? YOU WOULD HAVE GOTTEN IT, TOO, FOR NOT LOOKING AFTER ME!

DON'T YOU TRY TO MAKE THIS ABOUT ME. YOU'RE THE ONE WHO RAN OFF --AND INTO SPIKE'S LAIR, EVEN! WHAT WERE YOU THINKING?

HE'S FUN TO HANG OUT WITH. HE DOESN'T TREAT ME LIKE A KID, LIKE EVERYONE ELSE DOES. BESIDES, I DON'T CARE WHAT YOU SAY--THERE'S GOOD IN HIM.

VAMPIRE EQUALS EVIL CREATURE OF THE UNDEAD. SPIKE DOESN'T HAVE A *SOUL*...AND EVEN *WHEN* HE DID, I BET YOU COULDN'T TRUST HIM.

AND WHAT MAKES YOU THINK I WON'T DOUBLE-CROSS YOU?

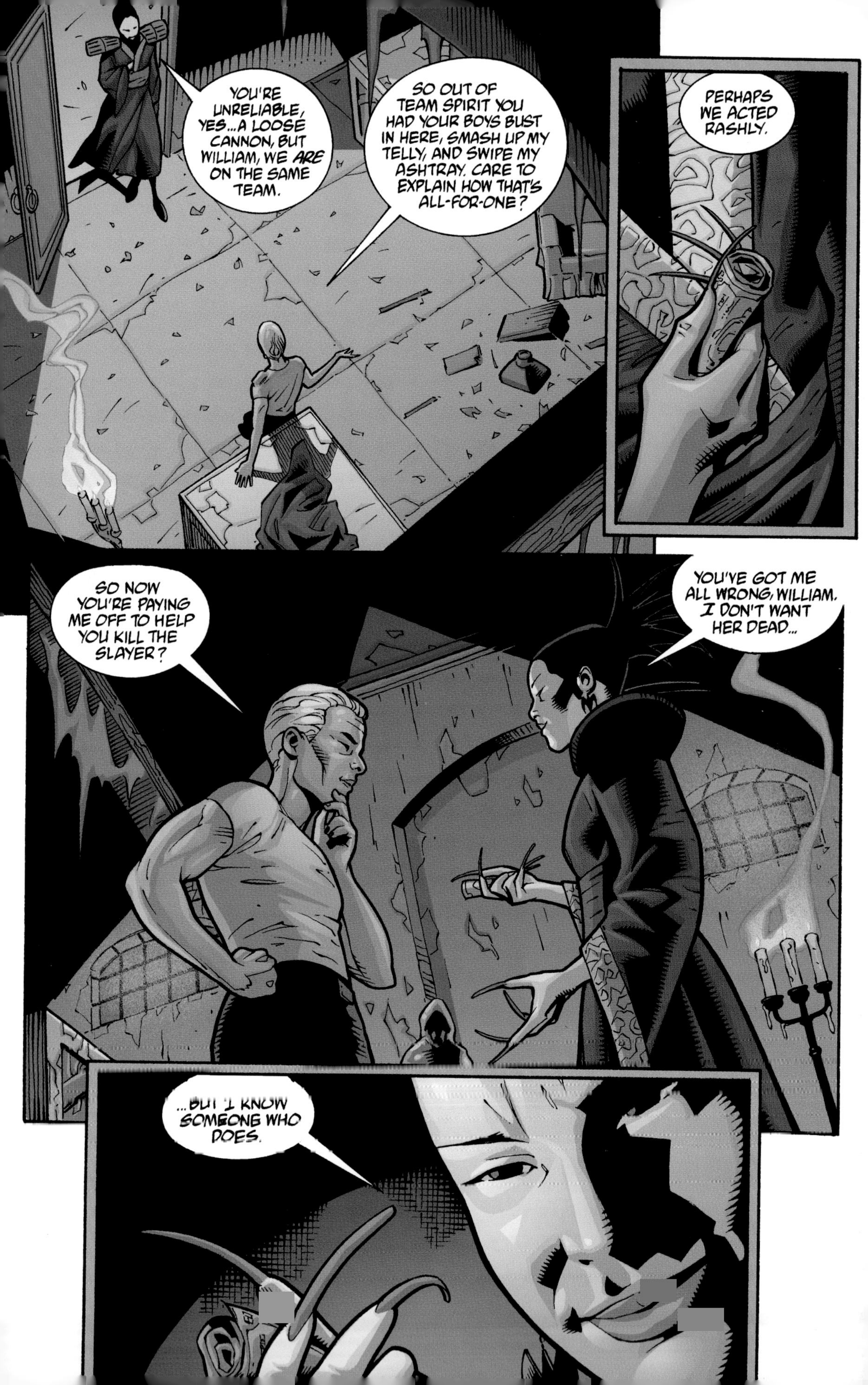
YOU'RE UNRELIABLE, YES...A LOOSE CANNON, BUT WILLIAM, WE *ARE* ON THE SAME TEAM.
SO OUT OF TEAM SPIRIT YOU HAD YOUR BOYS BUST IN HERE, SMASH UP MY TELLY, AND SWIPE MY ASHTRAY. CARE TO EXPLAIN HOW THAT'S ALL-FOR-ONE?
PERHAPS WE ACTED RASHLY.
SO NOW YOU'RE PAYING ME OFF TO HELP YOU KILL THE SLAYER?
YOU'VE GOT ME ALL WRONG, WILLIAM. I DON'T WANT HER DEAD...
...BUT I KNOW SOMEONE WHO DOES.

YOU *CAN TOO* TRUST SPIKE. HE MIGHT NOT HAVE A SOUL, BUT HE'S GOT A GOOD HEART.

GIVE ME A BREAK! WOULD YOU LISTEN TO YOURSELF! HE DOESN'T HAVE A HEART ANY MORE THAN HE HAS A SOUL!

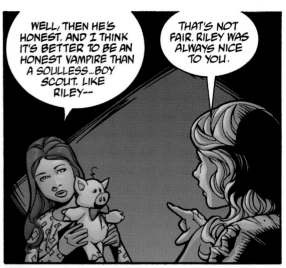

WELL, THEN HE'S HONEST. AND I THINK IT'S BETTER TO BE AN HONEST VAMPIRE THAN A SOULLESS...BOY SCOUT. LIKE RILEY--

THAT'S NOT FAIR. RILEY WAS ALWAYS NICE TO YOU.

PLEASE. HE NEVER LIKED ME. NOT FOR REAL. YOU DON'T REMEMBER.

REMEMBER WHAT? HE DID TOO LIKE YOU. WHERE'S THIS COMING FROM?

YOU'RE SO WRAPPED UP IN YOUR SLAYER WORLD YOU NEVER HAVE TIME TO BE A GOOD BIG SISTER...OR A GOOD GIRL-FRIEND. RILEY LOST *HIS* SOUL WHEN HE LET THAT SLUTTY VAMPIRE GIRL SUCK HIM DRY. AND WE ALL KNOW HOW ANGEL LOST HIS.

YOU ARE *NOT* MY SISTER.

WHATEVER. THANKS FOR LISTENING.

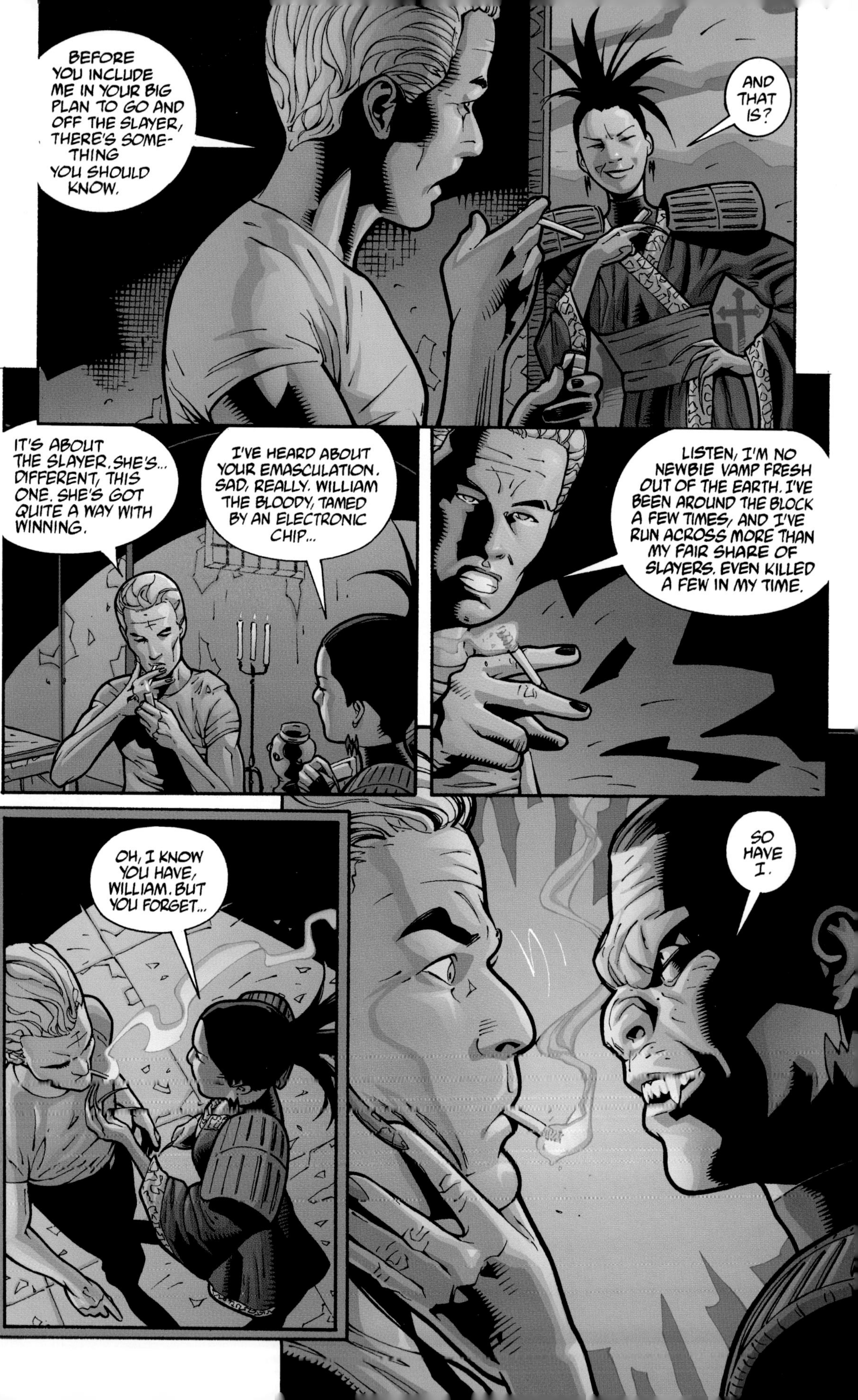
BEFORE YOU INCLUDE ME IN YOUR BIG PLAN TO GO AND OFF THE SLAYER, THERE'S SOMETHING YOU SHOULD KNOW.
AND THAT IS?
IT'S ABOUT THE SLAYER. SHE'S... DIFFERENT, THIS ONE. SHE'S GOT QUITE A WAY WITH WINNING.
I'VE HEARD ABOUT YOUR EMASCULATION. SAD, REALLY. WILLIAM THE BLOODY, TAMED BY AN ELECTRONIC CHIP...
LISTEN, I'M NO NEWBIE VAMP FRESH OUT OF THE EARTH. I'VE BEEN AROUND THE BLOCK A FEW TIMES, AND I'VE RUN ACROSS MORE THAN MY FAIR SHARE OF SLAYERS. EVEN KILLED A FEW IN MY TIME.
OH, I KNOW YOU HAVE, WILLIAM. BUT YOU FORGET...
SO HAVE I.

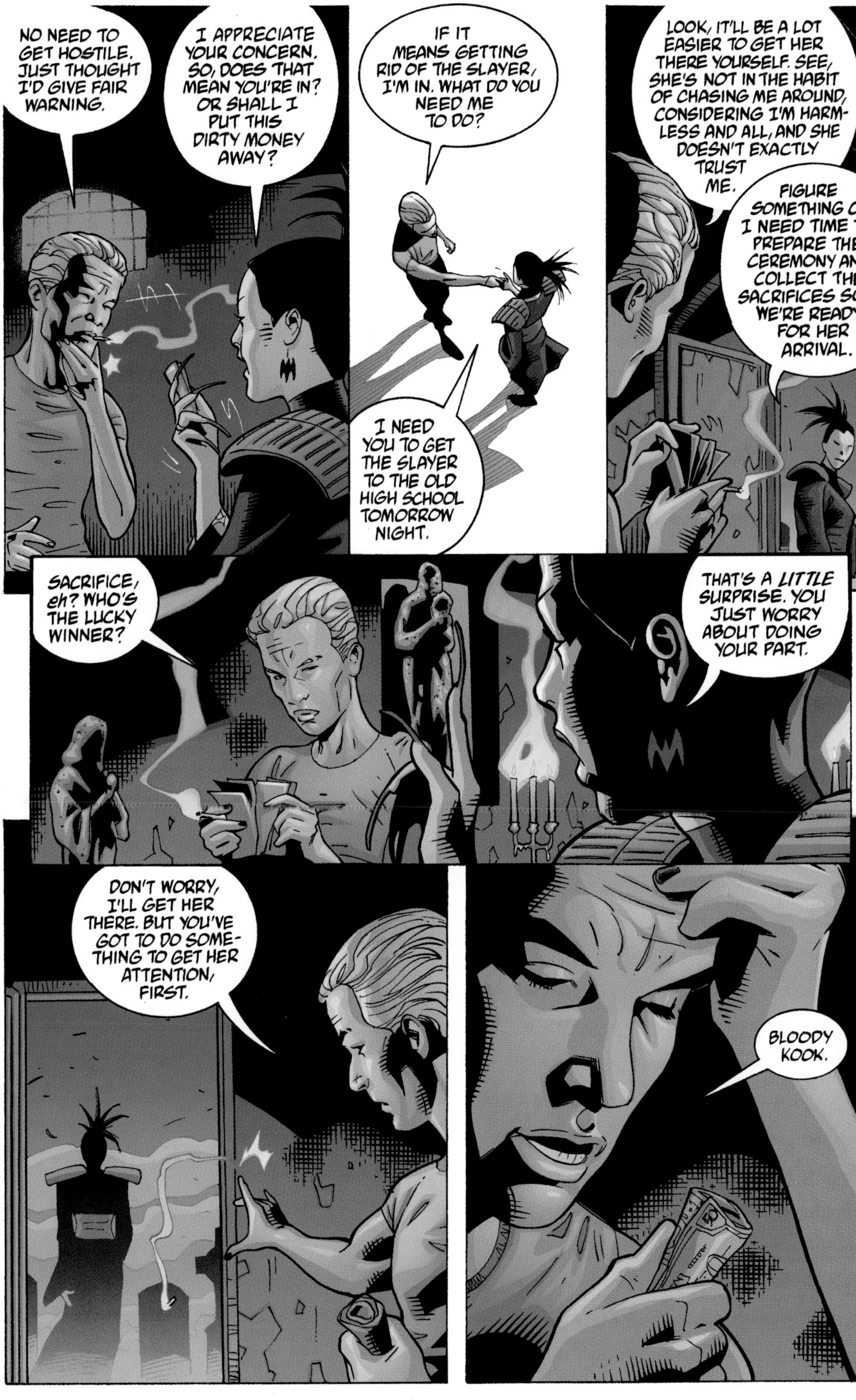
NO NEED TO GET HOSTILE. JUST THOUGHT I'D GIVE FAIR WARNING.
I APPRECIATE YOUR CONCERN. SO, DOES THAT MEAN YOU'RE IN? OR SHALL I PUT THIS DIRTY MONEY AWAY?
IF IT MEANS GETTING RID OF THE SLAYER, I'M IN. WHAT DO YOU NEED ME TO DO?
I NEED YOU TO GET THE SLAYER TO THE OLD HIGH SCHOOL TOMORROW NIGHT.
LOOK, IT'LL BE A LOT EASIER TO GET HER THERE YOURSELF. SEE, SHE'S NOT IN THE HABIT OF CHASING ME AROUND, CONSIDERING I'M HARMLESS AND ALL, AND SHE DOESN'T EXACTLY TRUST ME.
FIGURE SOMETHING OUT. I NEED TIME TO PREPARE THE CEREMONY AND COLLECT THE SACRIFICES SO WE'RE READY FOR HER ARRIVAL.
SACRIFICE, eh? WHO'S THE LUCKY WINNER?
THAT'S A LITTLE SURPRISE. YOU JUST WORRY ABOUT DOING YOUR PART.
DON'T WORRY, I'LL GET HER THERE. BUT YOU'VE GOT TO DO SOMETHING TO GET HER ATTENTION, FIRST.
BLOODY KOOK.

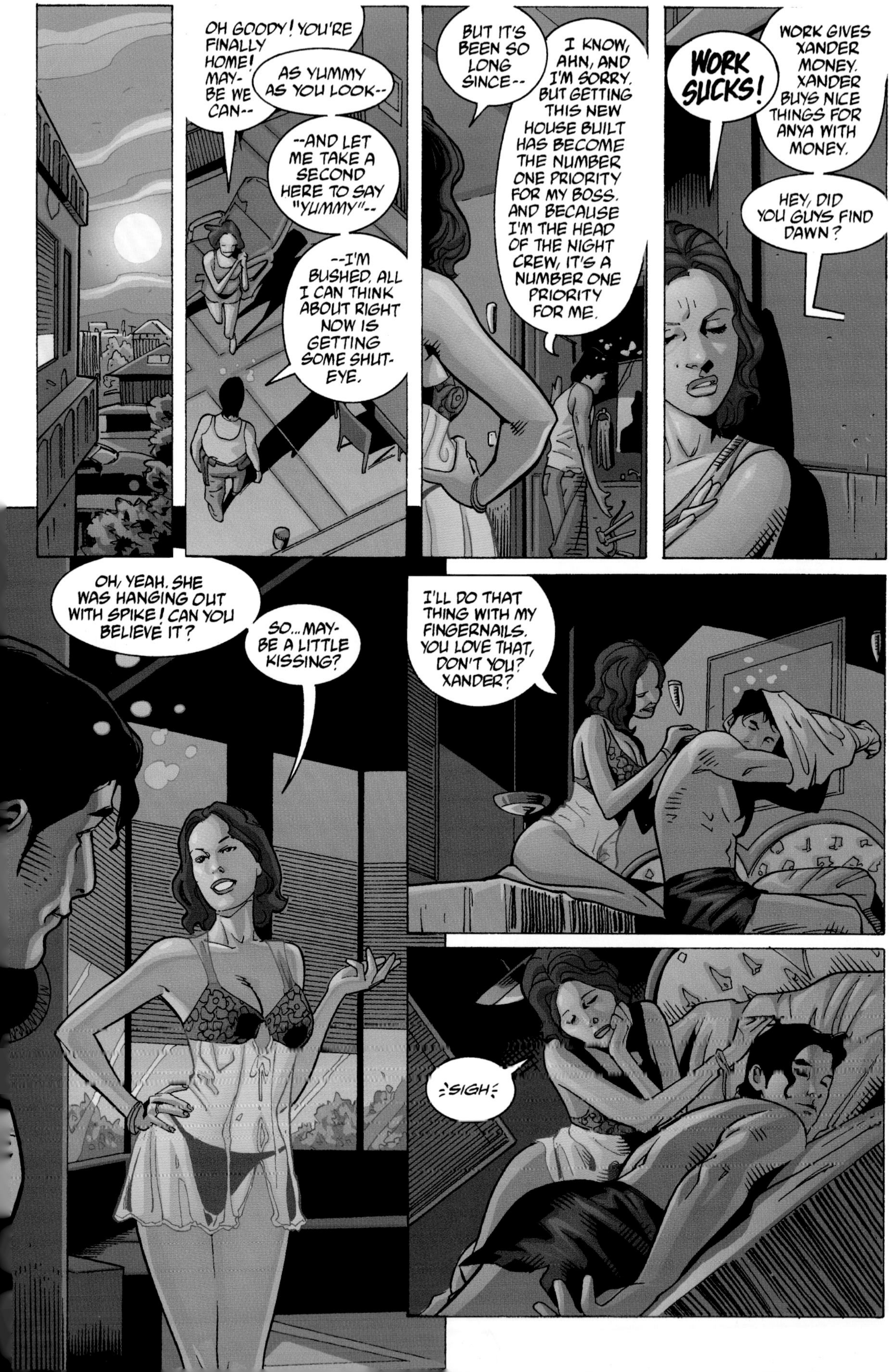
OH GOODY! YOU'RE FINALLY HOME! MAY-BE WE CAN--
AS YUMMY AS YOU LOOK--
--AND LET ME TAKE A SECOND HERE TO SAY "YUMMY"--
--I'M BUSHED. ALL I CAN THINK ABOUT RIGHT NOW IS GETTING SOME SHUT-EYE.
BUT IT'S BEEN SO LONG SINCE--
I KNOW, AHN, AND I'M SORRY. BUT GETTING THIS NEW HOUSE BUILT HAS BECOME THE NUMBER ONE PRIORITY FOR MY BOSS. AND BECAUSE I'M THE HEAD OF THE NIGHT CREW, IT'S A NUMBER ONE PRIORITY FOR ME.
WORK SUCKS!
WORK GIVES XANDER MONEY. XANDER BUYS NICE THINGS FOR ANYA WITH MONEY.
HEY, DID YOU GUYS FIND DAWN?
OH, YEAH. SHE WAS HANGING OUT WITH SPIKE! CAN YOU BELIEVE IT?
SO...MAY-BE A LITTLE KISSING?
I'LL DO THAT THING WITH MY FINGERNAILS. YOU LOVE THAT, DON'T YOU? XANDER?
SIGH

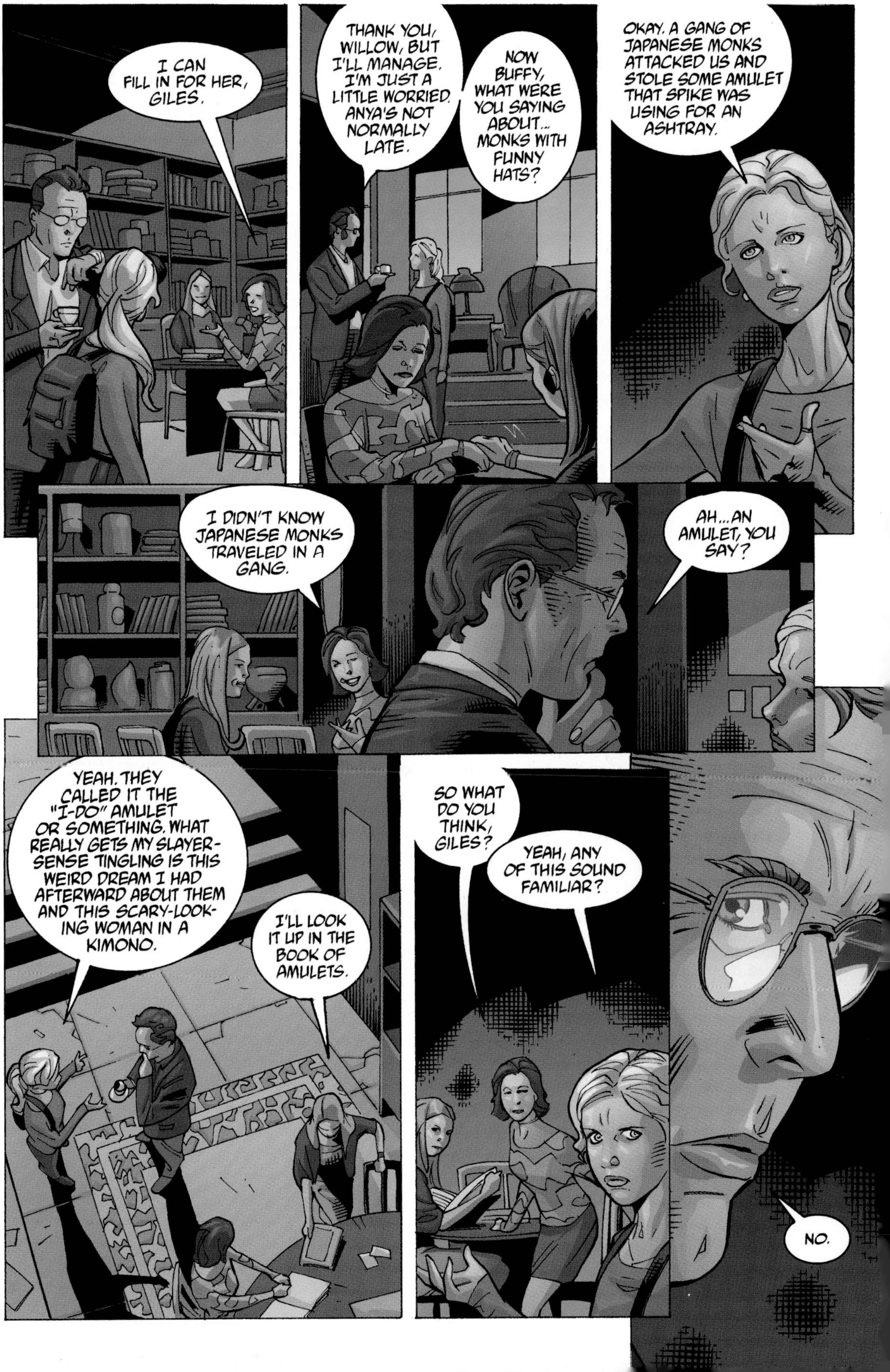
I CAN FILL IN FOR HER, GILES.
THANK YOU, WILLOW, BUT I'LL MANAGE. I'M JUST A LITTLE WORRIED. ANYA'S NOT NORMALLY LATE.
NOW BUFFY, WHAT WERE YOU SAYING ABOUT... MONKS WITH FUNNY HATS?
OKAY. A GANG OF JAPANESE MONKS ATTACKED US AND STOLE SOME AMULET THAT SPIKE WAS USING FOR AN ASHTRAY.
I DIDN'T KNOW JAPANESE MONKS TRAVELED IN A GANG.
AH...AN AMULET, YOU SAY?
YEAH. THEY CALLED IT THE "I-DO" AMULET OR SOMETHING. WHAT REALLY GETS MY SLAYER-SENSE TINGLING IS THIS WEIRD DREAM I HAD AFTERWARD ABOUT THEM AND THIS SCARY-LOOKING WOMAN IN A KIMONO.
I'LL LOOK IT UP IN THE BOOK OF AMULETS.
SO WHAT DO YOU THINK, GILES?
YEAH, ANY OF THIS SOUND FAMILIAR?
NO.

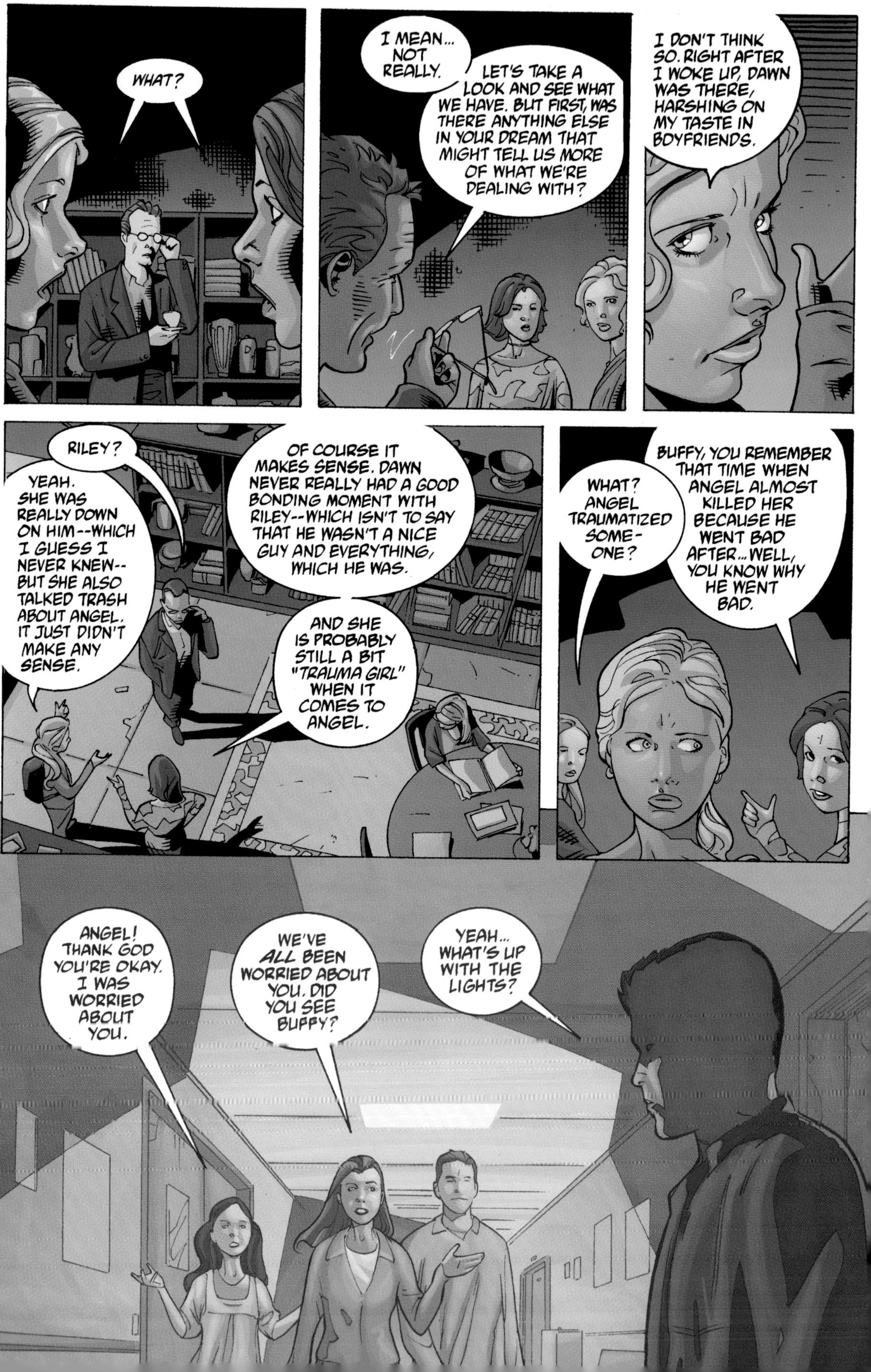
WHAT?
I MEAN... NOT REALLY.
LET'S TAKE A LOOK AND SEE WHAT WE HAVE. BUT FIRST, WAS THERE ANYTHING ELSE IN YOUR DREAM THAT MIGHT TELL US MORE OF WHAT WE'RE DEALING WITH?
I DON'T THINK SO. RIGHT AFTER I WOKE UP, DAWN WAS THERE, HARSHING ON MY TASTE IN BOYFRIENDS.
RILEY?
YEAH. SHE WAS REALLY DOWN ON HIM--WHICH I GUESS I NEVER KNEW--BUT SHE ALSO TALKED TRASH ABOUT ANGEL. IT JUST DIDN'T MAKE ANY SENSE.
OF COURSE IT MAKES SENSE. DAWN NEVER REALLY HAD A GOOD BONDING MOMENT WITH RILEY--WHICH ISN'T TO SAY THAT HE WASN'T A NICE GUY AND EVERYTHING, WHICH HE WAS.
AND SHE IS PROBABLY STILL A BIT "TRAUMA GIRL" WHEN IT COMES TO ANGEL.
BUFFY, YOU REMEMBER THAT TIME WHEN ANGEL ALMOST KILLED HER BECAUSE HE WENT BAD AFTER... WELL, YOU KNOW WHY HE WENT BAD.
WHAT? ANGEL TRAUMATIZED SOME-ONE?
ANGEL! THANK GOD YOU'RE OKAY. I WAS WORRIED ABOUT YOU.
WE'VE ALL BEEN WORRIED ABOUT YOU. DID YOU SEE BUFFY?
YEAH... WHAT'S UP WITH THE LIGHTS?

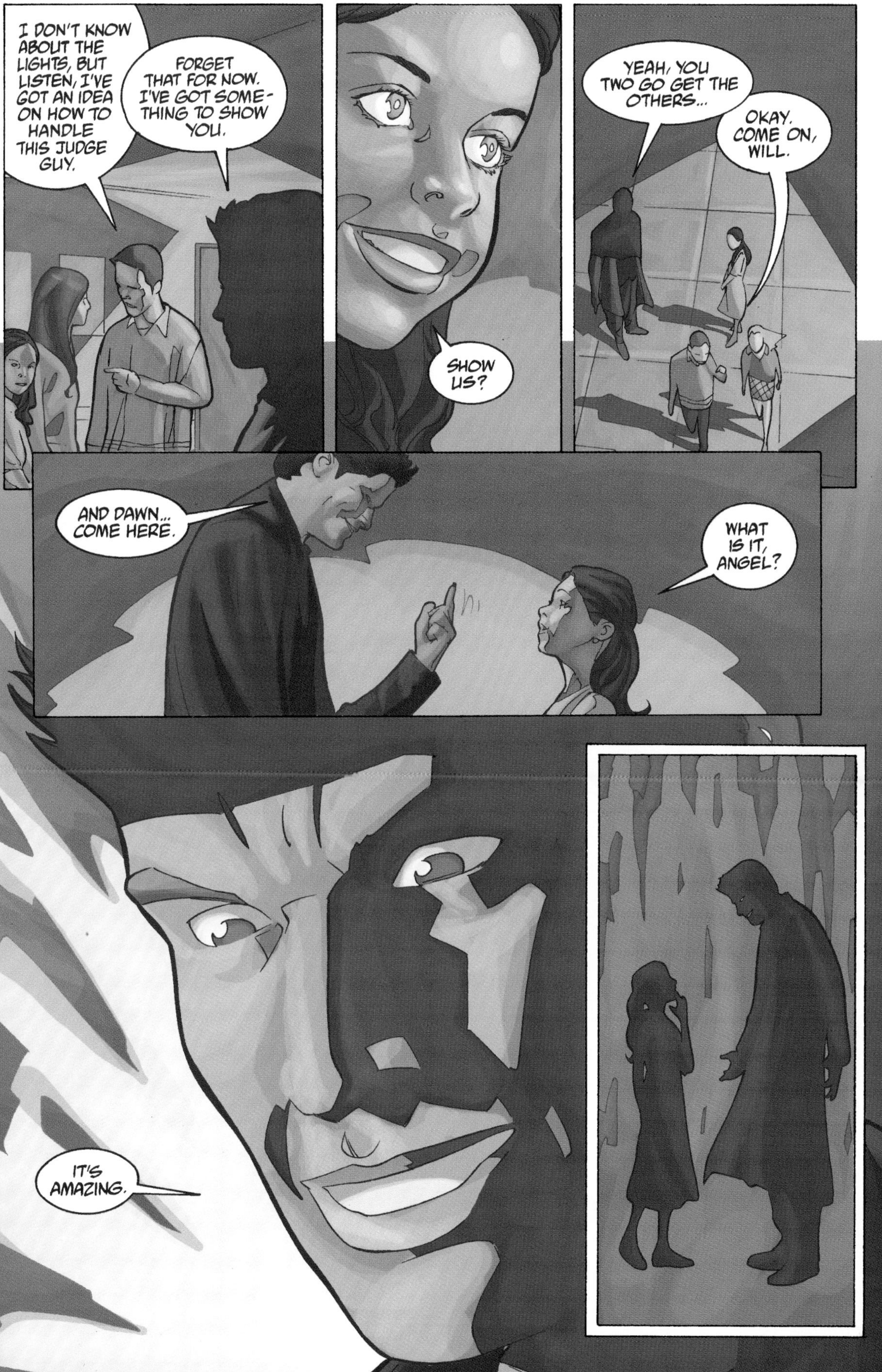

I DON'T KNOW ABOUT THE LIGHTS, BUT LISTEN, I'VE GOT AN IDEA ON HOW TO HANDLE THIS JUDGE GUY.
FORGET THAT FOR NOW. I'VE GOT SOME-THING TO SHOW YOU.
SHOW US?
YEAH, YOU TWO GO GET THE OTHERS...
OKAY. COME ON, WILL.
AND DAWN... COME HERE.
WHAT IS IT, ANGEL?
IT'S AMAZING.

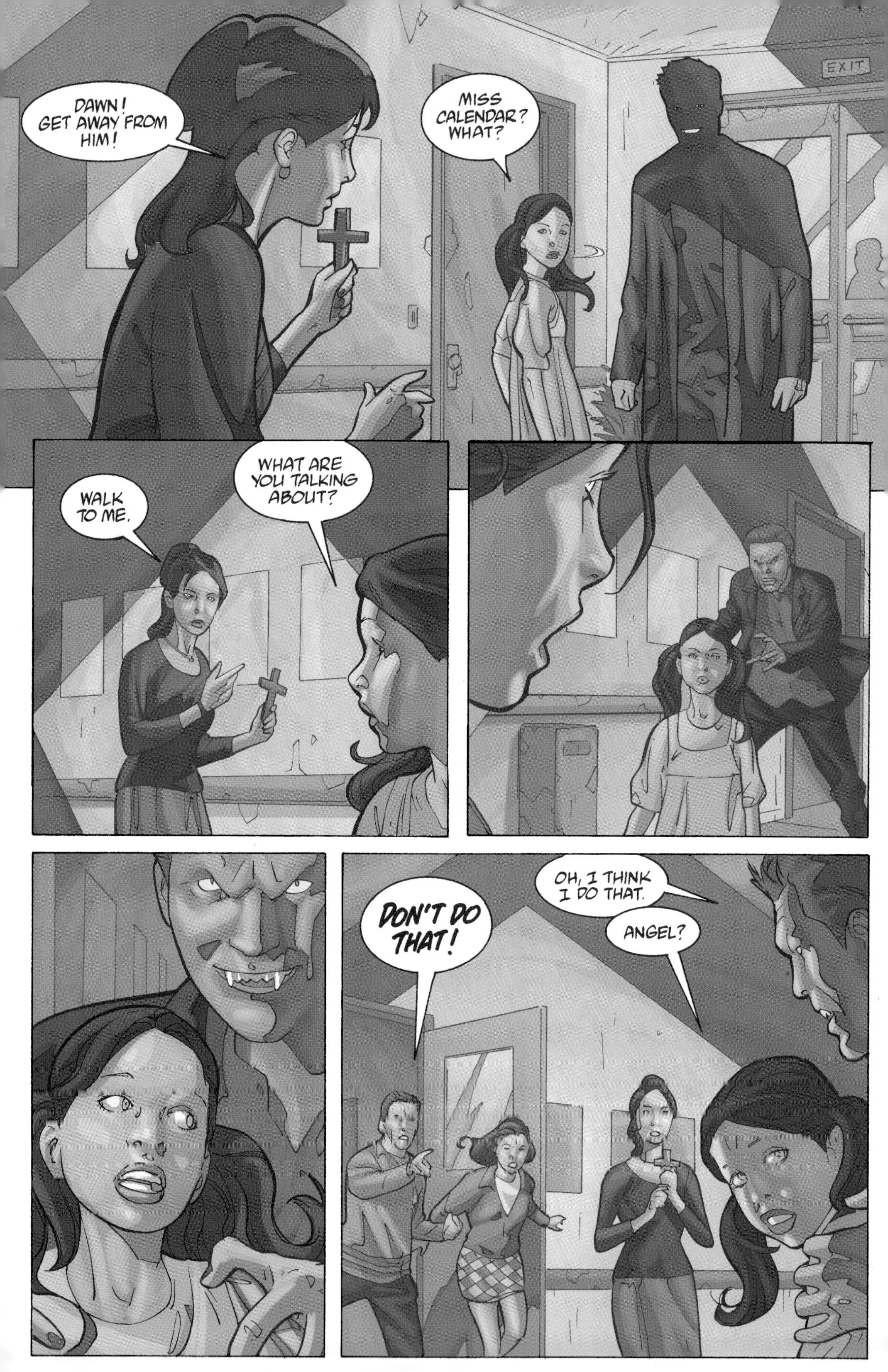
DAWN! GET AWAY FROM HIM!
MISS CALENDAR? WHAT?
WALK TO ME.
WHAT ARE YOU TALKING ABOUT?
DON'T DO THAT!
OH, I THINK I DO THAT.
ANGEL?
EXIT

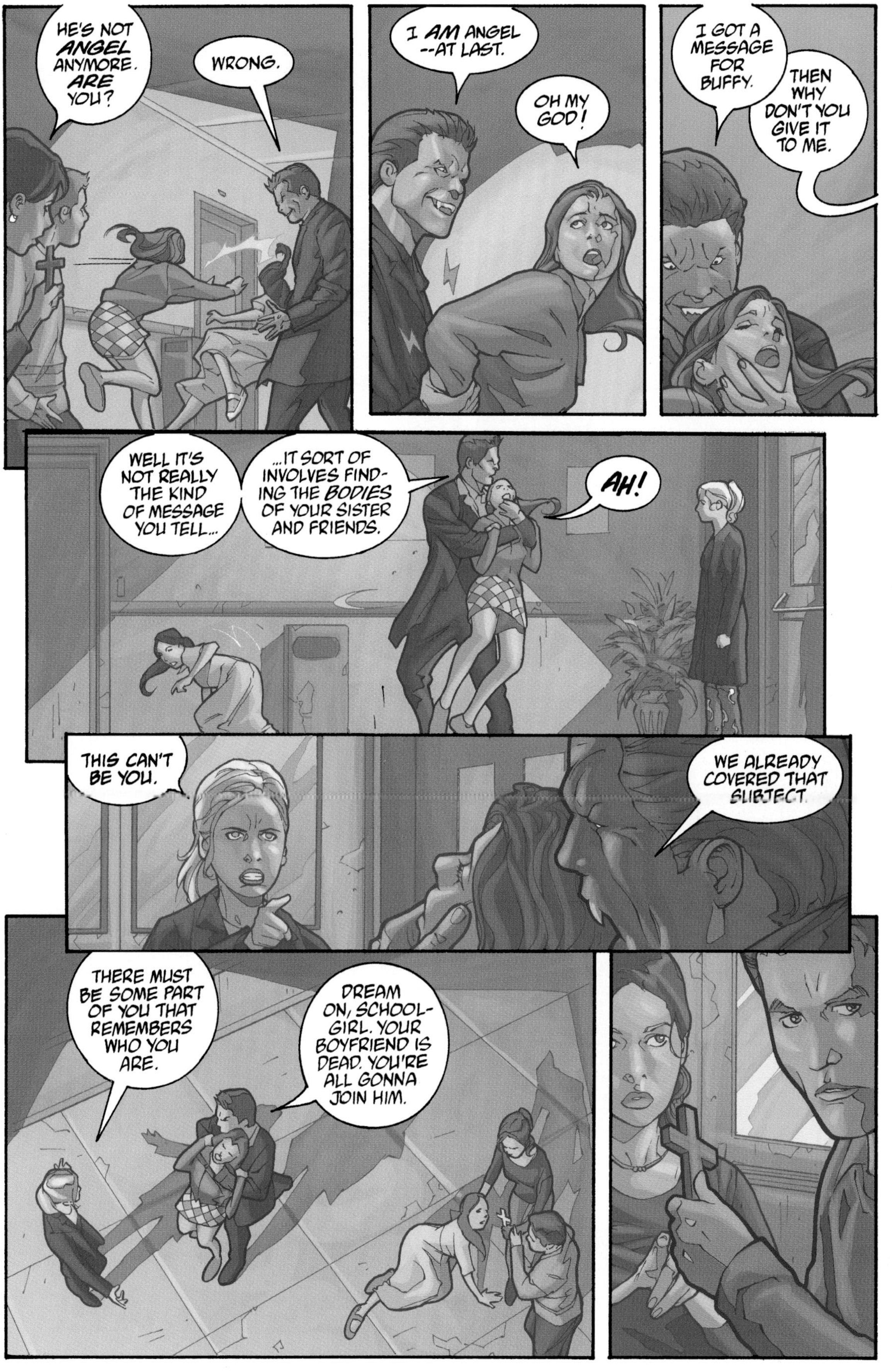

HE'S NOT ANGEL ANYMORE. ARE YOU?
WRONG.
I AM ANGEL --AT LAST.
OH MY GOD!
I GOT A MESSAGE FOR BUFFY.
THEN WHY DON'T YOU GIVE IT TO ME.
WELL IT'S NOT REALLY THE KIND OF MESSAGE YOU TELL...
...IT SORT OF INVOLVES FINDING THE BODIES OF YOUR SISTER AND FRIENDS.
AH!
THIS CAN'T BE YOU.
WE ALREADY COVERED THAT SUBJECT.
THERE MUST BE SOME PART OF YOU THAT REMEMBERS WHO YOU ARE.
DREAM ON, SCHOOLGIRL. YOUR BOYFRIEND IS DEAD. YOU'RE ALL GONNA JOIN HIM.

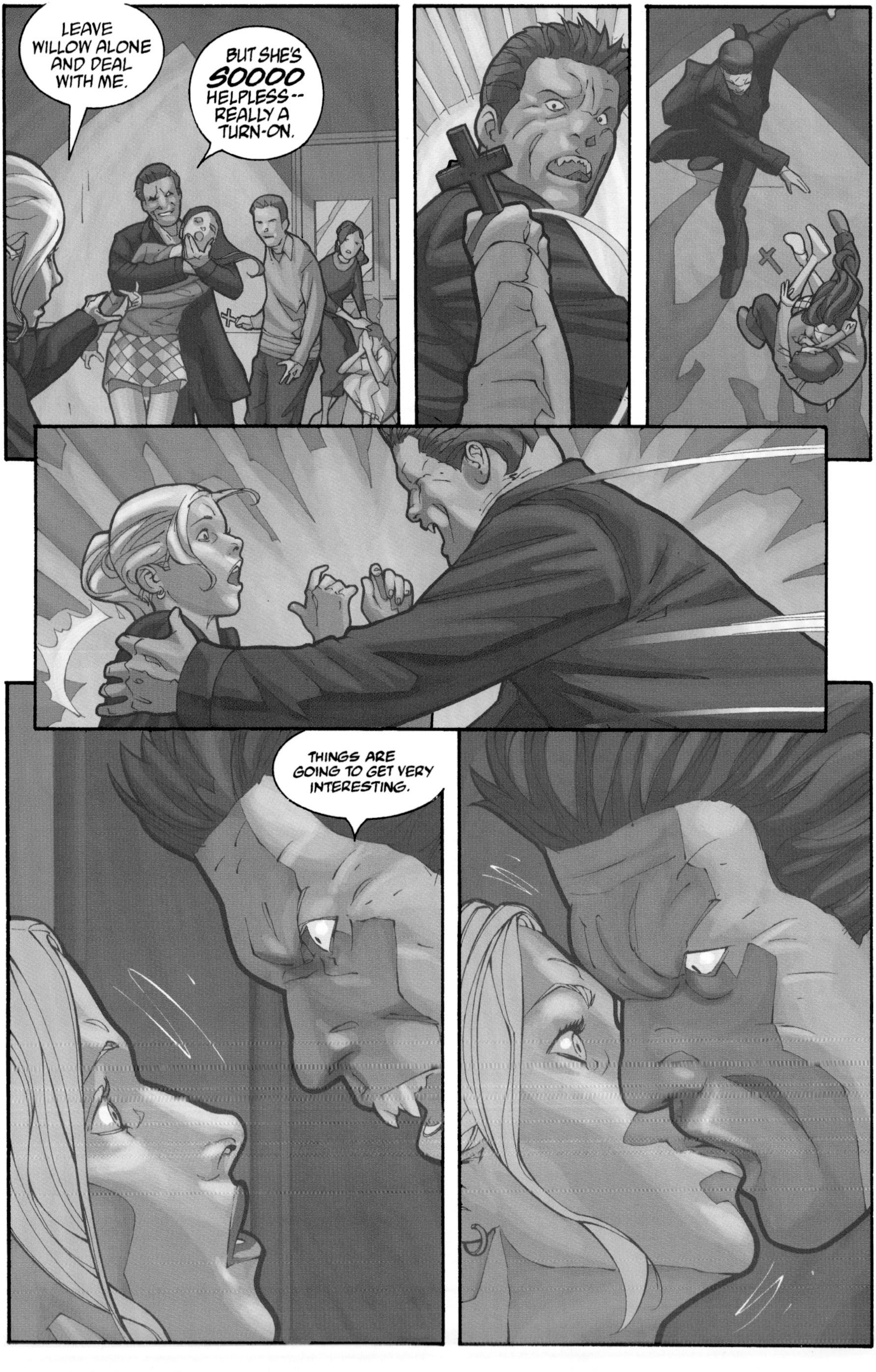
LEAVE WILLOW ALONE AND DEAL WITH ME.
BUT SHE'S SOOOO HELPLESS-- REALLY A TURN-ON.
THINGS ARE GOING TO GET VERY INTERESTING.

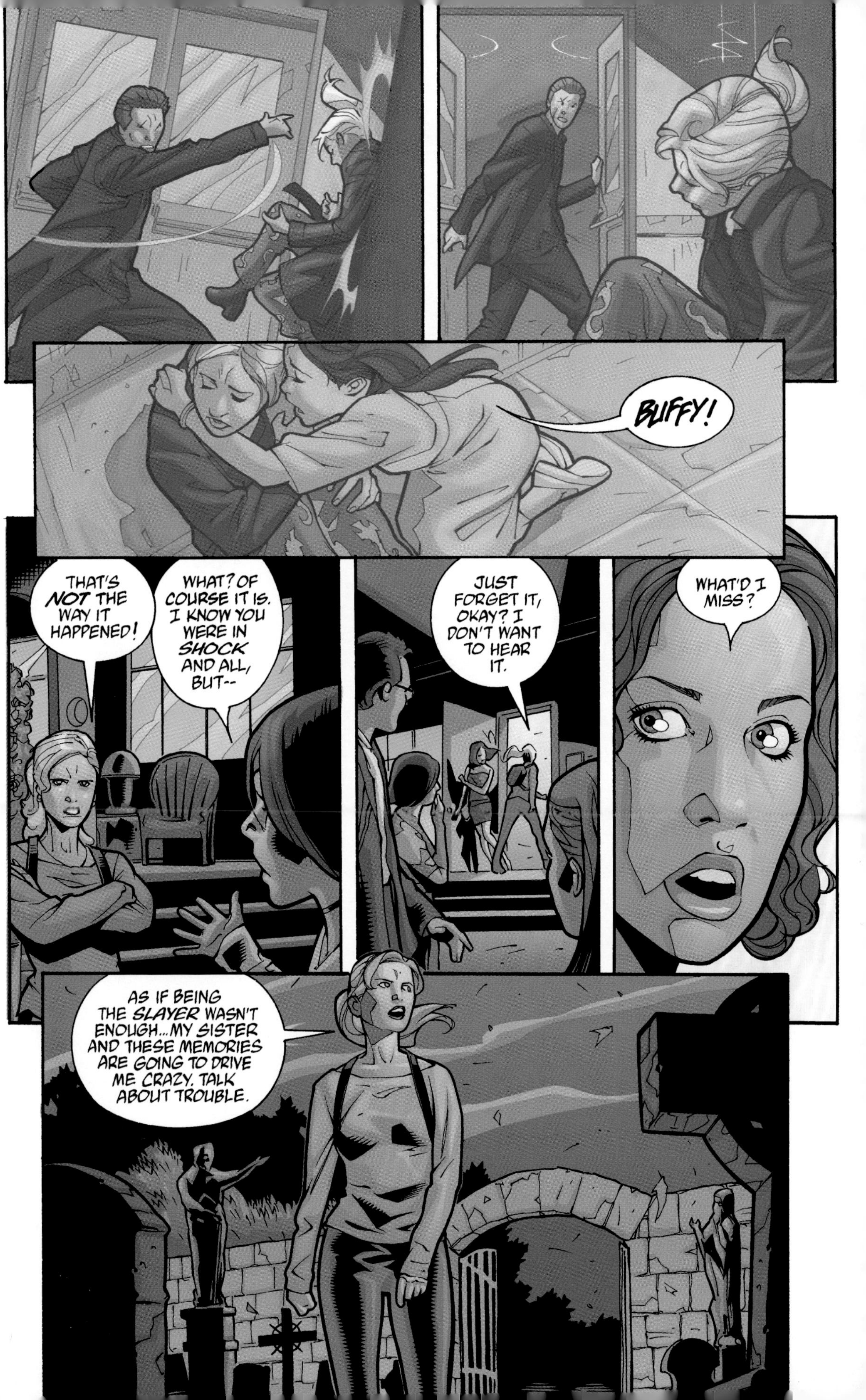
BUFFY!
THAT'S NOT THE WAY IT HAPPENED!
WHAT? OF COURSE IT IS. I KNOW YOU WERE IN SHOCK AND ALL, BUT--
JUST FORGET IT, OKAY? I DON'T WANT TO HEAR IT.
WHAT'D I MISS?
AS IF BEING THE SLAYER WASN'T ENOUGH...MY SISTER AND THESE MEMORIES ARE GOING TO DRIVE ME CRAZY. TALK ABOUT TROUBLE.

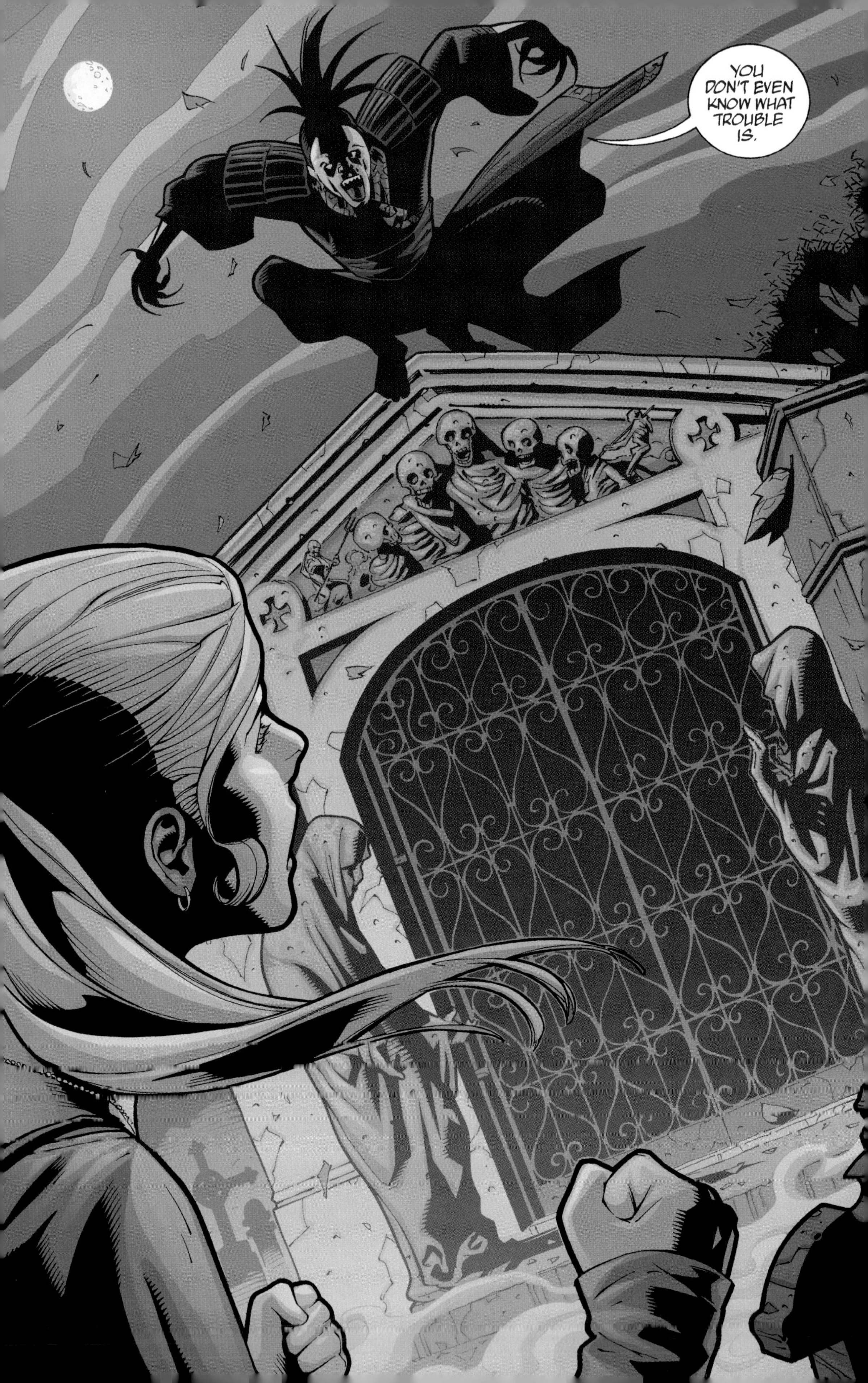
YOU DON'T EVEN KNOW WHAT TROUBLE IS.

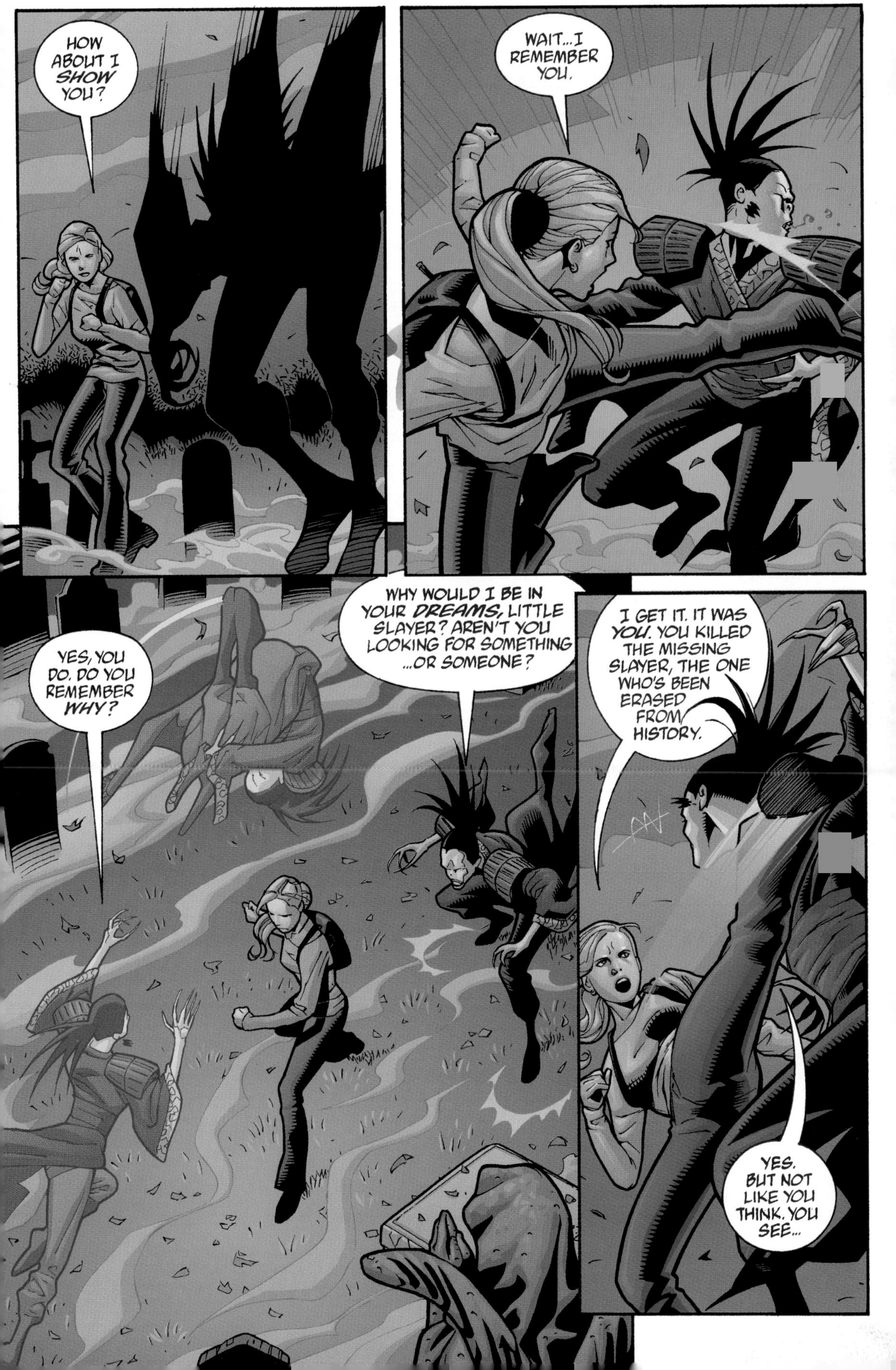
HOW ABOUT I SHOW YOU?
WAIT... I REMEMBER YOU.
YES, YOU DO. DO YOU REMEMBER WHY?
WHY WOULD I BE IN YOUR DREAMS, LITTLE SLAYER? AREN'T YOU LOOKING FOR SOMETHING ...OR SOMEONE?
I GET IT. IT WAS YOU. YOU KILLED THE MISSING SLAYER, THE ONE WHO'S BEEN ERASED FROM HISTORY.
YES. BUT NOT LIKE YOU THINK. YOU SEE...

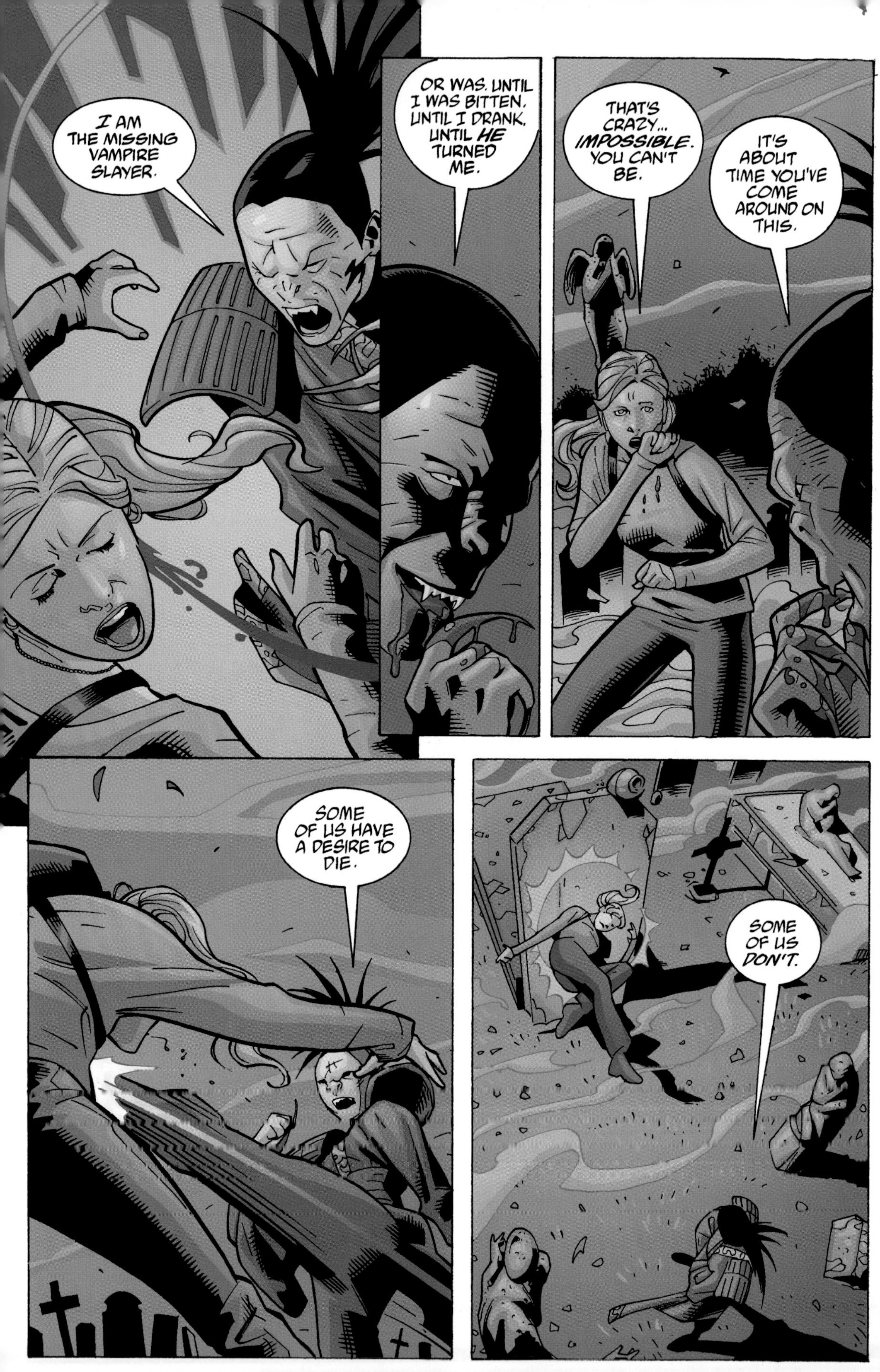
I AM THE MISSING VAMPIRE SLAYER.
OR WAS. UNTIL I WAS BITTEN. UNTIL I DRANK. UNTIL HE TURNED ME.
THAT'S CRAZY... IMPOSSIBLE. YOU CAN'T BE.
IT'S ABOUT TIME YOU'VE COME AROUND ON THIS.
SOME OF US HAVE A DESIRE TO DIE.
SOME OF US DON'T.

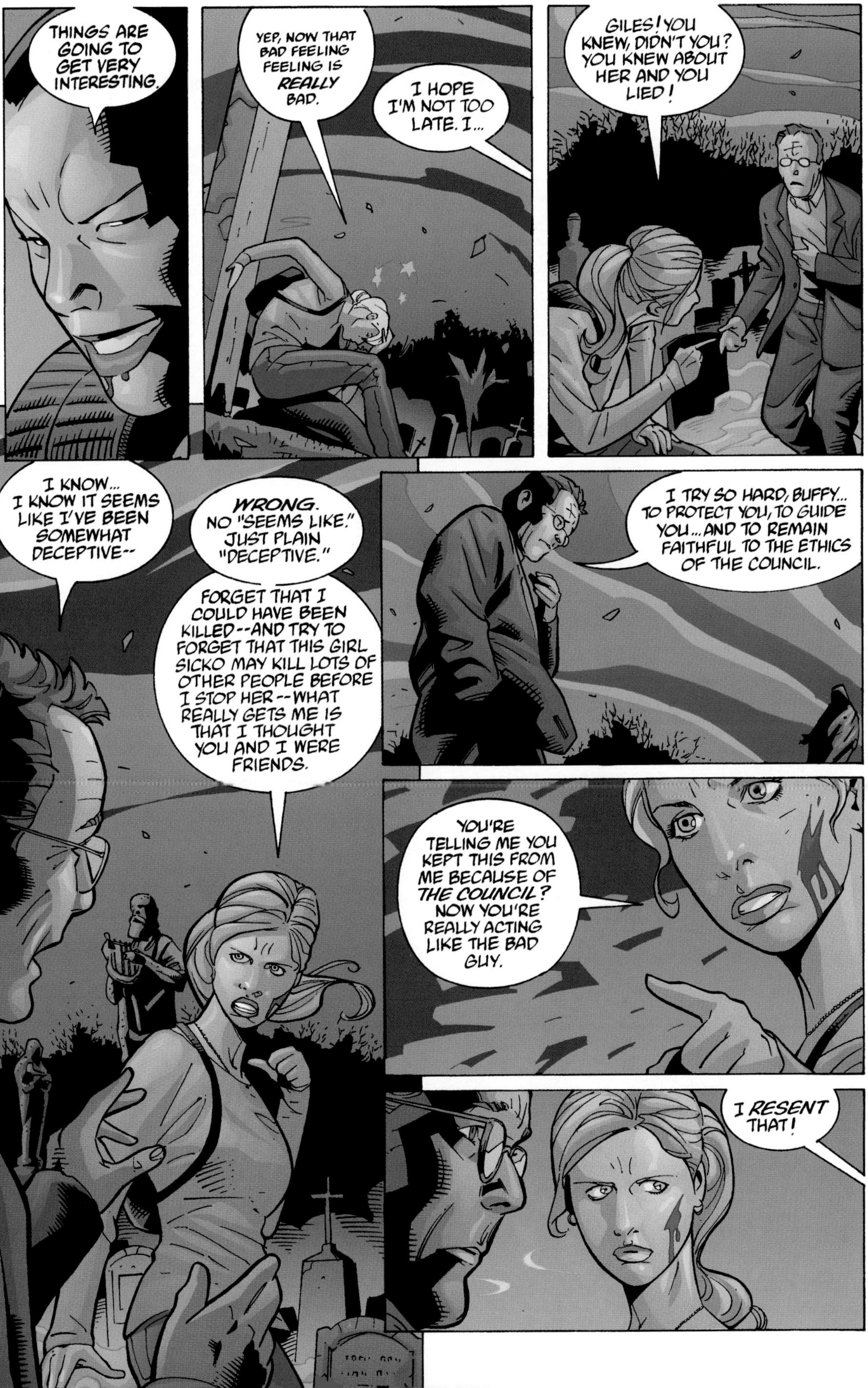
THINGS ARE GOING TO GET VERY INTERESTING.
YEP, NOW THAT BAD FEELING FEELING IS *REALLY* BAD.
I HOPE I'M NOT TOO LATE. I...
GILES! YOU KNEW, DIDN'T YOU? YOU KNEW ABOUT HER AND YOU LIED!
I KNOW... I KNOW IT SEEMS LIKE I'VE BEEN SOMEWHAT DECEPTIVE--
WRONG. NO "SEEMS LIKE." JUST PLAIN "DECEPTIVE."
FORGET THAT I COULD HAVE BEEN KILLED--AND TRY TO FORGET THAT THIS GIRL SICKO MAY KILL LOTS OF OTHER PEOPLE BEFORE I STOP HER--WHAT REALLY GETS ME IS THAT I THOUGHT YOU AND I WERE FRIENDS.
I TRY SO HARD, BUFFY... TO PROTECT YOU, TO GUIDE YOU... AND TO REMAIN FAITHFUL TO THE ETHICS OF THE COUNCIL.
YOU'RE TELLING ME YOU KEPT THIS FROM ME BECAUSE OF *THE COUNCIL*? NOW YOU'RE REALLY ACTING LIKE THE BAD GUY.
I *RESENT* THAT!

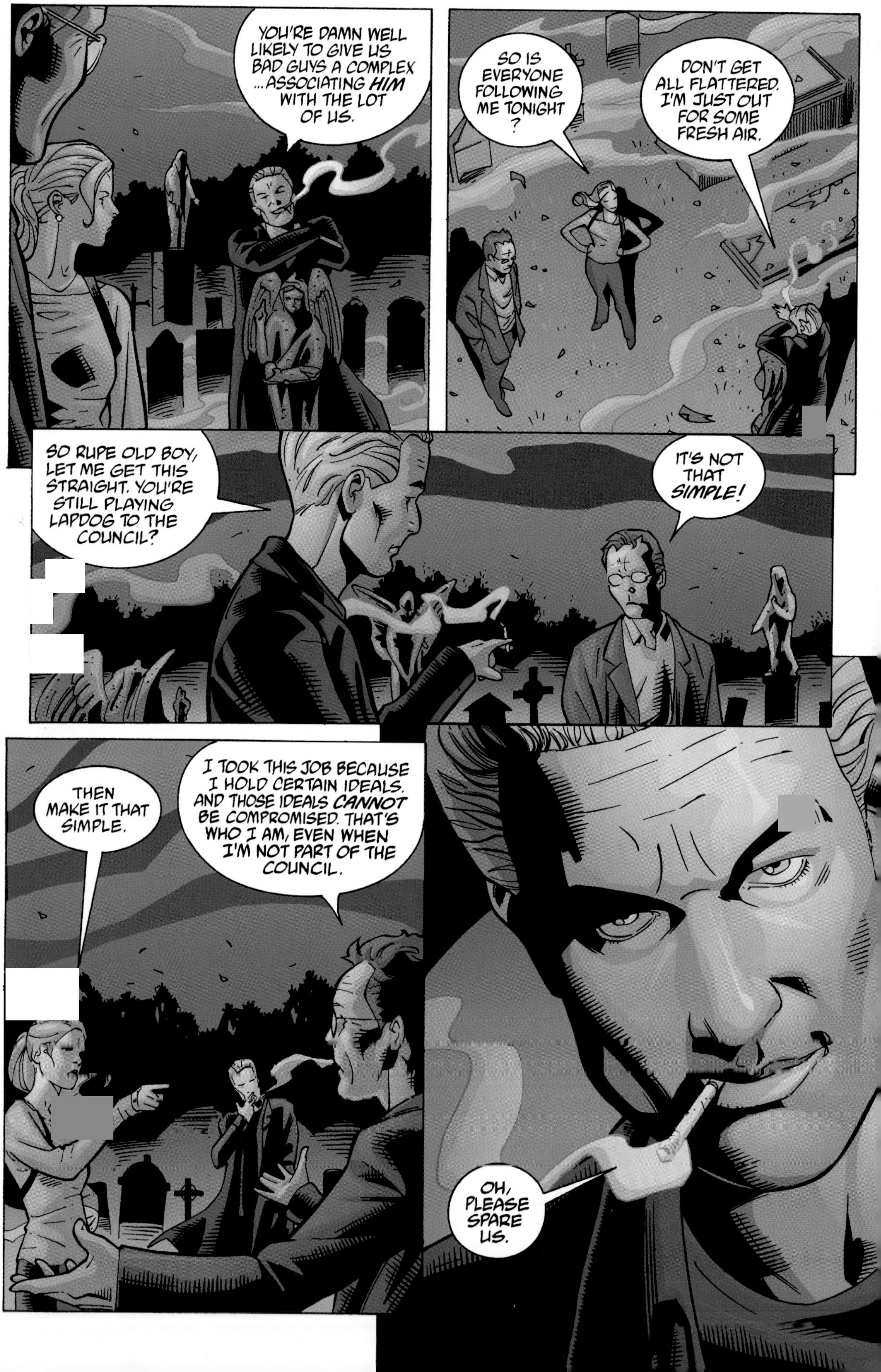
YOU'RE DAMN WELL LIKELY TO GIVE US BAD GUYS A COMPLEX ...ASSOCIATING HIM WITH THE LOT OF US.
SO IS EVERYONE FOLLOWING ME TONIGHT ?
DON'T GET ALL FLATTERED. I'M JUST OUT FOR SOME FRESH AIR.
SO RUPE OLD BOY, LET ME GET THIS STRAIGHT. YOU'RE STILL PLAYING LAPDOG TO THE COUNCIL?
IT'S NOT THAT SIMPLE!
THEN MAKE IT THAT SIMPLE.
I TOOK THIS JOB BECAUSE I HOLD CERTAIN IDEALS. AND THOSE IDEALS CANNOT BE COMPROMISED. THAT'S WHO I AM, EVEN WHEN I'M NOT PART OF THE COUNCIL.
OH, PLEASE SPARE US.

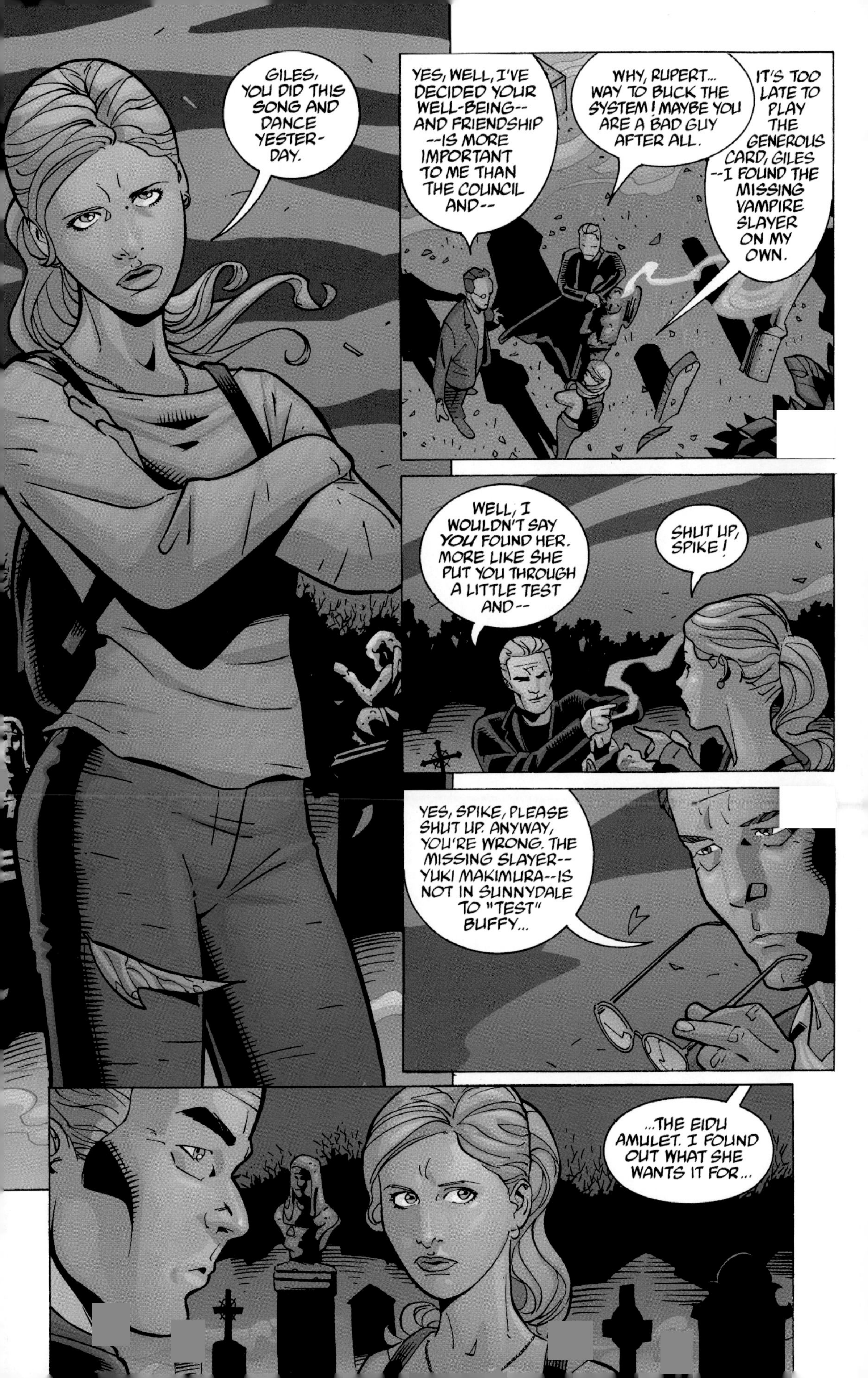
GILES, YOU DID THIS SONG AND DANCE YESTER-DAY.
YES, WELL, I'VE DECIDED YOUR WELL-BEING-- AND FRIENDSHIP --IS MORE IMPORTANT TO ME THAN THE COUNCIL AND--
WHY, RUPERT... WAY TO BUCK THE SYSTEM! MAYBE YOU ARE A BAD GUY AFTER ALL.
IT'S TOO LATE TO PLAY THE GENEROUS CARD, GILES --I FOUND THE MISSING VAMPIRE SLAYER ON MY OWN.
WELL, I WOULDN'T SAY YOU FOUND HER. MORE LIKE SHE PUT YOU THROUGH A LITTLE TEST AND--
SHUT UP, SPIKE!
YES, SPIKE, PLEASE SHUT UP. ANYWAY, YOU'RE WRONG. THE MISSING SLAYER-- YUKI MAKIMURA--IS NOT IN SUNNYDALE TO "TEST" BUFFY...
...THE EIDU AMULET. I FOUND OUT WHAT SHE WANTS IT FOR...

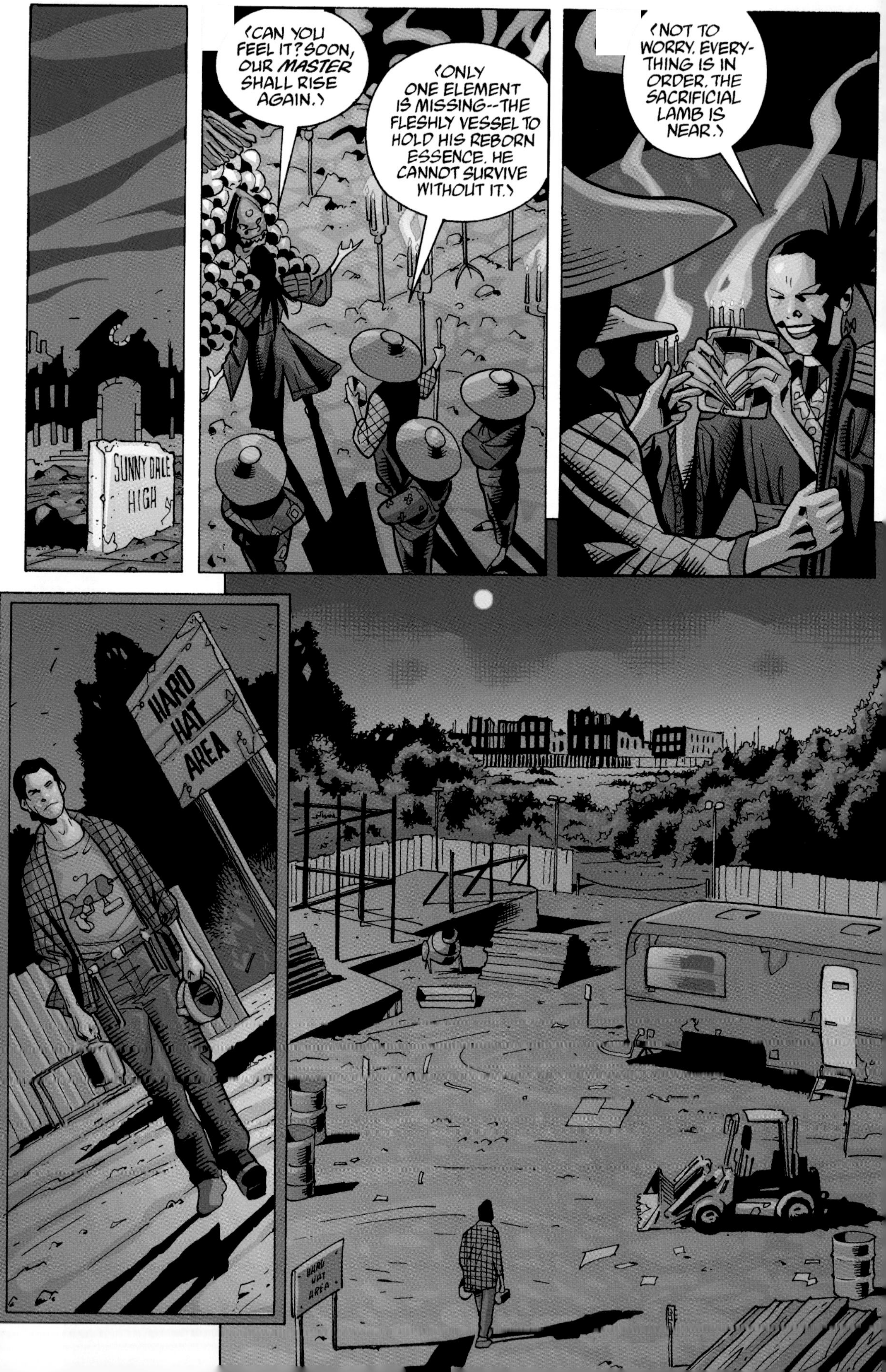
SUNNY DALE HIGH
‹CAN YOU FEEL IT? SOON, OUR *MASTER* SHALL RISE AGAIN.›
‹ONLY ONE ELEMENT IS MISSING--THE FLESHLY VESSEL TO HOLD HIS REBORN ESSENCE. HE CANNOT SURVIVE WITHOUT IT.›
‹NOT TO WORRY. EVERY-THING IS IN ORDER. THE SACRIFICIAL LAMB IS NEAR.›
HARD HAT AREA
HARD HAT AREA

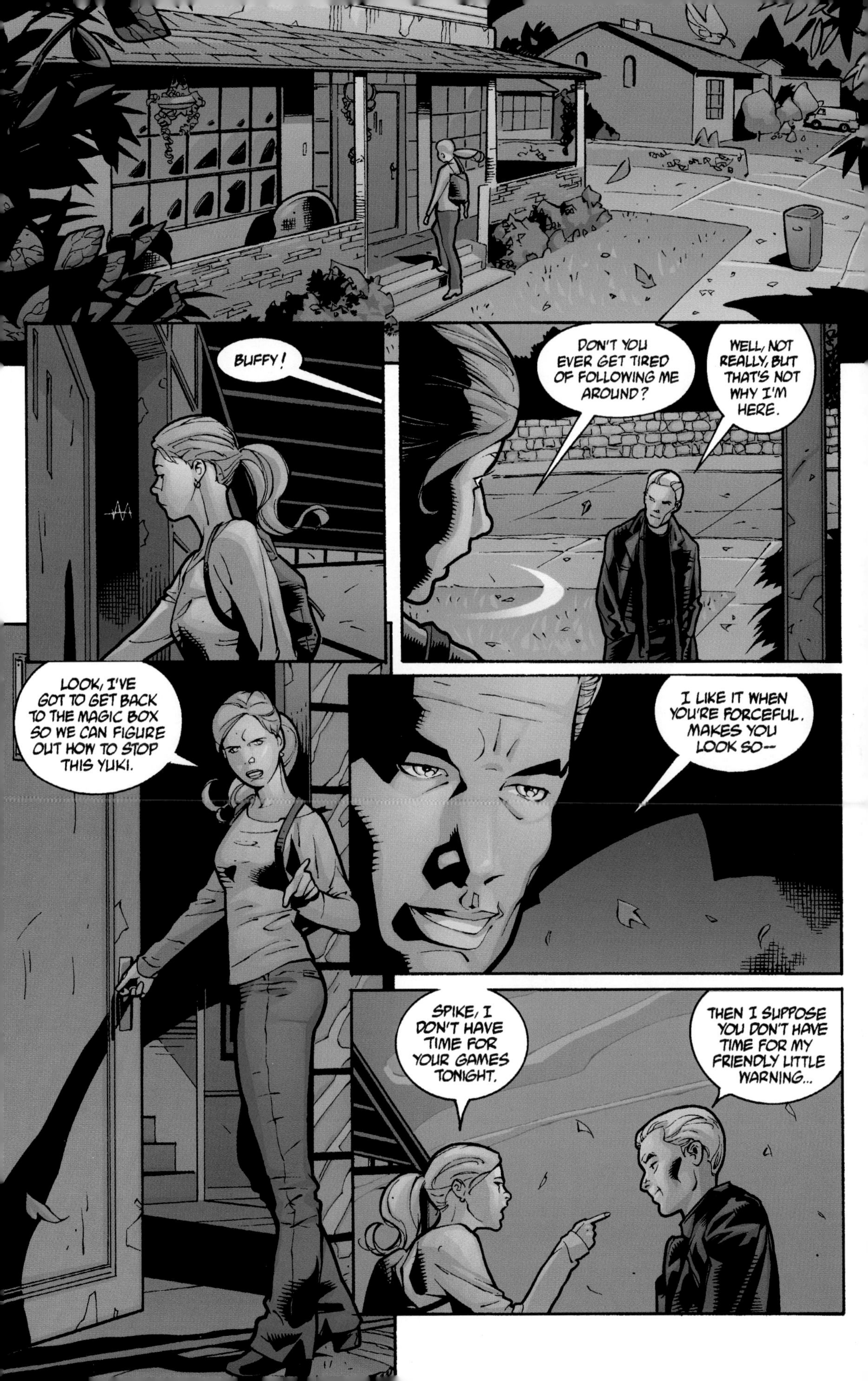
BUFFY!
DON'T YOU EVER GET TIRED OF FOLLOWING ME AROUND?
WELL, NOT REALLY, BUT THAT'S NOT WHY I'M HERE.
LOOK, I'VE GOT TO GET BACK TO THE MAGIC BOX SO WE CAN FIGURE OUT HOW TO STOP THIS YUKI.
I LIKE IT WHEN YOU'RE FORCEFUL. MAKES YOU LOOK SO--
SPIKE, I DON'T HAVE TIME FOR YOUR GAMES TONIGHT.
THEN I SUPPOSE YOU DON'T HAVE TIME FOR MY FRIENDLY LITTLE WARNING...

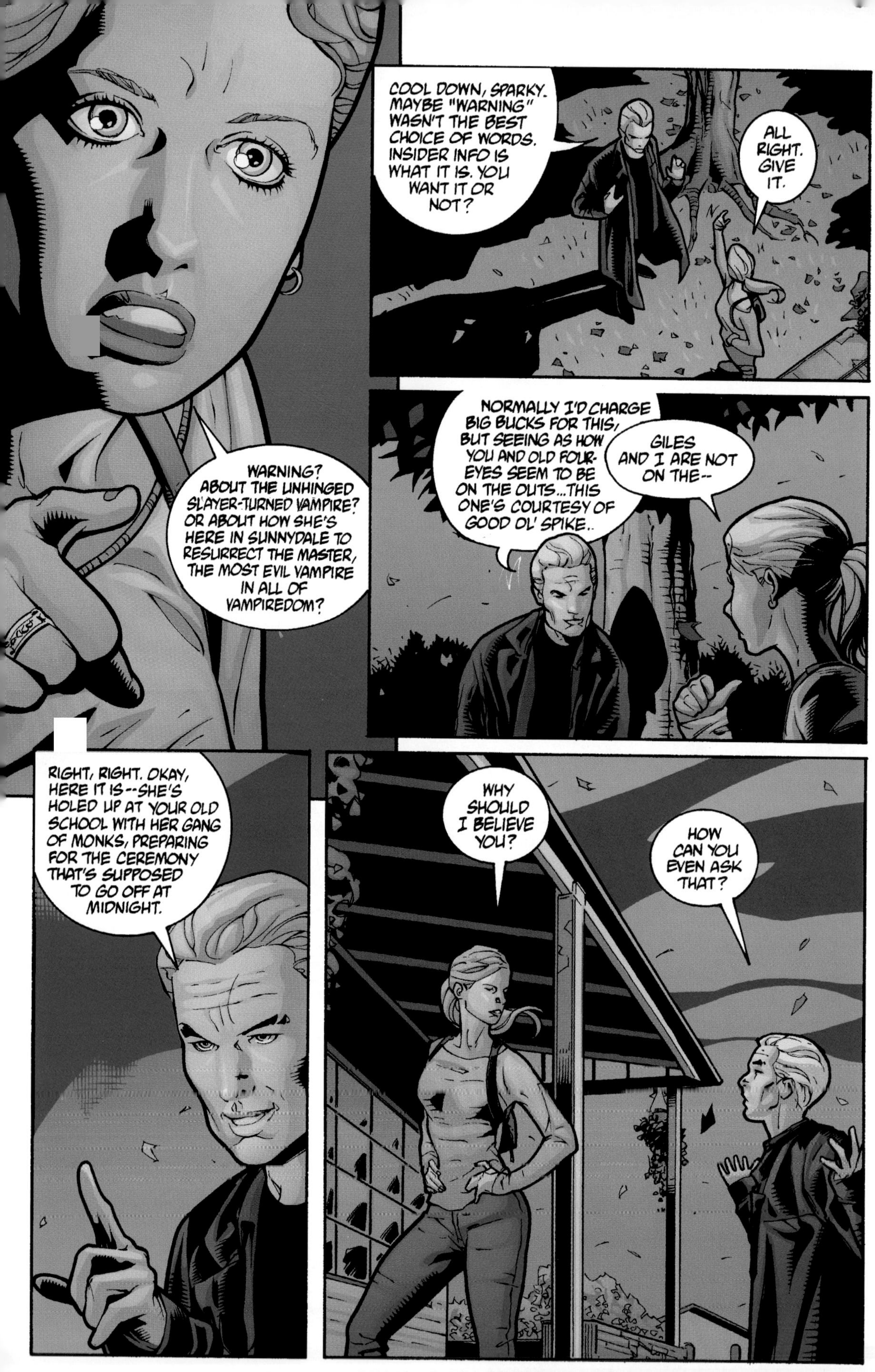
COOL DOWN, SPARKY. MAYBE "WARNING" WASN'T THE BEST CHOICE OF WORDS. INSIDER INFO IS WHAT IT IS. YOU WANT IT OR NOT?
ALL RIGHT. GIVE IT.
WARNING? ABOUT THE UNHINGED SLAYER-TURNED VAMPIRE? OR ABOUT HOW SHE'S HERE IN SUNNYDALE TO RESURRECT THE MASTER, THE MOST EVIL VAMPIRE IN ALL OF VAMPIREDOM?
NORMALLY I'D CHARGE BIG BUCKS FOR THIS, BUT SEEING AS HOW YOU AND OLD FOUR-EYES SEEM TO BE ON THE OUTS...THIS ONE'S COURTESY OF GOOD OL' SPIKE..
GILES AND I ARE NOT ON THE--
RIGHT, RIGHT. OKAY, HERE IT IS--SHE'S HOLED UP AT YOUR OLD SCHOOL WITH HER GANG OF MONKS, PREPARING FOR THE CEREMONY THAT'S SUPPOSED TO GO OFF AT MIDNIGHT.
WHY SHOULD I BELIEVE YOU?
HOW CAN YOU EVEN ASK THAT?

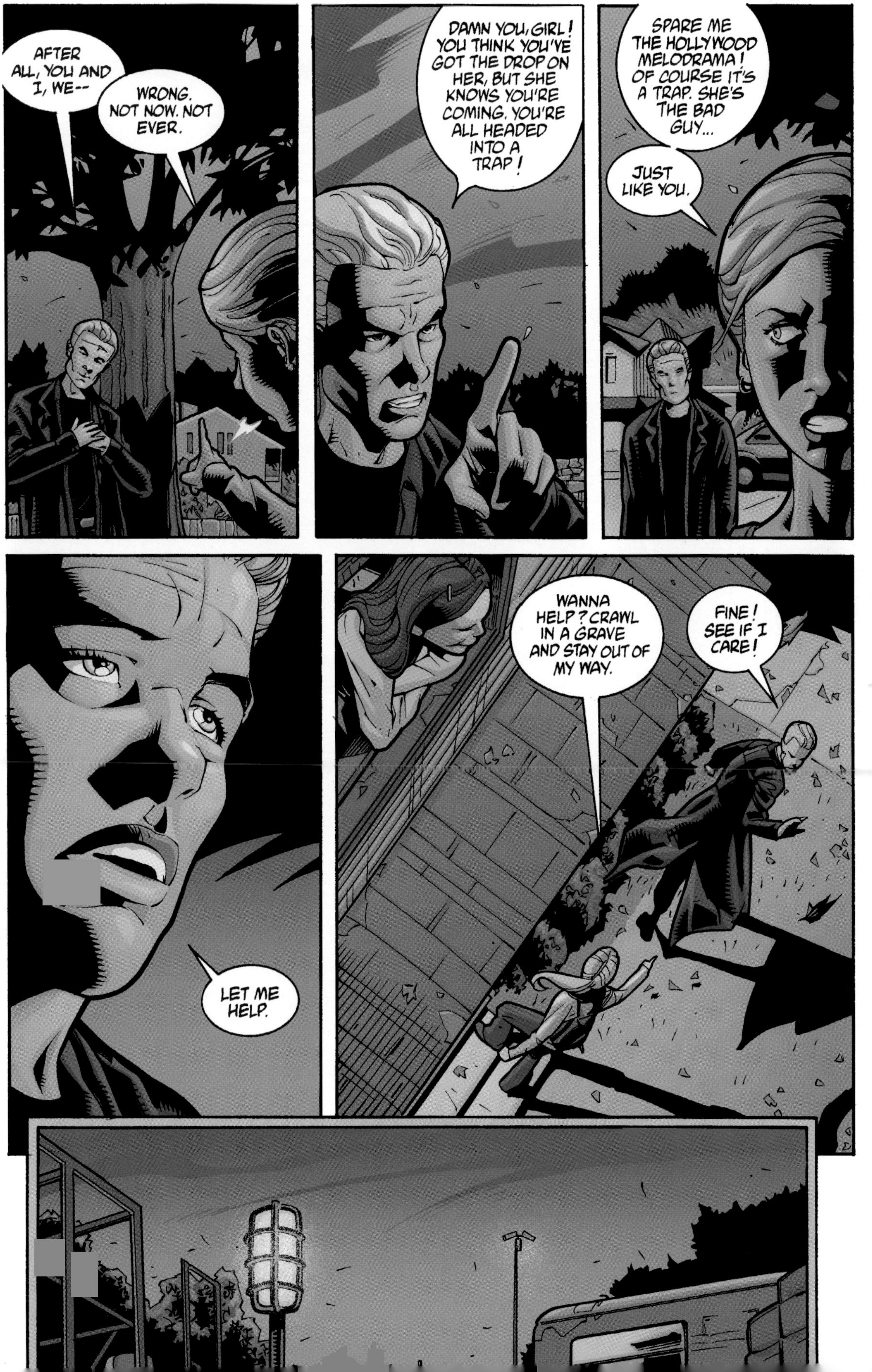
AFTER ALL, YOU AND I, WE--
WRONG. NOT NOW. NOT EVER.
DAMN YOU, GIRL! YOU THINK YOU'VE GOT THE DROP ON HER, BUT SHE KNOWS YOU'RE COMING. YOU'RE ALL HEADED INTO A TRAP!
SPARE ME THE HOLLYWOOD MELODRAMA! OF COURSE IT'S A TRAP. SHE'S THE BAD GUY...
JUST LIKE YOU.
LET ME HELP.
WANNA HELP? CRAWL IN A GRAVE AND STAY OUT OF MY WAY.
FINE! SEE IF I CARE!

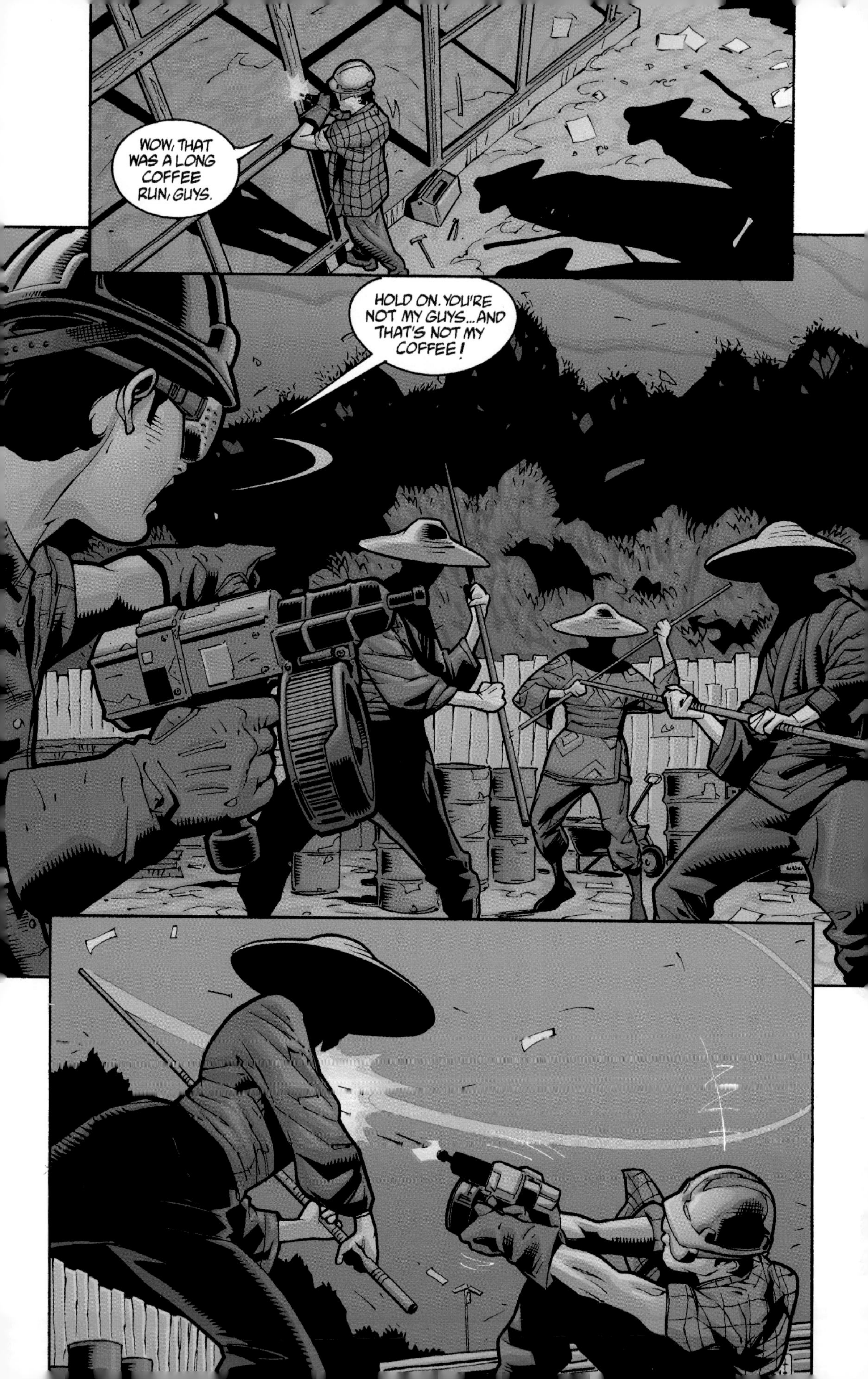
WOW, THAT WAS A LONG COFFEE RUN, GUYS.
HOLD ON. YOU'RE NOT MY GUYS... AND THAT'S NOT MY COFFEE!

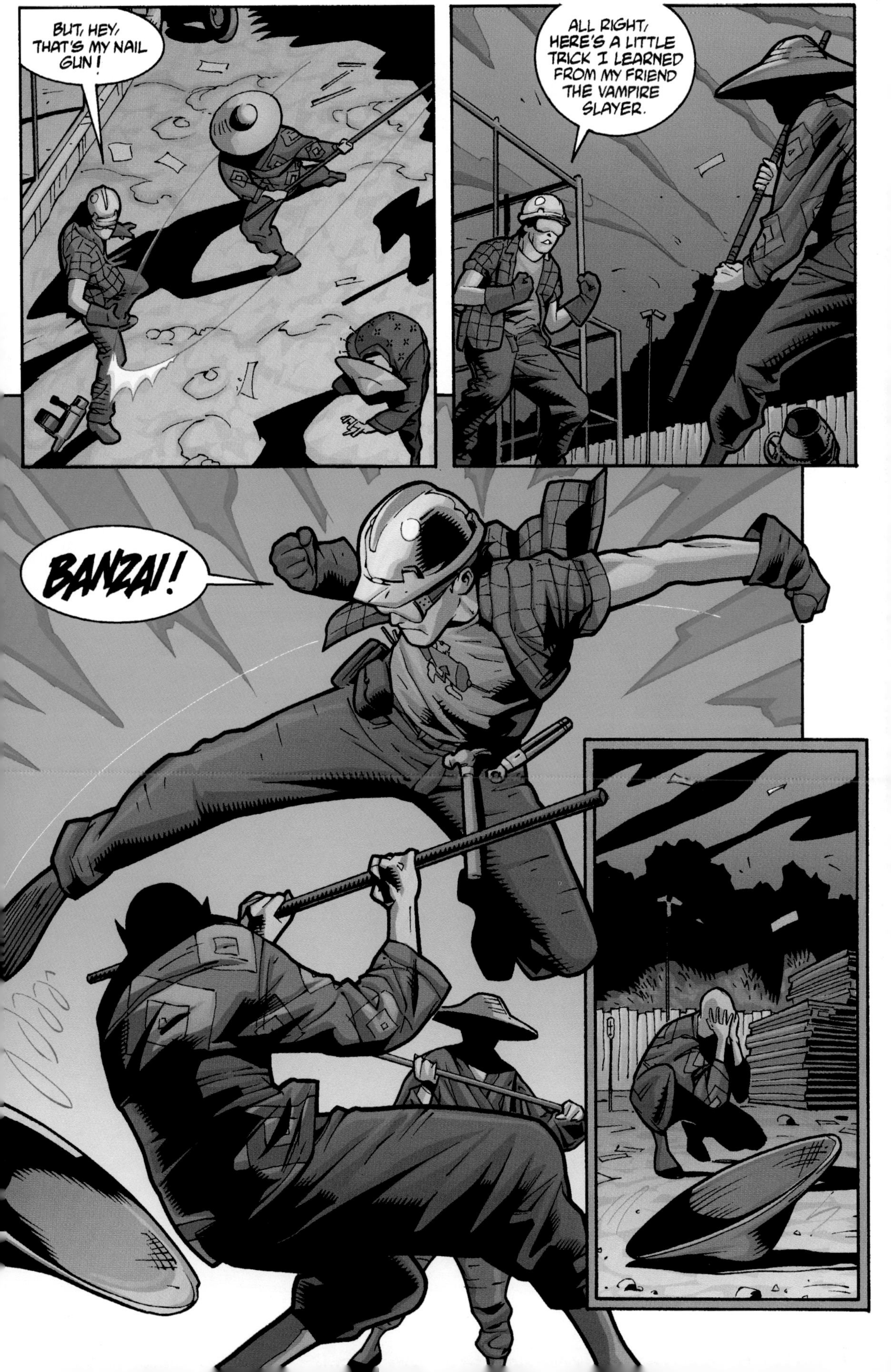
BUT, HEY, THAT'S MY NAIL GUN!
ALL RIGHT, HERE'S A LITTLE TRICK I LEARNED FROM MY FRIEND THE VAMPIRE SLAYER.
BANZAI!

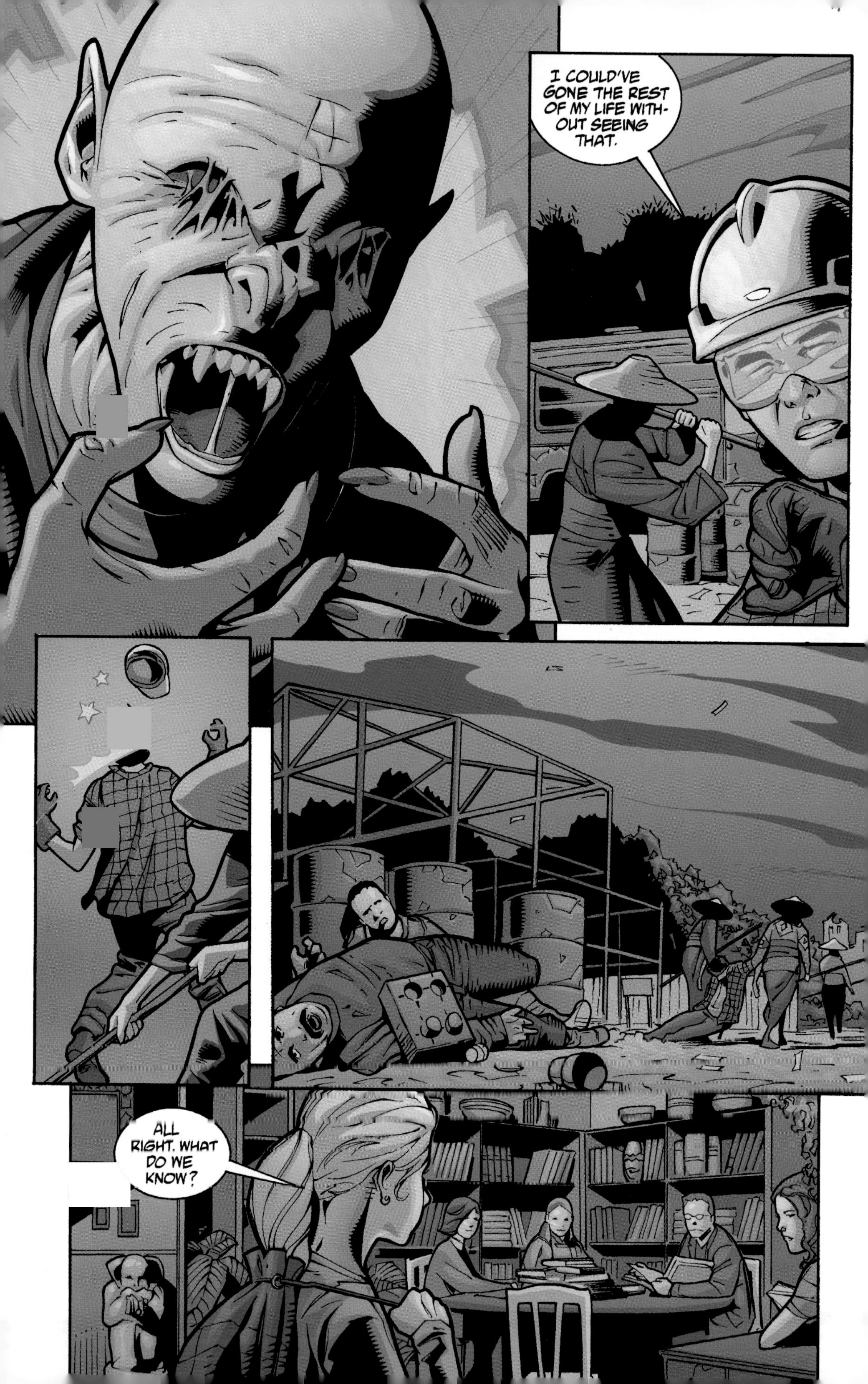
I COULD'VE GONE THE REST OF MY LIFE WITH-OUT SEEING THAT.
ALL RIGHT. WHAT DO WE KNOW?

WELL, AS WE MIGHT HAVE SUSPECTED, AGES AGO WHEN YUKI WAS A VAMPIRE SLAYER, SHE WENT UP AGAINST THE MASTER. HE WAS SOMEHOW ABLE TO GET TO HER MIND. IT WAS HE THAT TURNED HER.

I STILL CAN'T BELIEVE THAT ONE OF OUR TEAM JUST... SWITCHED OVER TO THE OTHER SIDE.

THERE HAS TO BE MORE TO IT THAN THAT. I'VE FACED OFF AGAINST BOTH THE MASTER *AND* DRACULA. AND WON. NO SLAYER LIFESTYLE CHANGES FOR ME.

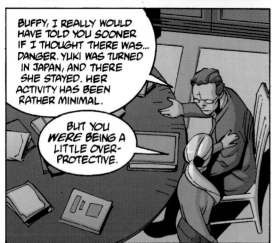

BUFFY, I REALLY WOULD HAVE TOLD YOU SOONER IF I THOUGHT THERE WAS... DANGER. YUKI WAS TURNED IN JAPAN, AND THERE SHE STAYED. HER ACTIVITY HAS BEEN RATHER MINIMAL.

BUT YOU *WERE* BEING A LITTLE OVERPROTECTIVE.

AND I TOTALLY UNDERESTIMATED THE EIDU.

AS IN AMULET?

AS IN EVIL SECT OF MONK-LIKE VAMPIRES WHO WORSHIP THE MASTER.

THEIR PERVERSION OF RELIGION IS ONLY EXCEEDED BY THEIR PERVERSION OF THEIR OWN SELVES. THEY BELIEVE THE MASTER HAS GIVEN THEM THE LEGACY OF SECOND SIGHT.

TO BECOME EIDU, YOUNG ACOLYTES, STILL HUMAN, ARE BROUGHT TO THE MONKS AND TORTURED. THEY ARE MADE TO BEG FOR THE BLOOD OF EVERLASTING LIFE.

THE FINAL IGNOMINY IS THAT ONCE THEY HAVE BEGGED FOR LIFE IN DEATH, THEY MUST BURN THEIR OWN EYES OUT. ONLY THEN ARE THEY BITTEN AND TURNED.

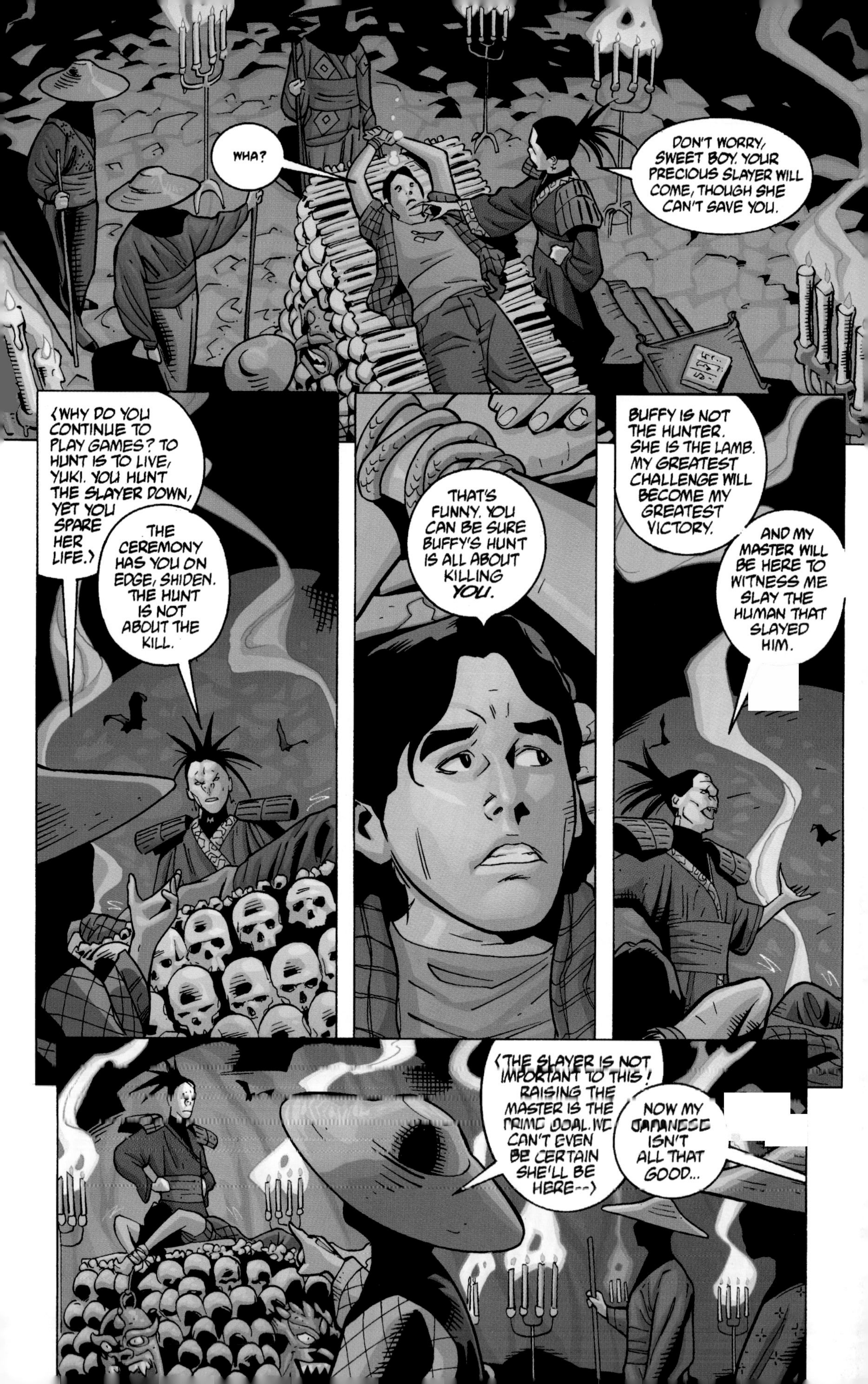
WHA?
DON'T WORRY, SWEET BOY. YOUR PRECIOUS SLAYER WILL COME, THOUGH SHE CAN'T SAVE YOU.
‹WHY DO YOU CONTINUE TO PLAY GAMES? TO HUNT IS TO LIVE, YUKI. YOU HUNT THE SLAYER DOWN, YET YOU SPARE HER LIFE.›
THE CEREMONY HAS YOU ON EDGE, SHIDEN. THE HUNT IS NOT ABOUT THE KILL.
THAT'S FUNNY. YOU CAN BE SURE BUFFY'S HUNT IS ALL ABOUT KILLING *YOU*.
BUFFY IS NOT THE HUNTER. SHE IS THE LAMB. MY GREATEST CHALLENGE WILL BECOME MY GREATEST VICTORY.
AND MY MASTER WILL BE HERE TO WITNESS ME SLAY THE HUMAN THAT SLAYED HIM.
‹THE SLAYER IS NOT IMPORTANT TO THIS! RAISING THE MASTER IS THE PRIME GOAL. WE CAN'T EVEN BE CERTAIN SHE'LL BE HERE--›
NOW MY JAPANESE ISN'T ALL THAT GOOD...

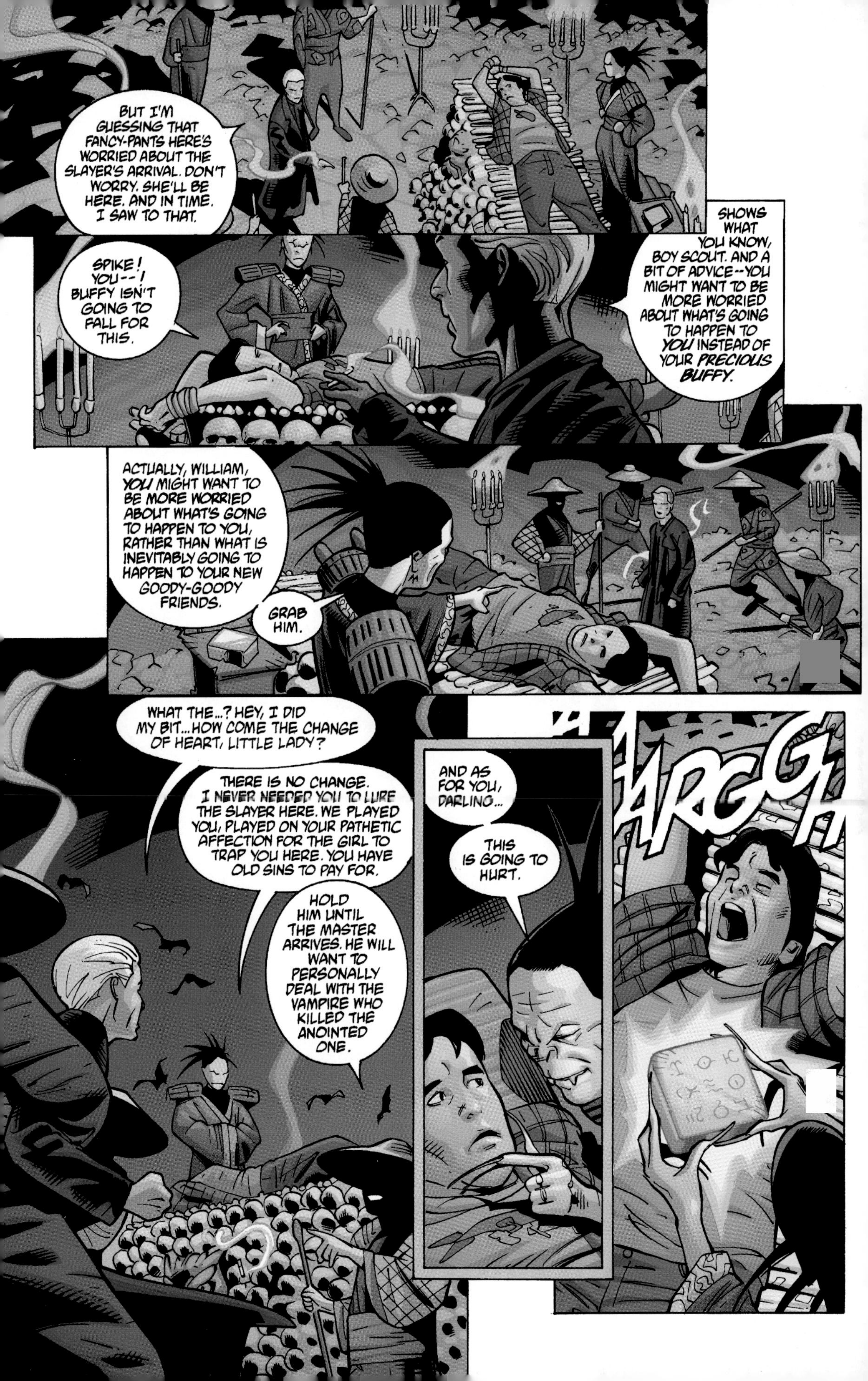
BUT I'M GUESSING THAT FANCY-PANTS HERE'S WORRIED ABOUT THE SLAYER'S ARRIVAL. DON'T WORRY. SHE'LL BE HERE. AND IN TIME. I SAW TO THAT.
SHOWS WHAT YOU KNOW, BOY SCOUT. AND A BIT OF ADVICE--YOU MIGHT WANT TO BE MORE WORRIED ABOUT WHAT'S GOING TO HAPPEN TO YOU INSTEAD OF YOUR PRECIOUS BUFFY.
SPIKE! YOU--! BUFFY ISN'T GOING TO FALL FOR THIS.
ACTUALLY, WILLIAM, YOU MIGHT WANT TO BE MORE WORRIED ABOUT WHAT'S GOING TO HAPPEN TO YOU, RATHER THAN WHAT IS INEVITABLY GOING TO HAPPEN TO YOUR NEW GOODY-GOODY FRIENDS.
GRAB HIM.
WHAT THE...? HEY, I DID MY BIT...HOW COME THE CHANGE OF HEART, LITTLE LADY?
THERE IS NO CHANGE. I NEVER NEEDED YOU TO LURE THE SLAYER HERE. WE PLAYED YOU, PLAYED ON YOUR PATHETIC AFFECTION FOR THE GIRL TO TRAP YOU HERE. YOU HAVE OLD SINS TO PAY FOR.
HOLD HIM UNTIL THE MASTER ARRIVES. HE WILL WANT TO PERSONALLY DEAL WITH THE VAMPIRE WHO KILLED THE ANOINTED ONE.
AND AS FOR YOU, DARLING...
THIS IS GOING TO HURT.
ARRGGH

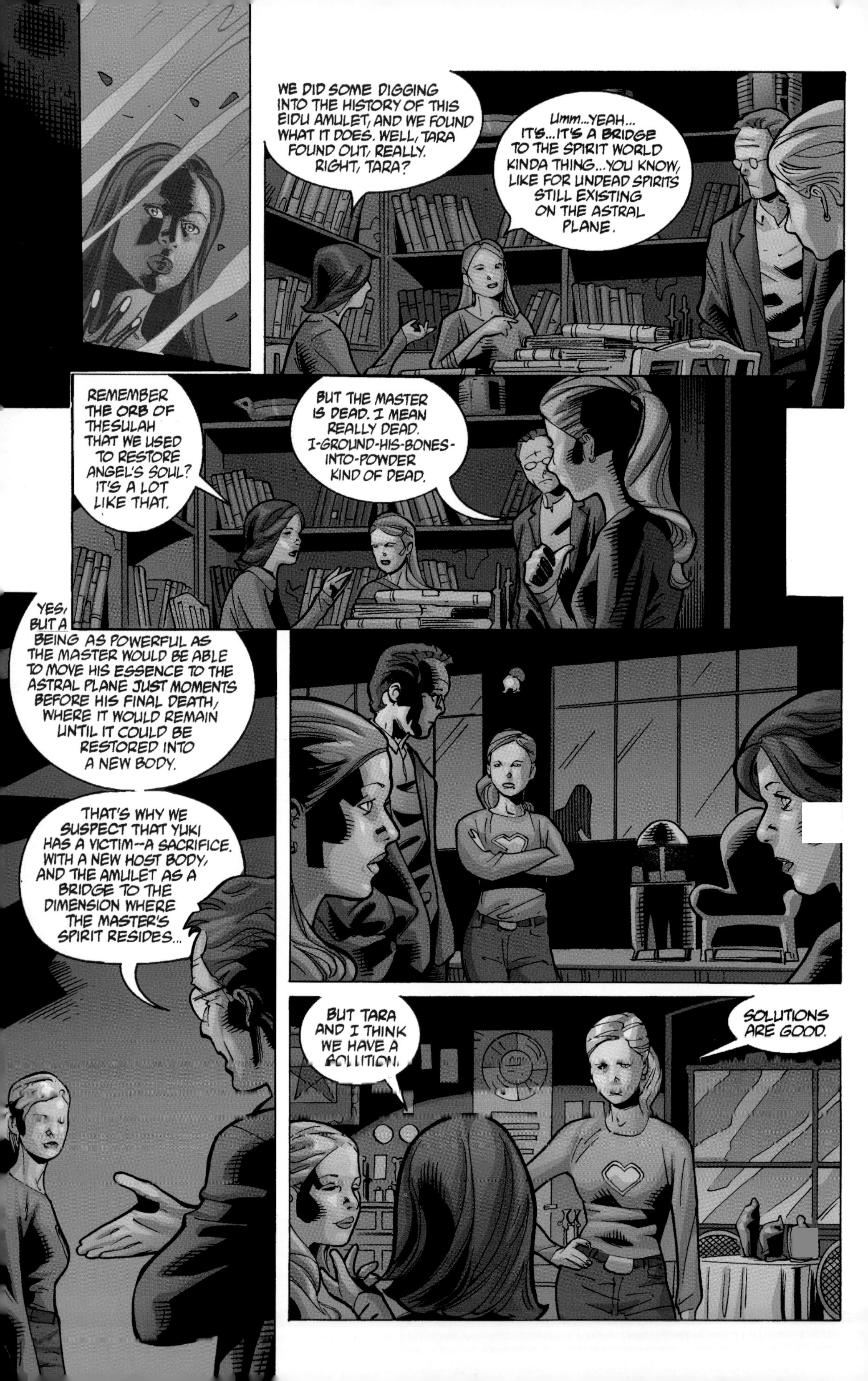
WE DID SOME DIGGING INTO THE HISTORY OF THIS EIDU AMULET, AND WE FOUND WHAT IT DOES. WELL, TARA FOUND OUT, REALLY. RIGHT, TARA?
Umm...YEAH... IT'S...IT'S A BRIDGE TO THE SPIRIT WORLD KINDA THING...YOU KNOW, LIKE FOR UNDEAD SPIRITS STILL EXISTING ON THE ASTRAL PLANE.
REMEMBER THE ORB OF THESULAH THAT WE USED TO RESTORE ANGEL'S SOUL? IT'S A LOT LIKE THAT.
BUT THE MASTER IS DEAD. I MEAN REALLY DEAD. I-GROUND-HIS-BONES-INTO-POWDER KIND OF DEAD.
YES, BUT A BEING AS POWERFUL AS THE MASTER WOULD BE ABLE TO MOVE HIS ESSENCE TO THE ASTRAL PLANE JUST MOMENTS BEFORE HIS FINAL DEATH, WHERE IT WOULD REMAIN UNTIL IT COULD BE RESTORED INTO A NEW BODY.
THAT'S WHY WE SUSPECT THAT YUKI HAS A VICTIM--A SACRIFICE. WITH A NEW HOST BODY, AND THE AMULET AS A BRIDGE TO THE DIMENSION WHERE THE MASTER'S SPIRIT RESIDES...
BUT TARA AND I THINK WE HAVE A SOLUTION.
SOLUTIONS ARE GOOD.

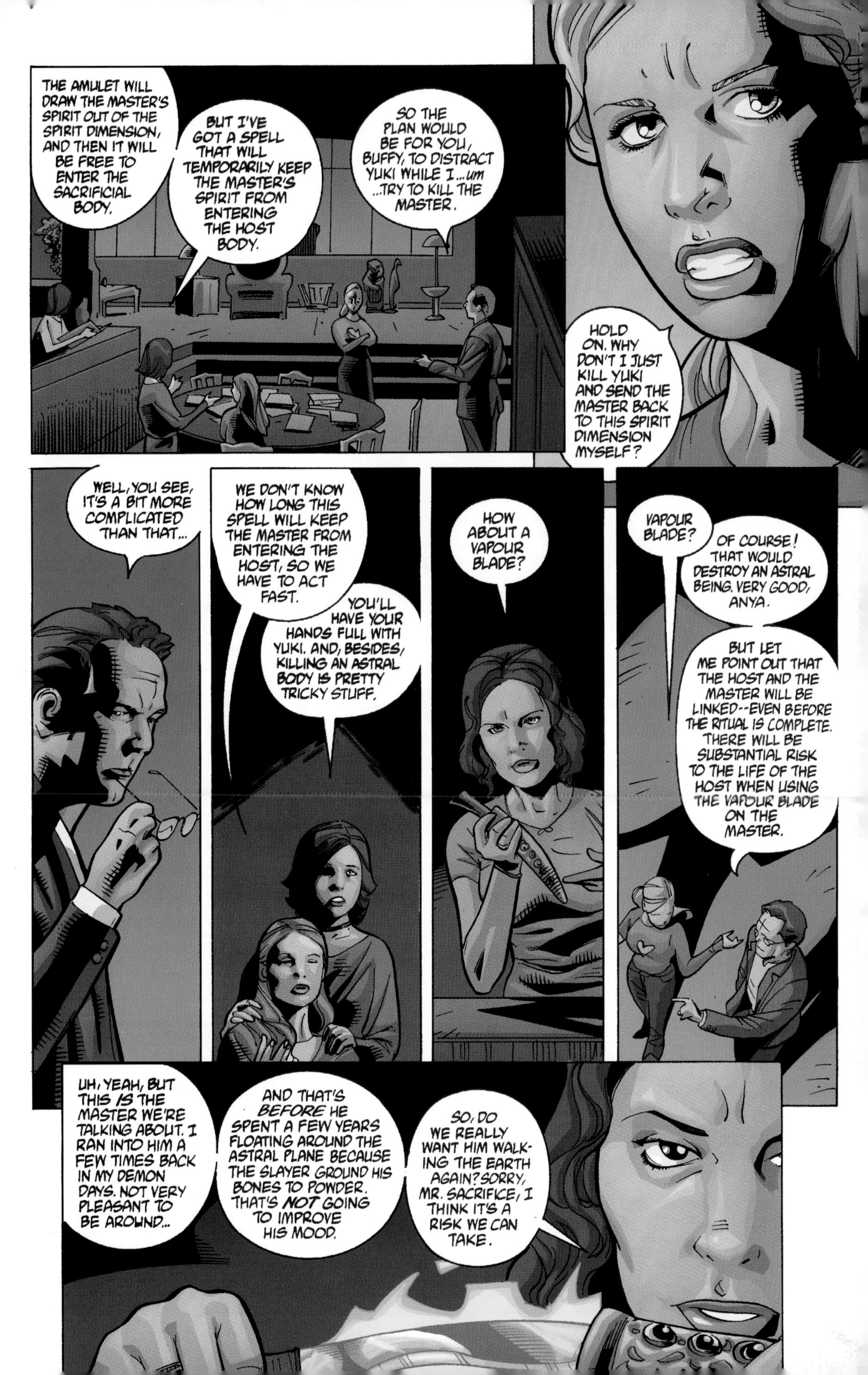
THE AMULET WILL DRAW THE MASTER'S SPIRIT OUT OF THE SPIRIT DIMENSION, AND THEN IT WILL BE FREE TO ENTER THE SACRIFICIAL BODY.
BUT I'VE GOT A SPELL THAT WILL TEMPORARILY KEEP THE MASTER'S SPIRIT FROM ENTERING THE HOST BODY.
SO THE PLAN WOULD BE FOR YOU, BUFFY, TO DISTRACT YUKI WHILE I... *um* ...TRY TO KILL THE MASTER.
HOLD ON. WHY DON'T I JUST KILL YUKI AND SEND THE MASTER BACK TO THIS SPIRIT DIMENSION MYSELF?
WELL, YOU SEE, IT'S A BIT MORE COMPLICATED THAN THAT...
WE DON'T KNOW HOW LONG THIS SPELL WILL KEEP THE MASTER FROM ENTERING THE HOST, SO WE HAVE TO ACT FAST.
YOU'LL HAVE YOUR HANDS FULL WITH YUKI. AND, BESIDES, KILLING AN ASTRAL BODY IS PRETTY TRICKY STUFF.
HOW ABOUT A VAPOUR BLADE?
VAPOUR BLADE?
OF COURSE! THAT WOULD DESTROY AN ASTRAL BEING. VERY GOOD, ANYA.
BUT LET ME POINT OUT THAT THE HOST AND THE MASTER WILL BE LINKED--EVEN BEFORE THE RITUAL IS COMPLETE. THERE WILL BE SUBSTANTIAL RISK TO THE LIFE OF THE HOST WHEN USING THE VAPOUR BLADE ON THE MASTER.
UH, YEAH, BUT THIS *IS* THE MASTER WE'RE TALKING ABOUT. I RAN INTO HIM A FEW TIMES BACK IN MY DEMON DAYS. NOT VERY PLEASANT TO BE AROUND...
AND THAT'S *BEFORE* HE SPENT A FEW YEARS FLOATING AROUND THE ASTRAL PLANE BECAUSE THE SLAYER GROUND HIS BONES TO POWDER. THAT'S *NOT* GOING TO IMPROVE HIS MOOD.
SO, DO WE REALLY WANT HIM WALKING THE EARTH AGAIN? SORRY, MR. SACRIFICE, I THINK IT'S A RISK WE CAN TAKE.

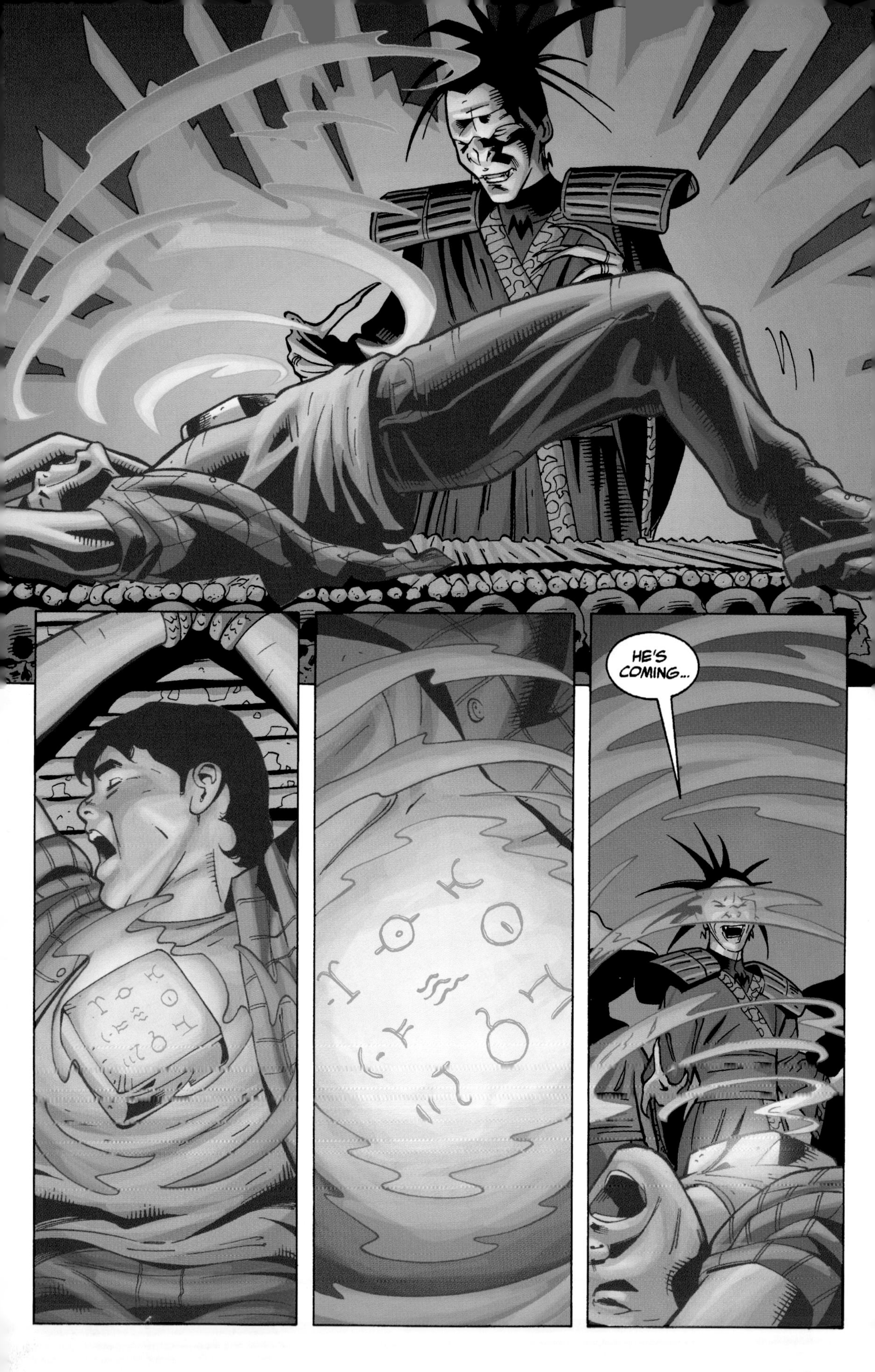
HE'S COMING...

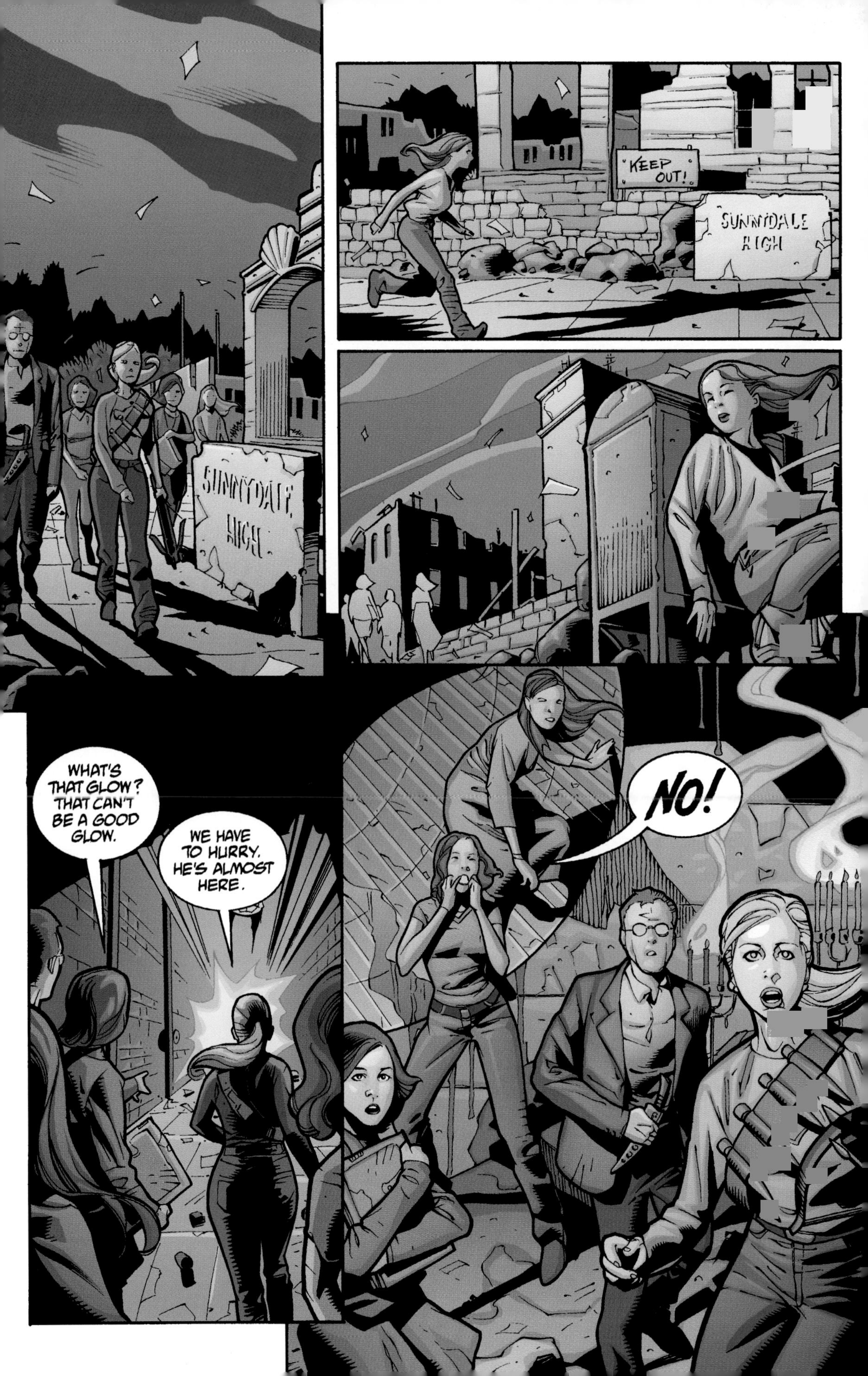
SUNNYDALE HIGH
KEEP OUT!
SUNNYDALE HIGH
WHAT'S THAT GLOW? THAT CAN'T BE A GOOD GLOW.
WE HAVE TO HURRY. HE'S ALMOST HERE.
NO!

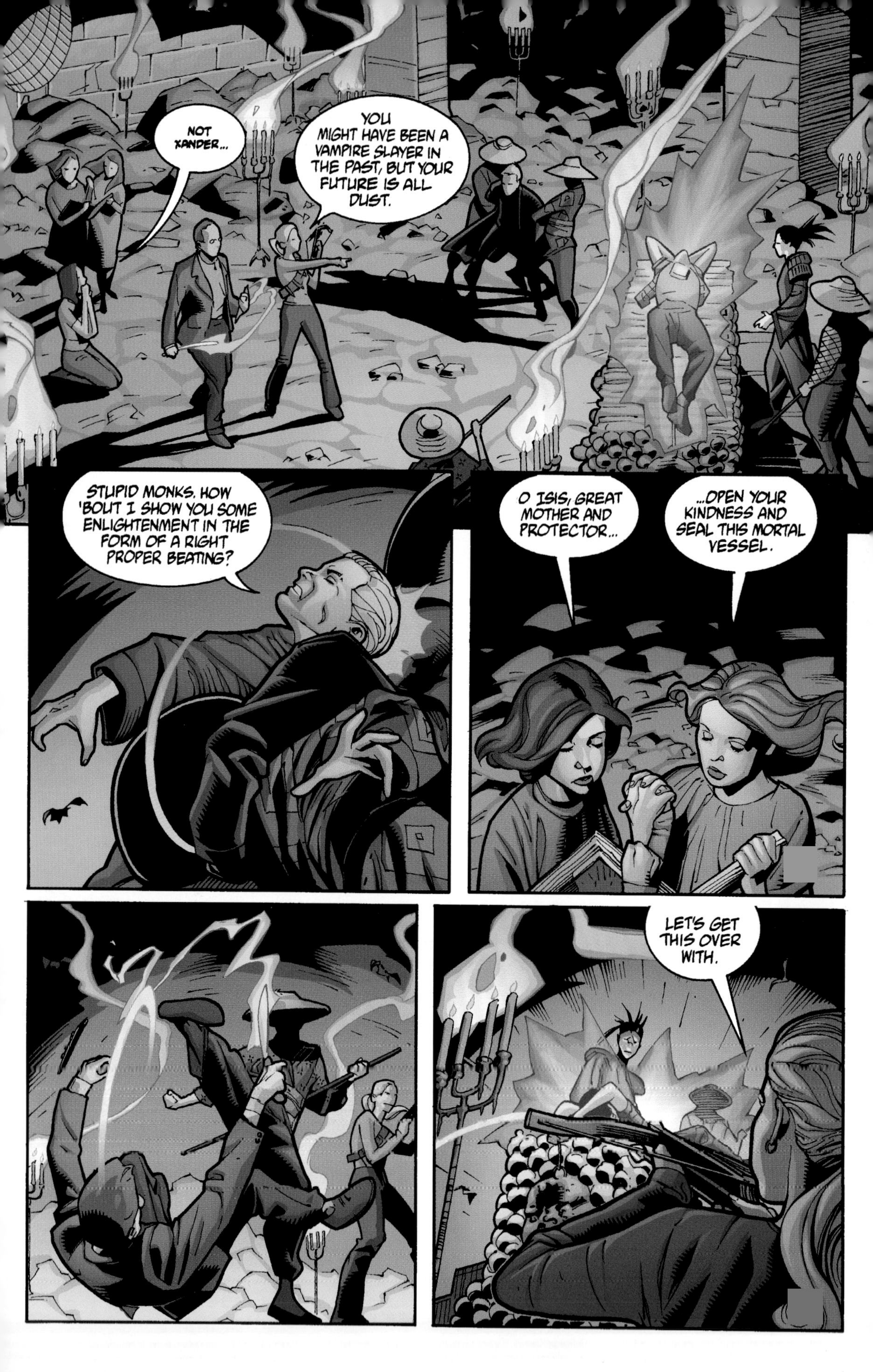
NOT XANDER...
YOU MIGHT HAVE BEEN A VAMPIRE SLAYER IN THE PAST, BUT YOUR FUTURE IS ALL DUST.
STUPID MONKS. HOW 'BOUT I SHOW YOU SOME ENLIGHTENMENT IN THE FORM OF A RIGHT PROPER BEATING?
O ISIS, GREAT MOTHER AND PROTECTOR...
...OPEN YOUR KINDNESS AND SEAL THIS MORTAL VESSEL.
LET'S GET THIS OVER WITH.

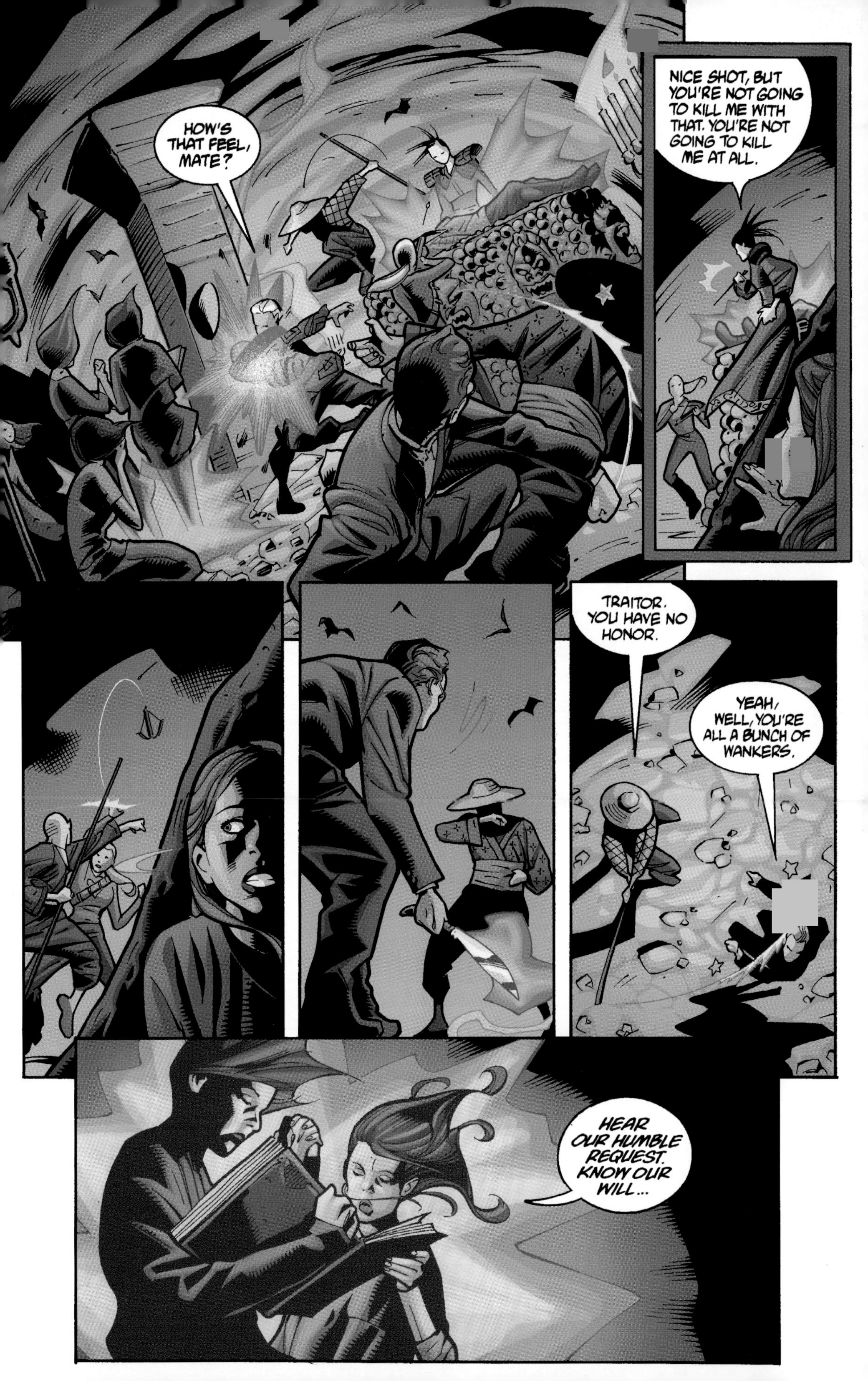
HOW'S THAT FEEL, MATE?
NICE SHOT, BUT YOU'RE NOT GOING TO KILL ME WITH THAT. YOU'RE NOT GOING TO KILL ME AT ALL.
TRAITOR. YOU HAVE NO HONOR.
YEAH, WELL, YOU'RE ALL A BUNCH OF WANKERS.
HEAR OUR HUMBLE REQUEST. KNOW OUR WILL...

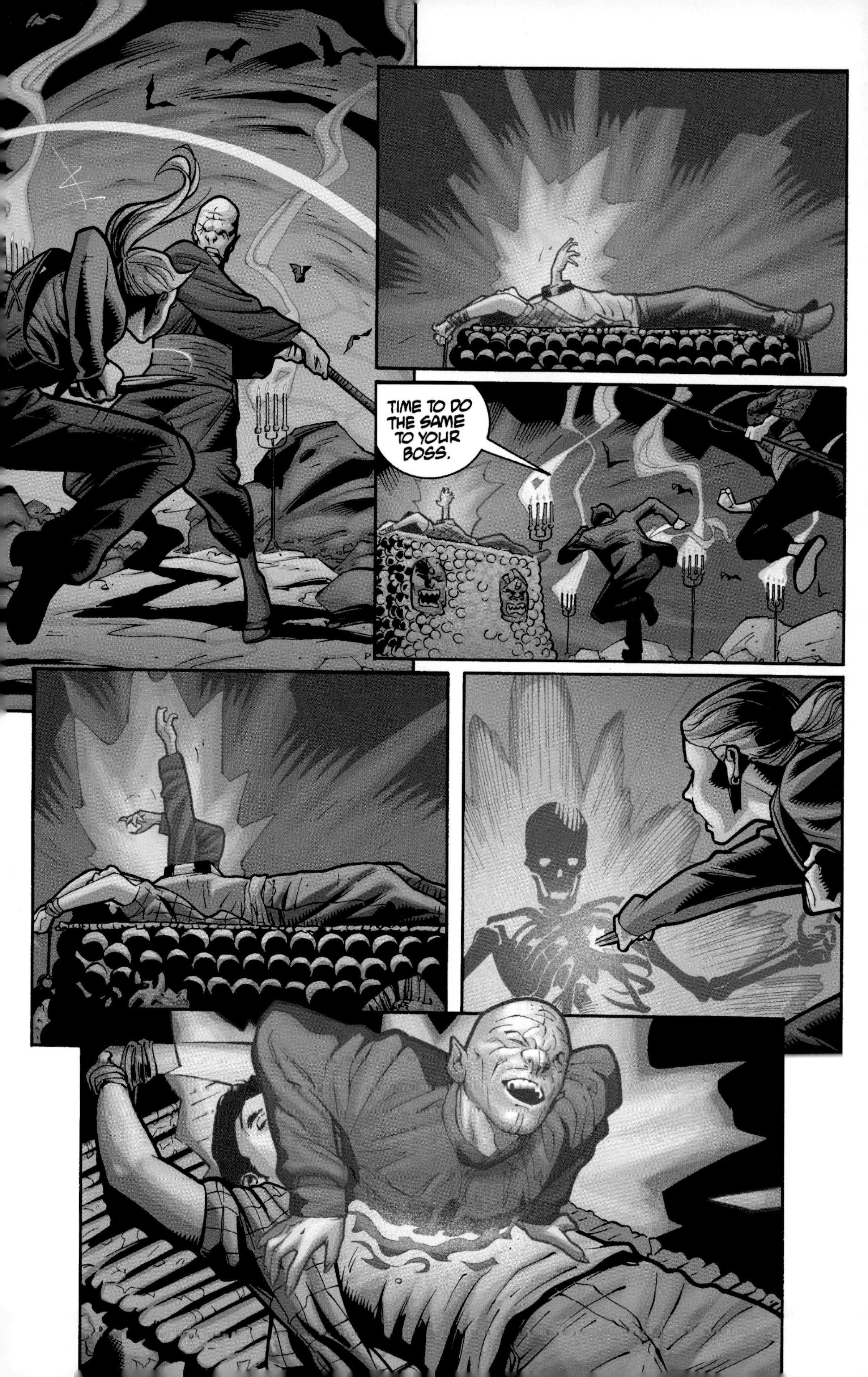
TIME TO DO THE SAME TO YOUR BOSS.

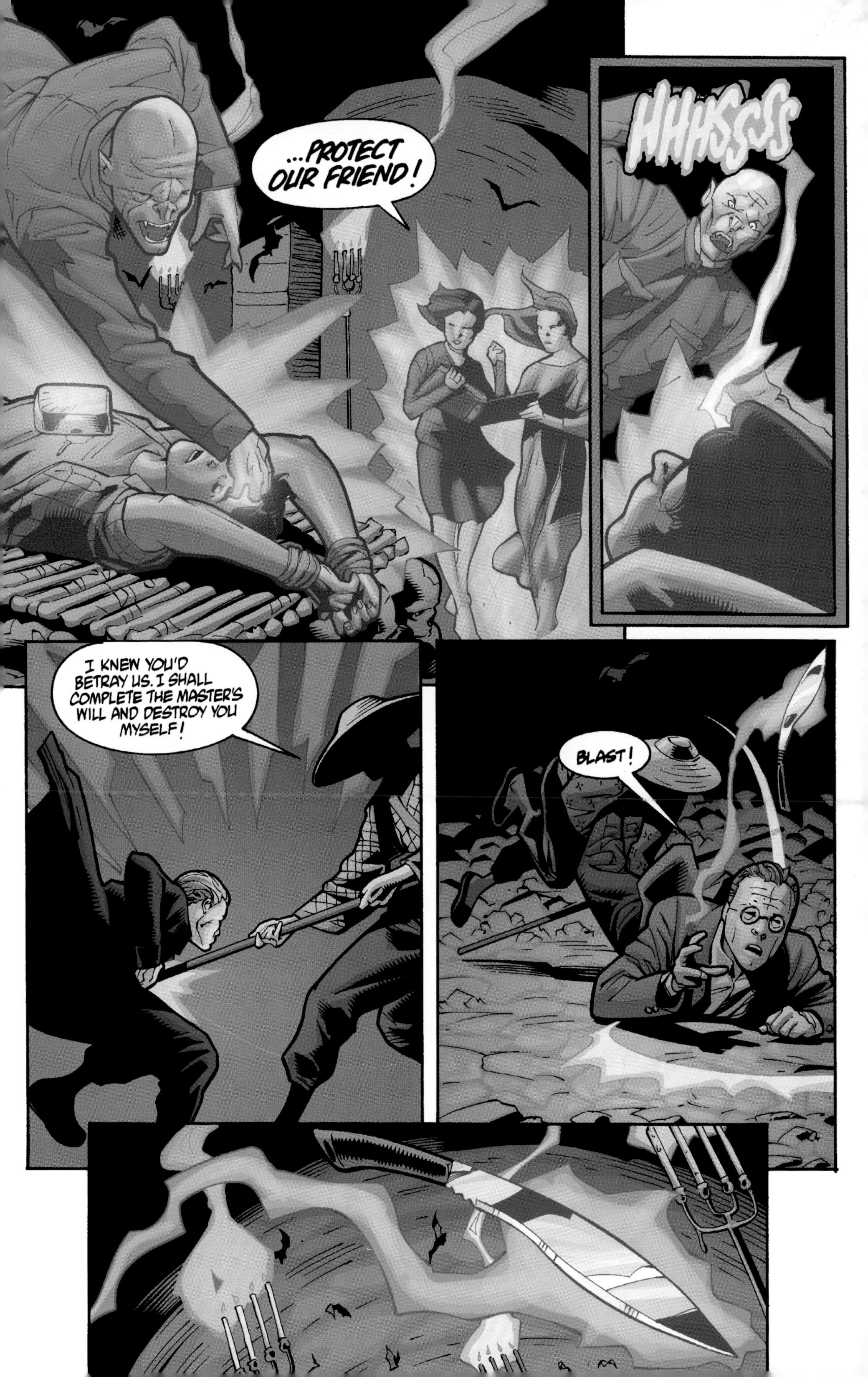
...PROTECT OUR FRIEND!
HHHSSSS
I KNEW YOU'D BETRAY US. I SHALL COMPLETE THE MASTER'S WILL AND DESTROY YOU MYSELF!
BLAST!

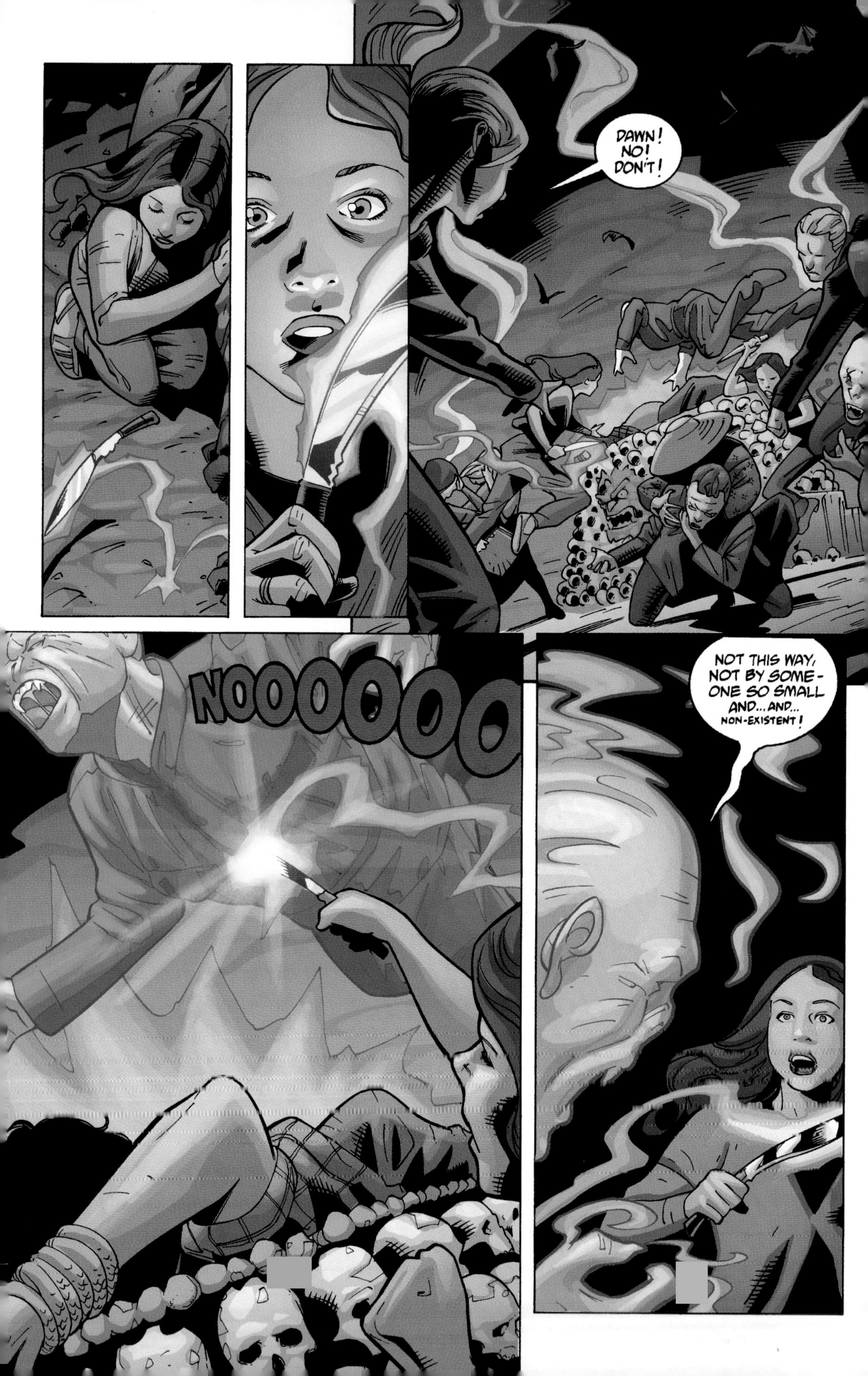
DAWN! NO! DON'T!
NOOOOOOO
NOT THIS WAY, NOT BY SOME-ONE SO SMALL AND...AND... NON-EXISTENT!

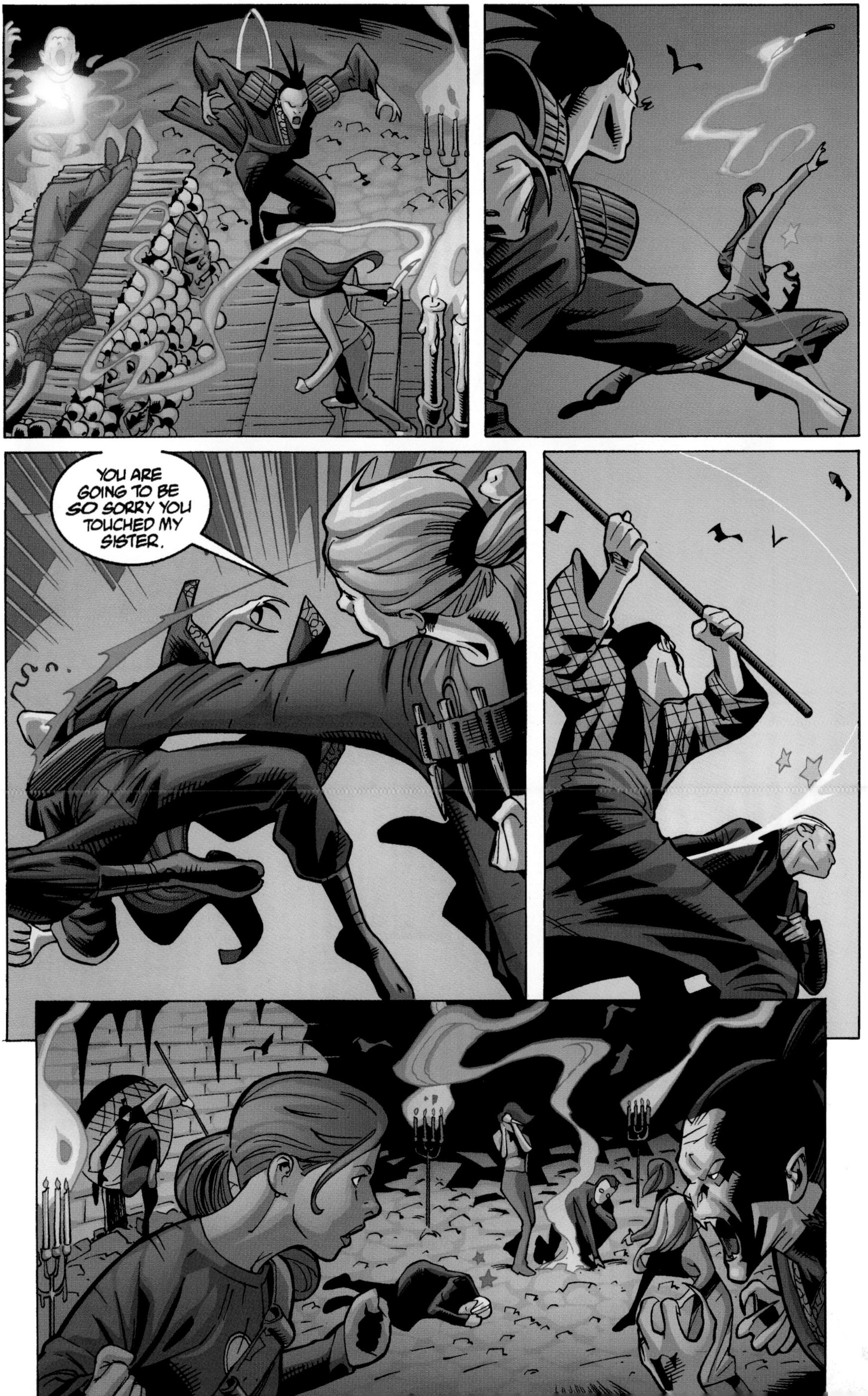
YOU ARE GOING TO BE SO SORRY YOU TOUCHED MY SISTER.

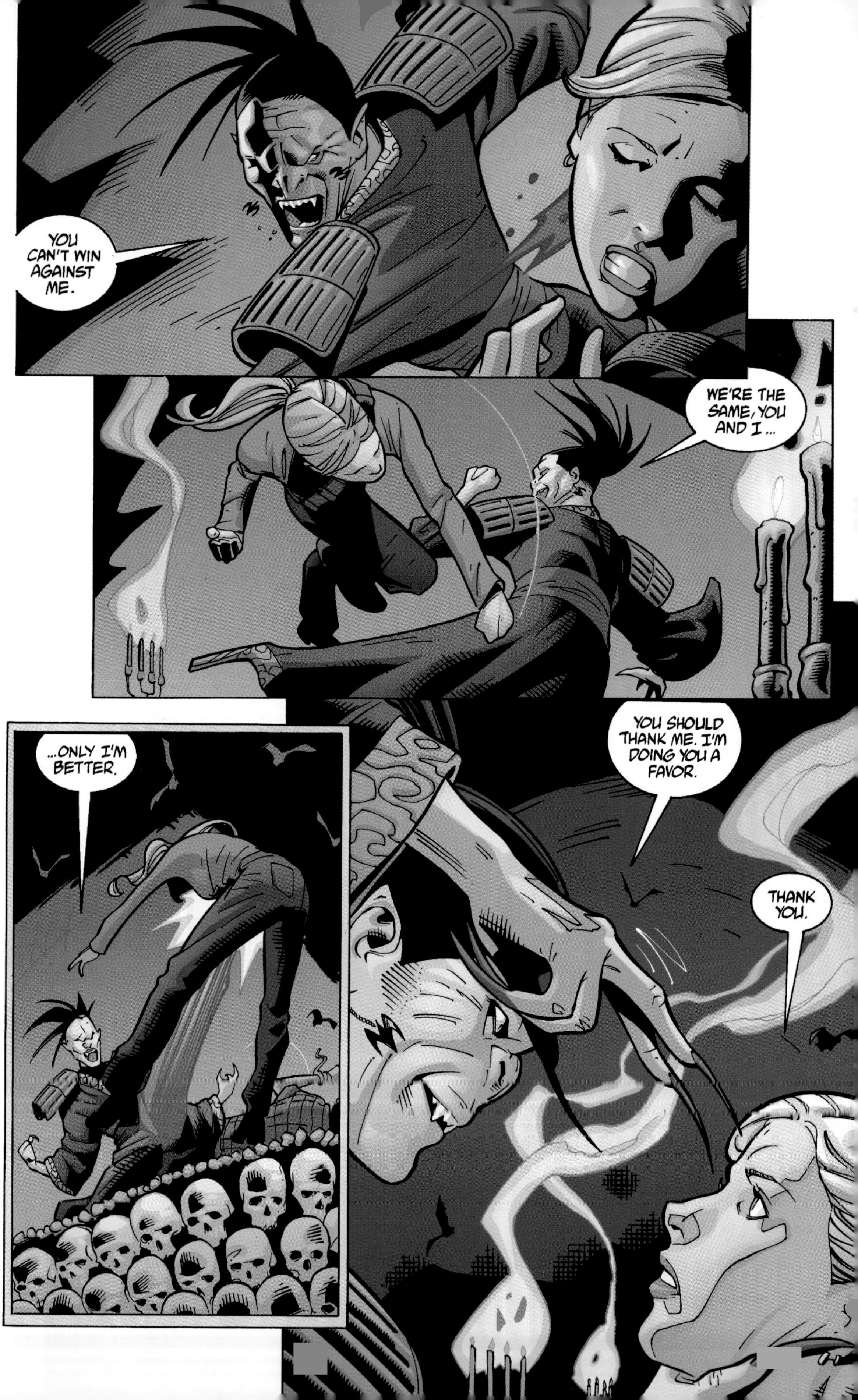
YOU CAN'T WIN AGAINST ME.
WE'RE THE SAME, YOU AND I...
...ONLY I'M BETTER.
YOU SHOULD THANK ME. I'M DOING YOU A FAVOR.
THANK YOU.

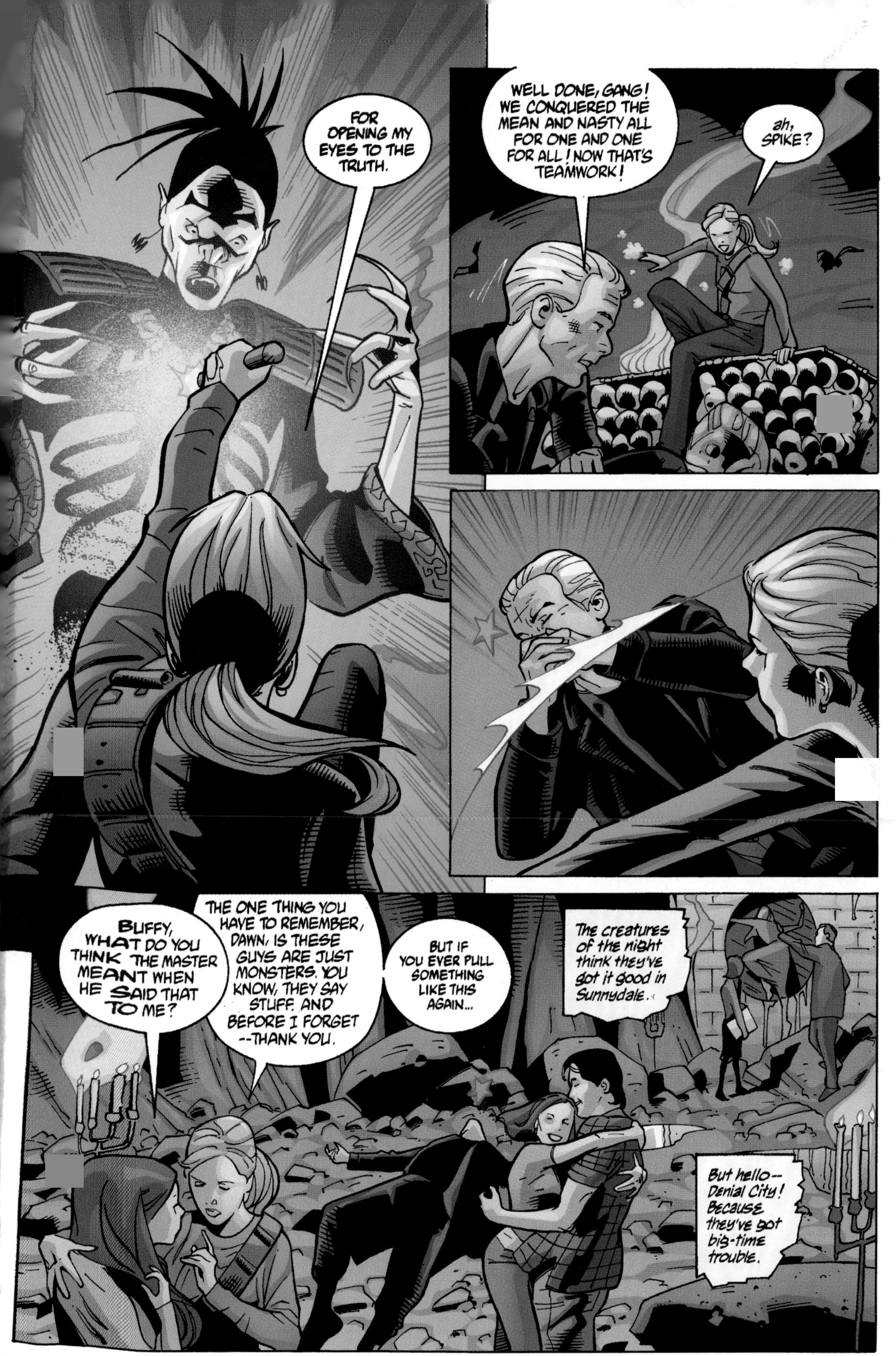
FOR OPENING MY EYES TO THE TRUTH.
WELL DONE, GANG! WE CONQUERED THE MEAN AND NASTY ALL FOR ONE AND ONE FOR ALL! NOW THAT'S TEAMWORK!
ah, SPIKE?
BUFFY, WHAT DO YOU THINK THE MASTER MEANT WHEN HE SAID THAT TO ME?
THE ONE THING YOU HAVE TO REMEMBER, DAWN, IS THESE GUYS ARE JUST MONSTERS. YOU KNOW, THEY SAY STUFF. AND BEFORE I FORGET --THANK YOU.
BUT IF YOU EVER PULL SOMETHING LIKE THIS AGAIN...
The creatures of the night think they've got it good in Sunnydale.
But hello-- Denial City! Because they've got big-time trouble.

The forces of evil don't stand a chance against the Slayer.

PARENTAL ADVISORY

She's the protector of the innocent, all right... and much more.

N'SINK

DAWN! HOW MANY TIMES DO I HAVE TO TELL YOU? NO BORROWING MY CLOTHES!

She's my sister.

THE END